Praise for *Midnight, Jesus & Me*

Gorgeous, brilliantly written, deeply moving, funny as f-bomb, life-affirming and just plain stunning. J.M. Blaine's debut will blow you away.

— **Augusten Burroughs, bestselling author of *Running With Scissors* and *This Is How***

If Christianity has become a stale institution, then Jamie Blaine's *Midnight, Jesus & Me* might be the perfect antidote. A raw reminder of the Gospel's power.

— **Philip Gulley, bestselling author of *If the Church Were Christian***

Blaine's got the gift that all great storytellers have — the ability to convey the crush of emotions in the tiniest of details. He renders otherwise ordinary people in resplendent detail, painting vignettes in heart-stopping strokes. Jamie is one of a handful of writers who makes me forget that I own a cell phone.

— **Joe Daly, *Classic Rock* magazine**

If a psychic cliff looms at midnight, pray it's Jamie Blaine rolling up to your door. Writing with grace, ease and kindness about the troubled and lost we push out of sight, Blaine shines a "there-but-for-the-grace-of-God-go-I" light on the hidden world of psychiatric crisis response — leavened with much-needed humor — in a manner that can't help but engender empathy and compassion.

— **Randy Susan Meyers, bestselling author of *The Murderer's Daughters* and *The Comfort of Lies***

A stupendous achievement. Exhilarating, hilarious, a virtuosic exploration of mental illness in America. Seething with fury and frustration, Blaine captures the reader with great conviction.

— Jeff Ragsdale, activist and author of *Jeff, One Lonely Guy*

In the vein of Donald Miller's *Blue Like Jazz*, Blaine's *Midnight, Jesus, & Me* uses everyday interactions to draw closer to the meaning of our existence. Unlike Miller, however, Blaine's interactions are with those who have not only lost their place in society, they have lost their place in the world. With pitch-perfect prose filled with raw heart and humor, *Midnight, Jesus & Me* reveals the hole in all of us that cannot be filled with anything but Divine love.

— Jolina Petersheim, author of *The Outcast*

Jamie's sharp writing takes us into the most intimate and dark moments of these vivid and truer-than-life characters. Super stylized but absolutely authentic, these stories are told visually and with a musicality that punctuates the humor and heartbreak of crisis work and its haunting side effects.

— Tony Shaff, filmmaker/television producer, MTV Networks

Blaine shares his sharp stories of grit and grace, faith and doubt, humor and heartbreak, details and depth. *Midnight, Jesus & Me* is a compelling, hopeful invitation for the reader to pay attention to life, to stay alive to the surprises and the search.

— Kent Annan, director of Haiti Partners and author of *Following Jesus through the Eye of the Needle*

If Jesus is really like Jamie says, I just might be a Christian after all.

— Eight-Ball Eddie from the alley off Lower Broad

MIDNIGHT, JESUS & ME

MISFIT MEMOIRS

OF A FULL GOSPEL

ROCK & ROLL

LATE NIGHT SUICIDE

CRISIS PSYCHOTHERAPIST

J.M. BLAINE

ECW Press

Published by ECW Press
2120 Queen Street East, Suite 200, Toronto, Ontario, Canada M4E 1E2
416-694-3348 / info@ecwpress.com

LIBRARY AND ARCHIVES CANADA CATALOGUING IN PUBLICATION

Blaine, J.M.
    Midnight, Jesus & me : misfit memoirs of a full gospel, rock &
roll late night suicide crisis psychotherapist / J.M. Blaine.

5155 0381 5/13

ISBN 978-1-77041-108-1
ALSO ISSUED AS: 978-1-77090-390-6 (PDF); 978-1-77090-391-3 (EPUB)

1. Blaine, J.M.   2. Psychotherapists—United States—Biography.
3. Evangelists—United States—Biography.   4. Psychotherapy—Religious
aspects—Christianity.   5. Psychology and religion.   I. Title.

RC438.6.B53A3 2013   616.890092   C2012-907512-4

FSC
www.fsc.org
MIX
Paper from
responsible sources
FSC® C016245

Editor for the press: Michael Holmes
Cover design: Troy Cunningham
Cover illustration: Sergio Cariello
Text design: Tania Craan
Author photo: Carter Andrews
Typesetting and production: Carolyn McNeillie
Printing: Friesens 1 2 3 4 5

PRINTED AND BOUND IN CANADA

"I didn't come for the religious people. I came for the misfits."
— Luke 5:32 (BLE translation)

Foreword

After reading Jamie Blaine's notorious new work, this collection of true tales of a rockin' ride of a life, of being everything from a roller-rink DJ to a late-night psych guy trolling the streets amid the freaks and forgotten, I wanted to write an endorsement. I wanted to say, "You must read this book because it is ugly and raw and beautiful and forlorn and hopeful and all those things about the human race that make me proud to be counted a part of that clan." But I was struck with a peculiar challenge. Words kept escaping me or kept rising to the surface out of order and untrue. Elusive. Lacking the depth of what I was feeling or the wisdom of what I wanted to say. So, here, listen now.

It's come to me like the backside of a jungle tree where the ghost orchid grows silent and unseen. A place you must discover in dreams with your heart's eye. And that's the way I would have you discover Jamie's book *Midnight, Jesus and Me*. In the secret places where you let few enter but you must begin.

I've been pondering a few things in today's mish-mash angry culture of snark and sarcasm, where rote diatribes have replaced true believing. I was wondering lately where I'd find my red-letter Jesus. Where would he be hanging out these days if this were "his first time around"?

And I was thinking . . .

If I had reached the end of my rope, the edge of my hope, and darkness was prevailing. If I stood there on the ledge of lost and losing still — and somehow I managed to crawl to some dark barstool corner of the world for one last shot before I gave it all up and caved in, I hope it would be this Jamie and Jesus that walked in behind me. That they pulled up a seat and told me a story and that their telling of it found me right where I was, drowning in this sea called life. And that their story would perform its magic, one funny, dark, raw, honest, loving, wild word at a time and in so doing — revive my soul.

And so they did.

This is that book.

Read it.

— River Jordan, bestselling author of *The Miracle of Mercy Land* and *Praying for Strangers*

Disclaimer

Midnight, Jesus & Me is a work of creative nonfiction and features stories from rehabs, mental hospitals, counseling centers, emergency rooms and prisons. Names, places, faces and sexes have been changed and in some cases combined in the interest of protecting myself and others. Any resemblance to persons living or dead is purely coincidental and unintentional.

From Texas to Louisiana to Georgia to Tennessee, begins as high school ends, through college and grad school. God and psychosis and the glory of rock and roll . . . dive bars and psych wards and Sunday night church . . . jail cells to bridge rails . . . roller rinks to single-wide trailers at the far end of the gravel lane . . . late-night grocery stores and that place over the levee where Jesus laughs and walks through the cool, dark night . . .

"Is it fiction?" a friend asks after reading. "This really happened?"

"Well," I tell her, "the end of the rope gets a little surreal. But yeah, it's true."

"Your people sure do smoke and drink and curse and talk about God a lot."

"Yeah," I answer, after giving it some thought. "That sounds like my people."

Rhythm & the River of Words

Anytime I read a piece that rings true or moves me, I wonder what music the author listened to while they worked the words. Everything is lyrical. I write and read out loud, to the cadence and feel of a song. So I included the soundtrack in a separate section at the end of this book.

Follow along if you wish. Cue up the accompanying song and read to the beat to which the words were originally conceived.

PART I

Fall Back

"We are here and it is now. Further than that all human knowledge is moonshine." — H. L. Mencken

Plan G | Life Is What Happens

Sunday, 9:35 p.m.

36 y/o white male, history of paranoid schizophrenia and intermittent explosive disorder. Staff unable to control client's outbursts and request assistance.

I'm sitting in my car in the parking lot of a group home for the mentally impaired near Darby's Mini-Mart, far back in the hills of Tennessee.

Earlier tonight, the client threw a TV through the bedroom wall, brandished a kitchen knife and told Jena, the night tech, he wanted to cut both wrists and die. She called the crisis line and dispatch sent me to intervene.

The drive up was pleasant enough: horse farms, hay fields and rolling hills. Alabama singing about Tennessee River and the changes coming on. Soon as I pulled into the driveway, I saw shadows waving wildly behind the blinds.

What am I doing here?

Fifteen years now on late-night psychiatric crisis. Suicide, homicide, psychosis, addiction. Jail cells, bridge rails, emergency rooms, rehabs. Group homes.

Why am I in the middle of this? I was just the DJ at the skating rink. . . .

There's a crashing sound and shouts from the house. I'm tempted to leave. I'm always tempted to leave. The Mini-Mart has a Subway inside and their fountain cokes are crisp and super-cold. *Just come back later.* A man with broken teeth and hound dog jowls stares at me like a jack-o-lantern from the bedroom window. I breathe deep, say a prayer and walk up the front steps to ring the bell.

"This is Mr. Ralph," Jena says, pointing to a patient with bird-nest hair, a Viking's beard and the physique of an off-season Santa. He's leaning against the wall with both arms behind his back, rocking and lightly banging his head. I hold out my hand to shake and suddenly he seems fearful and meek, his eyes shining back at me from the shadows of the hall. I keep my hand out, the way a stranger approaches a stray dog. When he finally steps towards the doorway, I notice his bloody arm.

"Accidentally scratched him," Jena says, "taking away the knife."

She's late teens/early twenties, wearing carpenter jeans and a stiff denim shirt. Built like a fire hydrant with the same haircut as Ricky Schroder in *Silver Spoons*. "Uh, good work," I tell her, "Sorry it took so long to get here."

"That's okay," she says. "Do you need the knife?"

"I don't need it," I reply.

A smaller man with a furious unibrow storms the hall with his fists balled and bottom lip poked out. The cable of a hearing aid trails down his left shoulder into the pocket of his shirt.

"And this is Geof, Ralph's roommate," Jena says. "Geof's upset about the TV through the wall thing. When Ralph gets out there, he's bad about throwing stuff."

Geof walks to Ralph until the tips of their shoes touch. "I hate you," he seethes.

"Geof," Jena says, in a schoolteacher voice. "This man is from Crisis."

"Good!" Geof shouts to Ralph. "He's gonna lock you up in the crazy house and stick an ice pick in your brain!"

Shoulda gone to Darby's.

Ralph throws out his arms and makes a panicked face, like he's playing to the cheap seats in a small-town production of *Oklahoma!* There's a bookcase in the hall filled with old encyclopedias. Grabbing a thick one, he smashes the den's sliding glass door, jumps through the hole and vanishes into the night.

"Ralph, no!" Jena cries.

Caught in the adrenaline, I give chase and tackle him in the tall grass past the gate. He screams like a panther and elbows my nose. I've got him in a half-nelson when I feel another arm throttling my neck. Geof. We flounce around the pasture like the Three Stooges at a UFC free-for-all. Finally, Jena grabs a roll of Geof's belly fat and pinches it until he rolls away crying, "Oww!"

"Don't hurt him, Jena," Ralph pleads, slack now. "Geof ain't done nothin' to you."

Jena pulls Geof to his feet. I release Ralph and we lie back in the weeds and catch our breath. There's blood and sweat and broken glass and ants. . . .

"Ants!" I shriek, scrambling to my feet. Ralph and Geof and Jena slap at my clothes until the crawling is under control. I've got one sentence with fourteen curse words ready to spew but after a big breath all that comes out is laughter. And Ralph laughs. And Geof laughs.

"I don't see how you do this all the time," Jena says, laughing too.

"Beats working in an office," I reply.

With a little guidance, Geof is back in bed and Ralph is ready to go, meeting me out front in too-short sweatpants, topsiders with white socks and a Cactus Jack t-shirt. A plastic sack with spare socks, boxers and a toothbrush dangles from his hand.

We sit on the trunk of Jena's car and wait for Ralph's ride to the psych ward, bandaging his arm and assuring him everything's gonna be all right.

"Sorry about the door," he says, in a big scared Pooh Bear voice. "I thought you'd send me to that crazy place where those mean people pick out your brain."

"Fair enough," I say, "but why'd you throw the TV?"

Ralph laughs behind his hand, not evil or deviously, more like the laugh of a mischievous child. "It was telling me lies," he says. "But I'm tired now. Can I lay down?"

"Sure," I tell him. "Car's on the way but might take awhile." Ralph climbs into the passenger side, ratchets the seat back and clasps his hands across his chest.

"What do you think is goin' on?" Jena asks.

"I don't know. What do you think?"

"Meds out of whack?" she offers.

"That's what I was thinkin' too," I say.

It's November and the moon is full, orange and fat like it is in the country. The group home is on a hill and there's a platform built in a big hickory near the car.

"Y'all let 'em climb in that treehouse?" I ask.

"Yeah," Jena says. "The patients love it up there. Hey, you wanna see something?"

"Sure."

She plants one foot on the bottom rung and pulls herself into the loft. "Come on up." When I get to the top she turns me around and points. Looking over the tree line, there's ridge after ridge and the river far away.

"Wow," I tell her. "You spend a lot of time up here?"

"I come and chill after my people are sleeping," she says. "Work on my songs. Are you a musician?"

"Sort of, why?"

"You look like one. What do you play?"

"Little bit of everything. Grew up playing gospel and rock and roll and blues. Guitar, bass, drums. DJed for a long time. Played in church a lot. I love everything."

"Everything?" she says.

"'War Pigs.' 'White Lines.' 'What a Friend We Have in Jesus.' Everything."

"You like classical?" she asks.

"Classical. Opera. I'd stand in this treehouse and sing 'Nessun Dorma' to the stars, if I could."

"How about country?"

What the heck. I'll probably never see her again. I stand to the rail, hold forth my hand and sing the intro to "The Gambler."

"Dang, you do love everything," she says.

"I don't particularly love that Billy Joel song about the uptown girl."

"Yeah, me neither," Jena replies. "I'd like to do music full time but I know you gotta have something to fall back on. Is mental health what you wanted to do or was this like your plan B?"

"More like a Plan G," I confess. "Ever hear that saying *Life is what happens while you make other plans?*"

"I think so," Jena says. "Who said that?"

"Jesus."

"Really?"

"No."

"But you went to college, right?" she asks.

"College kinda came to me," I tell her.

We stand there staring out over the land until she clears her throat. "Can I ask you something else? How'd you get started?" she says, chewing at her thumbnail. "I'm, um, thinking about doing what you do? I'd like to."

"You can see how glamorous it is," I say, pointing to the blood on my shirt and my beat-up old Saturn parked in the drive. "And the money. I've made tens of dollars in mental health."

"Seriously," she says, "I thought you'd be a good person to ask. You seem real good at it."

"Aw, I don't know about that. . . ." I hesitate, look off. There's a set of three radio towers, maybe ten miles east, their red lights glowing one by one. The sheriff's car is at least half an hour away. "You really wanna know?"

"Ralph's fine, we can see him from up here," Jena says.

We sit cross-legged on the treehouse floor and lean against the branches. "So," she says, "how *did* you become the midnight crisis guy?"

"The hardest part of a story," I tell her, "is finding a place to start."

Lumberyards & Bars

"All personal theology should begin with the words: Let me tell you a story. . . ." — Sue Monk Kidd

I stare across the lumberyard at the Central Bank Time and Temperature sign.

9:45 a.m. 101 degrees.

I am fifteen years old, working in my father's mill. Trustees from the local prison and me. Sawdust. Sweat. Murderous summer sun.

"Blaine," says the inmate on the other side of our pallet of loose lumber. Armed robbery, liquor store, nine years ago. Every day at lunch, he sits in the shade of the boxcar and eats a cheese sandwich from a greasy paper sack.

"Blaine."

I grab my end of a twenty-foot cottonwood slab, nod to the convict and together we heave it onto the conveyer chain and grab the next board down. And the next.

And the next. Another forklift with more pallets pulls in behind the first.

"When do they stop?" I ask.

"Them forklifts," says the prisoner, "they don't ever stop."

9

"You niggas get ya hustle on," the black driver on the second forklift shouts to us. "Ain't got all day."

On the Central Bank Time and Temp sign, the clock flashes *9:49 a.m. 101 degrees.*

9:49 a.m. 101 degrees.

I stare down my father when he makes his bossman pass. He motors over on his ATV, shaking his head. "Working man's day is eight hours, son," he says.

Sweating it out through a long, miserable summer, I save my money and buy a silver-on-black Fender Strat guitar and three hundred dollars' worth of DJ gear.

"Baby," Aunt Mimi suggests, "find a way to get paid doing what you love. Doing what you would do anyway for free. That's the best job you'll ever have. 'Specially if it's in the air conditioning."

I get hired on at the mall record shop and DJ freelance on the side. Sock hops and proms, gospel, hip hop and rock and roll radio stations. Nightclubs. Give me a bar over the lumberyard any day. Long as I am up high in the DJ booth looking over the crowd. I like to study people's behavior, watching how the liquor makes them change, how some turn sad while others get happy or mad. I love making them feel sexy or silly or sentimental just with the songs and the ways that I play them. And it's not for free by far. Ten to twenty bucks an hour. Cash, plus tips.

Fools & Roosters |

A pack of young men in matching clothes swaggers through the club, shoulders swaying and jaws clenched tight. Their leader is a short but wide guy with a spray-on tan, tribal tattoos and too much mousse in his hair. He trades threatening gestures with a drunken knot of freshmen on the other side of the dance floor. Foolish roosters looking to fight are nothing new in a college dive, it happens almost every Thursday night.

"Watch this," I tell Jenn, the girl tending bar.

I play a song whose time has passed, that radio has run into the ground. With the bass and treble pulled flat and the sound low enough for voices to be heard over the mix.

Roosters and fools exchange words from a distance. The matching pack moves purposely through the crowd. Just as they get close, I cut straight into the hottest song of the night, with the bass stacked and volume pumping. The people scream, swarm the dance floor and both fools and roosters are swallowed in the rush.

At the song's end I mix in a classic, match the beat faster and one notch louder. Hands are in the air like they just don't care about tomorrow or anything but tonight and the energy in the room ramps up higher. The matching men retreat to a corner and brood. I spotlight them in red and release the fog.

The song dies down and the matching men march the

perimeter, rattled but still with blood in their eyes. I hit the season's slow jam, the love song that makes everyone sway and fumble for sloppy kisses. A girl appears, the leader's crush, she pulls him away by the fingers, their center fades, the men disperse.

"Tempo, timing," I say with my hand fanned out over the room. "Bow down, peoples. I run this place."

"Fool," Jenn snorts, "You ain't even old enough to get in here."

"Oh yeah . . ."

"See that chick in the polka-dot tube top?" Jenn laughs and points to a girl in mid-sway. "She's real self-conscious about her smile but the more shots she drinks, the less she covers her mouth with her hand. Gave her two already, on the house. Tempo, timing, tequila. We run this place."

Some time later, a drunk Women's Studies student waves two dollars and asks me to please, please play "Funky Cold Medina." "Like, right now," she begs.

"I'll play it," I tell her. "But lemme wait and hit it at the right time."

"You DJs," she slurs with a tipsy contempt. "Y'all are all just voyeurs and control freaks." She shoves the bills deep into my front pocket and leans in close with her fingertips lingering. "Play my song, okay, Mr. DJ?"

"I'm a storyteller," I yell after she's walked away. "An artist!"

"Hey, MC Van Gogh," Jenn says. "Some kid puked in the back hall. Watch the bar."

I wave her off and tweak the bass, creeping the beats down into the pocket, one song becoming another, at one with the peoples.

"Tempo," I murmur. "Timing. Little stories, one into the other. . . ."

Dancing in the corner, there's a green-eyed blonde, skin dark under black lights and the taste of sweat on her lips as she loses herself in the music. She raises one hand, points to the sky and closes her eyes.

Everywhere the Music Takes You

"I'm not saying it's wrong for you to work in bars, little brother," the pastor suggests. "Just that a young man has to be careful."

As college begins, I turn loose of the nightclub scene and take the weekend shift at a full gospel radio station. Most Charismatics I meet seem pretty flaky but the few that are genuine touch my heart and I often find myself visiting their places of worship.

I like the way a good church service teeters between chaos and ecstasy, the overflow of emotion into tears and laughter and shouts of tongues and Hallelujah. Holy Rollers have the best music by far, that electric mix of country, soul and rock and roll, slain in the Spirit and Jericho march. I love their Jesus too, earthy and concerned and always so very close.

I grew up in the passive brand of Catholicism. No emotion. Rote prayers. Distant God. Always wanted more. Leaving the religion of my youth, I convert to the full-on apostolic bombast of Pentecostals.

My church buddy Caleb is a tiny fellow with a flat-top haircut and a hole in his heart who's been through a lot of sickness and tragedy in his life. Though small in stature, he's an old soul with faith like a mighty oak. I'm just a lapsed Catholic with a bad case of magical thinking, a scatterbrained mystic who looks like a roadie for Foghat.

There's an interfaith campus mixer held at the home of two flirty Baptist sisters with long legs and short skirts. Caleb and I sing a little for the co-eds then slip out to the back porch swing to swap blues licks.

"We oughta start us a gospel band," Caleb says. "Somewhere between Southern rock and country."

"Like a Pentecostal Skynryd," I reply.

"Like if Hank showed up at Sun Studio to sing hymns with Elvis and Cash and Jerry Lee."

"Like all of 'em together," I come back, "with a bit of Little Milton and Jimmy Martin thrown in."

"Misfits for Jesus," says Caleb, with his apple pie smile. "The world could always use a few more, come on."

We recruit a drummer and lead guitarist and perform at youth rallies and church fairs and all-night sings — anywhere they'll have us, really. With the radio voice and fundamental unction, I am elected preacher of the group. Sometimes I speak from the heart but mostly I stick to the evangelical script, the notion that God can be earthy and concerned and close — as long as you are one of us. A lot Charismatics like their message mixed with a good measure of arrogance and at my worst I am all ego, flash and Amway Jesus. To tell the truth, in church circles, success comes easier when you follow the script.

I'm still DJing in various venues, playing rhythm guitar in a black Southern gospel group, lead in a punk outfit with some art school kids and bass/vocals in the Christian country band.

My attention span is limited to say the least. One genre, one project, I can never keep my scope too focused. I want to meet all the sweet crazy people and go to all the outrageous places music can take you, to watch the way art changes lives and songs bring people together. I want to be in the mix of it all and not miss a thing.

Within the span of six weeks, I play a Power and Holy Ghost Revival in a converted service station on the south side

of town, an all-ages punk gig where our singer pulls pantyhose over his head with oranges for eyes and sings the Cramps'
"Human Fly" — and a church cakewalk that nearly turns Klan
rally. *Plus*, DJ a gay Sadie Hawkins dance where I don't figure
out what's going on until an hour into the set and perform an
improv set of Beethoven fakes at a ladies-only cocktail cotillion.
There's a gold-leaf harpsichord in a back room at the college
music hall and I've been sneaking back there to teach myself
the "Moonlight Sonata." If a heavy metal polka band needs a
drummer, I'm there.

I change my major from Astronomy to Music to Radio/TV/
Film. Algebra is kicking my *a* double *s* to the power of *x*. College
is just something to fall back on anyway.

The local rock radio station gives me an afternoon shift and
says my stock is rising. I have a hard time getting female listen-
ers off the request line. They tell me I'm easy to talk to and have
a nice voice.

Dr. Strong |

"You a college student?" the woman asks. I'm spinning records at a local roller rink when she approaches.

"Yes ma'am," I reply.

"*Ma'am*, I like that," she says. "I'm charge nurse out at Forest Hills Psychiatric Facility. You seem pretty good with people, kids and all. I'm looking to hire a new tech, if you're interested. It's a great college job."

I ask Pastor Reddy — the same one who good-naturedly warned me about liquor and bars and temptations of the flesh — what he thinks about working at the psych ward.

"I feel a peace about it, brother," he says. "You can help teach those people. God can use you to change hearts."

Forest Hills is a big sprawling estate, like the Southfork Ranch on *Dallas*. We have horses and a swimming pool and a full-sized gym. Awesome job for a college kid. Psych techs get free meals, use of laundry, study time, paid to watch movies and play dominoes and volleyball. Punctuated by occasional naked anarchy, screaming word salad and free-for-all psychotic wrestling matches.

Straitjackets have just been banned, labeled inhumane, so when something breaks loose, it's up to the techs to lock it down with physical restraints. I know some wrestling holds from buddies in the business and an old cowboy bouncer teaches me this secret: *Keep your cool, make it your goal that nobody gets hurt and things will almost always end well.* Other than the occasional carpet burn, he's right.

There's a rush of static before the announcement breaks over the psych ward PA system.

"*Dr. Strong, PICU.*"

There are four units at Forest Hills Psych. Adult, Addiction, Adolescents and PICU: Psychiatric Intensive Care Unit. A super-lockdown for severely violent or psychotic patients.

"*DR. STRONG, PICU.*"

Code Blue calls resuscitation, Code Red is for fire. Code Black for severe weather. Dr. Strong means combative patient/assault, all staff arrive stat.

I sprint down the long hall from Adolescents, past Addiction and take a right through the adult unit. There's a narrow pane in the PICU door. Through it I see a Morgan Freeman–looking man in green and white striped pajamas. He shouts *F*ck off, Satan!* and throws an end table into the Plexiglas.

"*DR. STRONG, PICU!*"

The RN has barricaded herself in the nurses' station. She bugs out her eyes and waves me in. I turn and scan the East Hall. The West. The wall clock reads 1:13 a.m. No one else is coming. Psycho Morgan Freeman growls about Uncle Sam's camera and kicks out the drywall. The nurse has spotted me; it's too late to slip away. The patient turns, his arms and chest bowed; we stare at each other through the pane. He's bigger than me, older and slower maybe but infused with the power of psychosis. *Help*, I pray, paralyzed but too curious to turn away. The acid smell of adrenaline is in the air. No one else is coming. I fumble for my key and open the door.

No Rock and Roll |

Caleb picks me up from the psych ward Sunday afternoon and takes me to a Holiness church out past the mill where we are scheduled to play two songs before the evangelist speaks.

We're off to the side tuning up when the Reverend steps to us, his countenance stern. "Talk to you boys in my office a minute?"

The music minister trails behind him, his lightbulb head bald and shiny on top, the sides and back ringed with brown baby-fine hair. He narrows his lizard eyes and throws us a look of disgust, like a man who just discovered someone took a leak in his lemonade.

The Reverend shuts the door behind us and shakes his head. He's Andy Rooney with Roosevelt's mustache. "We don't allow rock and roll in this church," he says.

"Well, uh, no sir," Caleb explains. "We play a, um . . . a good old *gospel* sound. With a country flavor. But you know," — pats me on the back — "*really* sold out for church."

"For church," I agree, my arm slung around Caleb's skinny neck. There's a mirror on the back wall and I steal a glimpse. We look like Opie and Slash.

The music minister stands with hands on his hips, beaming like a snitch. The Reverend leans in, speaking to Caleb but leering at me. "There will be no rock and roll in this house. You all understand, now?"

Caleb nods. "Yes sir," I answer.

Scalded, we head back to the sanctuary. The church is packed with old school holy rollers, men with crewcuts in long-sleeve white shirts and high-water slacks, women with no makeup or jewelry, hair pinned and piled high, dresses to the floor showing not even an ankle for lust.

"Welcome to 1955," Caleb says.

The youth pastor announces us and we take the stage, backed by the house praise band. I step to the mic. Feedback shrills. A legion of eyeballs gives me the stink. Caleb leans in and whispers, "Do your thing, Jamie. You sing first."

I count it down and we kick hard into "I Saw the Light," double time from Hank, heavy on the backbeat, driving guitars. Thirty seconds pass. A minute. The Reverend stands and starts to jig. People spill out into the aisles, clapping on the two and four, shouts go up, a woman with a big gray bun begins to keen; the church breaks loose, speaking in tongues, pogo-ing, gripping the pew backs, praising the Lord and wailing red-faced at Satan to get thee behind.

As Caleb takes the verse, a small dark-skinned man steps into the space between the altar and pews. He raises both hands, jerks and glossolalia gushes forth.

SHALA CORO-DEH BO-SEEKIA OH SHAMBACH ELA CON HI

Another man moves in, just behind him to the right. He slips off his shoes, lies facedown on the floor and starts to weep.

We pick up the pace and medley into "Jesus on the Mainline." I sing it with full-on fever, sweating through my coat jacket, hair in my eyes. A woman in a denim skirt and white Keds runs full speed from front to back with one finger lifted high. *Hoah!* She shouts at the corners. *Glo-ray!* A seventy-something-year-old man with a greasy black combover dances around the side rows and up past the platform. As he passes, he pulls out a harmonica and blows furious notes, every one in time and tune.

Caleb shoots up his eyebrows, grins wide and we lean back to back while he slings a flurry of notes from his flattop guitar.

I search the crowd for the music minister. He stands to the side swaying, hands held high, eyes tightly shut, his bald dome shining in the light.

We shamble and crash to an end. The evangelist storms the pulpit and motions for us to jump back in. We find the groove again as the little firecracker of a man with orange flame hair and a forest green suit paces the platform, down into the aisles, shouting his riff like Coltrane against the beat.

"*Jesus* is here. . . ."

"Jesus *is* here."

"Jesus is *here!*"

Then like a cross between Jimmy Swaggart and Muhammad Ali: "*Get up on your feet and make welcome the Alpha and Omega, the First and Last, Rose of Sharon, Lily of the Valley, Lion of Judah, Lamb of God, Prince of Peace, King of Kings and Lord of Lords, the Bread of Life and Bright Mornin' Star . . . !*"

The evangelist pauses; a sound like tornadoes fills the room.

"***JESUS! IS! HERE!!!***"

The congregation goes apocalyptic; we wait for the roof to blow, for blood red moons and crashing stars, for lightning to split the eastern sky and rapture us over the Jasper Wall. . . .

After the service, Caleb and I sit behind the baptismal pool, dazed and quiet. The Reverend slips into the tiny space, lays his palm on Caleb's shoulder and presses his hand into mine.

"Hal-le-lu-jah," he says. "The Lord bless and keep you both."

He leaves the room. I open my hand. There is a thick wad of bills.

Caleb laughs and sweeps the air with the flat of his hand. "There'll be *no rock and roll* in this house."

Together for the Good |

At times, late nights on the psych ward can be peaceful. Just after meds, out on the porch for the last smoke of the night, passing around the pack of community cigarettes, lighting them end to end, people at the end of their rope talking about God and family and love and sex and work and making it through one day at a time.

This being the South, the group often holds little non-religious reprobate Bible studies before bed. They read verses about still waters and green pastures and the peace that passes understanding, about where sin abounds grace abounds more and forgiveness not seven but seventy times seven.

Fifteen cigarettes glowing in the dark, flashlight and a motel Bible. Old drunks and outlaws, loose women, outcasts, losers, dope fiends, failed suicides, schizophrenics.

I enjoy sitting, listening, having a laugh at how tricky and senseless and *totally unfu*king fair* life can be. (A jilted booze-hound once marched into the courtyard, determined to chant that phrase a thousand times or until she wasn't so angry anymore. "March on," I told her.)

I learn that you can't judge a book by its cover and that first impressions are often wrong. Some of the most down-to-earth good-hearted people I meet are drug addicts and deviants and manically depressed. It feels like good church to me.

"Religion is what we do. Everything else is just a bunch of religious talk." A bankrupt riverboat gambler with a five-star smack habit tells me this.

As my mind begins to open to different ideas about grace and goodness, my ministry message starts to change. I drop the evangelical scripts and begin to speak more about mercy and humility and maybe not taking ourselves so seriously. I tell the church folks about the old drunks and the terminally depressed and how they teach me to look for the good, to not believe everything I think, to pray for help and to know that as long as you are alive there is always time to start making better choices. That God is close to the broken and the lost and confused and that it's okay to admit that we are all human and screwed up and clueless sometimes.

The shiny happy Bee Gees Jesus is dear to my heart but I have to talk about the other side — that dark-eyed Lord of Glory with dirt beneath his nails, the troublemaking Son of God who shows up when drunks march courtyards and cry that life is unfair, the Christ who is there when schizophrenics throw chairs and just want to go home, the Light of the World who loves people at gay bars and Klan rallies and Park Avenue garden parties, the King of Peace who turns over tables and makes water into wine, the Great High Priest whose Good News went something like this:

Those of you
so sure
you've got it together,
don't.
& those you call lost
are closer
to the Kingdom
than you.

Sometimes it goes over okay and other times it comes across as some long-haired heretic preaching Universalism in a redneck Bible Belt church. So you can imagine.

It's Sunday evening, a year or so after I started working at the psych ward. Old Pastor Reddy catches me in the church foyer after service and calls me over. With his curly wisp of hair and ear-to-ear smile, he reminds me of a middle-aged Charlie Brown.

"How's the mental health mission field?" he asks.

I try to find a way to sum it up, to compose the right words to where the pastor can understand. "Remember when you told me God could use me to change those people?" I ask him.

"Yuh," he says. "How goes it?"

"Pastor, I think God's using those people to change me."

Reddy looks at me kind of sideways a minute before sliding his arm around my shoulder. "Well," he says, "I guess we help change each other. Can I pray for you?"

"Yeah, sure," I say, closing my eyes.

He places his hand on the back of my neck and bows his head. "Father," he says. "Watch out for your boy here. Guide him with wisdom and protection and help him walk in kindness and bring light and life and goodness wherever he goes. We ask these things, in Your name, amen."

"Amen," I agree. There's a silence after genuine prayer, like Genesis again, like liquid peace poured over your soul. "So you, uh, think I oughta stick with it?"

"Son," he says, "we got too many preachers that can talk, not nearly enough that know how to listen."

"I don't know if I'm cut out for that preacher part."

"Ministry," Pastor Reddy says, pointing through the front glass to the *Git-R-Dunn* car wash and the laundromat just past the liquor store, "is out there."

"I'll try," I say.

"Just do your best," he says, giving me a quick hug before walking away.

"Hey Pastor," I call. "Is it wrong to ask for a sign or somethin'?"

"I got faith in you, brother," he calls back. "You'll find your way."

I change my major from Radio/TV/Film to Journalism. Grammar kills me. From Journalism to Biblical Archeology. Jews built the Sphinx. College is probably just something to fall back on anyway.

The psych ward asks me to come on regular. Bosses there tell me I have a reputation for being a good hand, that I am well liked by patients and staff and calm in the storm. I put them off, saying that right now, I've just got too much going on.

Fall Back | Until the Stars Steady Again

After a rock radio afternoon and seven to eleven shift at the psych ward, I swing by Caleb's house to talk about our band. Despite making a pretty bland record at a big shot Nashville studio, good things are happening. Tour buses, managers and major label deals are all in the works.

"You ready for this?" Caleb says as we ramble down the side streets of his neighborhood. He's wearing overalls with no shirt and looks so fragile it seems like the wind could just carry him away.

"Man, I don't know. Yeah. I guess. You?"

"I don't know," he says. It's one of those walks where you talk awhile and then you just walk and think before you say anything else.

"You ever wonder sometimes," he asks, "if the wanting ain't better than the having?"

"How you figure?" I say.

"I miss playing them little churches. Putting our stage clothes on in the truck out back. Playing jokes on each other. Laughing all the time. Sometimes I feel like maybe dreamin' is the best part."

"We don't have to lose that."

"I know. It ain't that. Guess I don't know how to say it," he says.

A shepherd trots up, his paws at my pockets and nose cold against the back of my hand. "Get on now, Luke," says Caleb.

Luke switches behind and walks at our heels, calm when Caleb scratches behind his ear.

"You ever think about Enoch?" Caleb says.

"Enoch . . . " I answer.

"Enoch in the Bible," he replies. "Enoch arrived. He walked with God." Caleb fishes through his pocket, pulling out a pinch of Red Horse Tobacco. "I like that part says *Enoch was, then he was not, for God took him.*"

"I like that part too," I say.

The night air carries the sweet smell of barbecue and laundry. Lights in the houses are dim and walking the block this late, it feels like we're the only two people alive.

"You gonna hold up okay on the road?" I ask.

He shoots me a look, like maybe I knew something he thought he was hiding better. "Havin' a hard time keeping my breath," he says, with a hand to his chest. "But I'll be all right."

"We'll strap you to a dolly if we have to," I tell him. "Roll you on stage."

Caleb laughs then lifts his skinny fist and points just over the trees. "You see that?"

"See what?"

"Shootin' star."

"Missed it," I say. "I always miss it. Never seen one."

"I've seen a million," he says, tossing his boots by the mailbox as we make another pass. "Keep looking. I bet we'll see another."

Boxcars collide in the downtown yard. Late night in the South, you can always hear faraway trains. "What would you do?" he asks. "If you could do what you wanted?"

"I kinda liked writing."

"What happened with that?" he says.

"Commas," I reply with a poker face.

"Hate them commas," he says. "The devil's tail."

Sprinklers swish over from fresh-cut grass, splashing the blacktop near our feet. Luke drifts away. "Ever see yourself settling down, kids and a house, regular job and all that?" he asks.

"Not really," I say, shaking my head. "You?"

His face takes on a different look, older and more serious than I've seen before.

"Naw."

A white trace of light streaks the sky. "Right there," Caleb says, tracking the path with his finger. "See it?"

"I saw it," I tell him.

"First one you ever seen?" he asks.

"First one," I say. "Guess I never paid attention."

Another falls, then another. Two at once, then three. "Jamie, look," he says low. For sixty seconds or so, showers of light fall, stars dying in the night sky.

"I ain't ever seen this many," he says.

We stand there with our heads pitched back until the stars steady again.

"Maybe that's Enoch," he says, spitting tobacco in the cattails and clapping his hands. "A whole carload of Enochs, goin' home."

"Maybe," I say. "Maybe so."

"I bet whatever happens," Caleb says, "we'll look back on this right here and it'll be the best part. This right now."

"You never know, do you?"

Then, for a long time, we just walk and watch the sky.

The art boys from the punk band move to Orlando. The black gospel brothers take time away. I show up to my radio job one day only to find out they switched us from rock to soft pop overnight. I am cut back to weekends, then let go.

On a Wednesday night before practice, the guitar player in our Christian group suggests I cut my hair, be more conventional and focus completely on the band.

"It's not fair," he says. "We all want to take this thing to the next level." I catch Caleb's eye but he's a million miles away.

"I understand," I tell them. "Call me gone."

I accept the regular shift at Forest Hills and change my major to Psych. I don't have much faith in college, but at least I can fall back and fake it until I figure something else out.

Caleb dies of a heart attack at age 21. He was, and then he was not. For God took him and he arrived.

PART II

Bothered by Bright Lights

"A watchman is an important person, but he doesn't do much. He knows the dawn is coming; there's no doubt concerning that. Meanwhile, he is alert to dangers, he comforts restless children and animals. He waits and he listens and he watches." — Eugene Peterson

Tiger Stripes & White Tires

There's something about fall nights on a college campus that makes you feel edgy and alive, like God hides in the magnolias at the water's edge and whispers *Psst. Hey. Hey you. This is the secret of life. Don't miss anything.*

Or at least it feels this way when you are trying to cram for a Botany exam with friends from class. Tombo's a Phys Ed major, a born instigator with a devilish Nicholson grin. Sheryl and Shanna are good-time girls, bused to college from the sticks, suitemates from the all-girl dorm across the way.

After a three-hour stint of cellular mitosis and plant systematics the four of us take a study break walk. Next to the stadium dumpsters, we find a Strawberry Shortcake bicycle with white tires and a basket on the bars.

"Dare you," Tombo says. "Ride to the quad and back. In your underwear."

"That's like, a mile," I reply.

"Double dare," says Sheryl.

It's October cold. I pull down the corner of my shorts. "I've got on tiger stripe boxers."

"Double *dog* dare," Shanna adds.

"If I do this," I tell them, "we go to the Pancake Shack and you guys are buyin'."

"Deal," says Tombo.

"Deal," says Sheryl while Shanna nods.

"I'm gone."

The air on bare skin feels freezing at first, then fresh, then free, like swimming without a suit. Cheers rise up from a balcony. A horn blows, laughter and hoots. The footfall of my friends as they chase from behind.

I pop a wheelie through the quad and turn back. Just as I pass the bookstore, a campus cop hits the lights.

Standing on the pedals, pumping, I tear through the grass, duck behind the natatorium, throw the bike in tall weeds and dive beneath the footbridge.

Sheryl, Shanna and Tombo tiptoe in from the other side and throw me my clothes. We hide there giggling, ten miles high while police spotlights scan the land around us.

"This is the best night ever!" Shanna whispers frantically.

"Shhh," we say, laughter spilling from the edges of our hands.

When all is dark and quiet we dash back to the car.

In the Pancake Shack booth there's blueberry waffles and scrambled eggs, ice-cold milk in metal cups.

"You know what?" says Sheryl. "I hope we don't ever get old and boring."

Shanna stabs her half-stack of pecan pancakes and holds forth the bite. "I hope we never stop having fun."

"Me too," says Tombo.

"Me too," says me.

"Forever young," says Sheryl. We clink cups and stare at our reflections in the front glass. Adventure-shabby hair and crooked clothes, midnight tired from mischief, a little bit drunk from laughing too hard. Sheryl frames our reflection with her fingers. "Take a picture" she says. "Young forever, let's never forget."

Not Yet Ready for the World |

I'm filling out the paperwork for graduation when my Psych advisor passes the office.

"Blaine, son, graduating, huh?" Stephens is a chubby little prof with woodpecker hair, thick gold-rimmed glasses and a voice somewhere between Mr. Haney and Yogi Bear.

"Guess so," I reply. "So — what can one do with a degree in Psychology?"

"All kinds of things," he exclaims in his Jellystone meets Green Acres tone. "You could . . . sell loafers, deliver papers, man a kiosk in the mall . . ." He slaps my back and his fuzzy eyebrows dance. "Have you thought about a future in cable TV installation?"

"Thanks for telling us this as we walk out the door."

". . . Or you could psych tech at the mental hospital," he suggests.

"Been there three years now."

"Well," he says, resting his chin in the web of flesh between his first finger and thumb, "you could always just keep on going."

"Seriously," I say.

"GRE is in two weeks," he says. "Give it a shot."

I have a vision: cubicle prisons, collared shirts. Riding the time clock until the rut closes in on both ends. I fear becoming the living dead, those zombie Americans sacrificing dreams and selling their souls for a white picket fence and a pension. So I do what bewildered, not-yet-ready-for-the-world students do. I apply to grad school.

"Son, be careful," Pastor Reddy tells me when I let him know of my plans. "Psychology is fine and good but don't let those crackpots get your mind all messed up."

"Pastor," I say, "they said the same thing about you." This he finds hilarious.

"Just stay close to Jesus," Reddy says. "Okay?"

Somehow, by grace, I blow out the GRE, even though I graduated with a 2.8 GPA. I pick up an application for grad school but the lady in Financial Aid informs me that my grants won't pay. "After you get that first diploma," she says, "they're done with you."

I'm walking back across campus trying to decide whether to join the circus or go back to rock radio when I run into the Head of Education, Dean Gage.

"Heard you're thinking about a Master's," he says. Gage's daughter hangs out in the roller rink DJ booth. Sometimes we couple skate.

"Nah, they just told me," I reply, jerking my thumb towards Financial Aid. "No more cash."

"Meet me in my office in thirty minutes," Gage says, "and let's see what we can do."

An hour later, I've got a full paid assistantship and a tag to park ten steps from the Psych department's front door.

Wolcott Hall stands on the water's edge. I sit in my car, watching paddleboats stream by, trying to decide how I should feel. Grateful? Surely. Conflicted? Yeah, that too. I'm not a counselor; I'm a goofball, the guy who told high school guidance his dream job would be playing Tigger at Disney. But what else am I gonna do? DJ the rest of my life? Sometimes you take the door that opens.

Closer to God with Cowgirl Strippers at the Coffee House College Bar

"Fifty bucks apiece plus tips, two one-hour sets, acoustic," says Spike. "We can play whatever we want. You in?"

Spike is bone-thin and brittle, legally blind and sits behind me in Abnormal Psych. Severely diabetic and unable to drive, he could draw disability but instead works two jobs, goes to college full time, parties like a frat boy and is the most live-life-to-the-fullest guy I know. He's got a regular Thursday night gig at a little hot spot near campus but says his stuff is getting stale and he needs a partner with new songs.

"Lemme think about it," I tell him. "But yeah, sounds good."

I've been pretty active with the church youth program lately and sort of gave up working in bars. But technically Spike's gig is not a bar. Just to be considerate, I let Marky, the youth pastor, know my plans.

"It's really just a coffeehouse," I explain. "In fact, that's the name. The Coffee House."

"Original," he says. "By the college, huh. They sell liquor?"

"Yeah. And uh, you know, burgers and stuff. Coffee."

He smiles, just a little. "Do they sell more liquor or coffee?"

"Liquor," I confess.

"You know, we could sure use someone to lead the singing

35

down at Grace Place, brother. If you wanna bless people with your talents. . . ." Marky's a good guy, just giving me a hard time. "Sing a little. Feed the hungry."

I pull the neck of my t-shirt over my face and fan away the heat, trying to think of a good reason not to sing at the soup kitchen.

"The whole hairnet thing," I say, gesturing around my curly mop.

"Go do your thing, man," Marky says, goosing my ribs until I giggle and run away.

The Coffee House is a dark, narrow space with low tables and couches around the edges, just down from fraternity row, right between Hairport Beauty Salon and E-Z Money Loans. Our stage is against the left wall by the door, about seven feet high and no bigger than a kitchen table at the top. A steep set of stairs with wrought-iron rails stands front and center.

"Who built our stage, the Mayans?" I ask.

"*Yes!*" Spike says, thrusting up his index and pinky fingers. "The Mayans!" He grabs a beer from the bar. "So what's the set list?"

"Side one of *Shotgun Willie*," I tell him, glancing over the meager crowd. "Side two of *G N'R Lies.*"

"Cool," he says.

"I'm joking."

We hike our gear to the summit and play Oasis and Otis Redding, Prince and Pink Floyd. Lenny Kravitz into Haggard into the Backstreet Boys. Anything really.

Customers watch from couches with heads pitched back like they're at a planetarium show. Between songs they clap politely. Someone yells out *Skynyrd!*

"Every f'n night," Spike says, rolling his eyes.

"I can fix this," I tell him.

I play a seven-minute version of "Simple Man" just to shut 'em up but sure enough not two songs later some other fool yells *Skynyrd!* again. To that we offer a long medley of "Mr.

Banker" and "Curtis Lowe" into "That Smell" and "Stairway to Freebird." Nobody yells *Skynyrd!* again.

It's two hours into the set, busier than usual and people are actually making a little ruckus for us between songs. A raven-haired beauty of uncertain ethnicity hauls herself up the stairs and pulls at my elbow.

"Hey, hey, you," she says. She's dressed in a tight black skirt and low-cut western blouse that strains to contain the amplitude of her curves. A sketchy-looking guy waits at the bottom, eyeing her backside as she leans into me and shouts, "Play 'Closer' by Nine Inch Nails."

I stare at her, then at her fellow. He grins and gives me two thumbs up. The girl braces herself against the rail and stifles a belch. "Whoa," she says. "I'm a little drunk. 'Closer,' you gotta play it for me, okay?"

"I've got, like, an acoustic guitar here." I lift it to prove my point.

Pushing herself upright and running both hands through her hair, she leers and swishes her hips. "'Closer' by Nine Inch Nails makes every girl want to get *naked*." She whispers this in my ear like it's a secret you'd climb a Chinese mountain to hear. The hem of her skirt creeps slowly up her thigh, her fingers pulling fabric over skin until the tattoo shows. Road Runner.

Two college girls at the table stage left start whooping. "Play it!" says a thin, tall blonde. "Hells yeah!" the smaller busty blond chimes in.

"If you play it, I'll do a three-piece," the girl on the stairs sings seductively.

"Three-piece?" I say.

Sketchy guy steps up, a five-dollar bill between his first two fingers. "Three-piece, dude." His right eyebrow rises. "Candie here's a dancer."

"Closer! Closer!" the co-eds chant. Sketchy Guy laughs and lays the cash on top of my guitar case. "Just play it, bro. . . ."

I look to Spike, deep into his fourth Zima Gold. He holds up the bottle and waggles his head, his binocular glasses refracting in the red and purple spotlights. "All *right!*" he says.

"Okay, okay, do this," I tell him.

boomp psst boomp psst boomp psst boomp psst

I nod as he mimics my beat box and Stripper Girl begins to sway.

"Just dance now, keep your clothes on," I tell her.

"Are you queer?" she shoots back.

"Don't wanna get in no trouble." I point to the owner, Ms. Becky, over at the bar.

"Get it *nek*-kid!" Ms. Becky yells, raising her wine and giving her rear a little shake. I bug out my eyes and make cutting motions to my neck. Sketchy Guy nods at me and says something in her ear. She nods back, pushes him away and starts a slow corkscrew towards the ground.

I wave the college girls on stage. "*Help me.*" They crawl up, smelling like two-for-one tap beer and Designer Imposters bodyspray.

"Who-ooo!" Tall Blonde croaks into the mic, knocking our guitars with her bony knees. Spike wobbles right and gestures for me to sing.

boomp psst boomp psst
you make me wanna chase you

Small Blonde eyes me from the side and punches my arm, hard. "That ain't the fruhggin' words!"

"Shut it, Blondie," I reply. "Or make up your own."

Spike finds his groove between beat box and acoustic guitar; Tall Blonde and Small bump their butts and boozily sing,

you make me bake a cake for you

A hush falls over the room as Stripper Girl arches back and tugs at the snaps of her blouse.

We make our fifty apiece and another forty in tips. Spike disappears while I'm playing out the night with "People Get Ready." Stripper Girl is too-much-Kahlua drunk and her fellow has to lead her away by the arm. At the door she breaks free, kisses her fingers and holds them out to me again and again. I catch her kisses and throw them out over the room as the last stragglers cheer. Sketchy gives me one last thumbs-up just before he tucks her into the car. Iroc-Z.

In the parking lot Tall Blonde watches as Small Blonde steadies herself against my shoulder and tries to get her shoes on. "I need to quit getting drunk every night," Tall says in a scratchy voice.

"Shua, me," Small agrees, poking a finger into her own chest.

"Girl," Tall tells her friend, with the sort of truthful tone that comes to Southern girls when the liquor begins to wane. "We need to start gettin' our asses back to church. Or somethin'."

"I know that's right," Small replies.

"Come on," I say. "I'll go with y'all."

Small Blonde flutters her lids and tries to focus on my face, her milk-cow eyes slitted now. The collar of her shirt is beer-soaked and the bottom rides up over her belly. She only has one shoe on. "I likes your hair," she says, reaching out to pet me like a spaniel. Covering her mouth, she makes a sudden sour face, then shakes it off and smiles. "What your name was again?"

I show up to Grace Place the next afternoon, tuck my hair under a hat and empty my tips into the offering box.

"Brother J! Glad you could make it!" Marky strides over, his bright Christian smile shining like the morning sun. "Your friends comin', huh?"

I point to the big picture window just past the serving tables. A silver pickup pulls up and parks. Two blondes in sweatpants and ponytails make their way through the door. When they spot me, the lanky one sashays her hips while the shorter busty girl bats her lashes and pulls open her shirt 'til we can see the color of her bra. Black.

"Oh, Lordy," Marky says and everybody laughs.

"Pastor," I reply, "meet my friends."

Gotta Run to Keep from Hidin' |

Forest Hills offers me a slot on intake and assessment. Three nights a week, from six p.m. to six a.m., I carry a pager for crisis calls that come in requesting on-site psychological evaluations.

Florentine is the intake manager. With his trim mustache and black helmet, of hair, he looks like a tough but smart-alec detective from an '80s cop drama. "The pager rarely goes off but if it does and you get stuck, call me," he says. "You know how to take vital signs, right?"

"Yeah, sure," I tell him. "Why?"

"If you get somebody in detox," he says, "stop at the liquor store. You don't want nobody dying on your watch."

"I'll call you," I reply.

"Just act like you know what you're doing," Florentine suggests. "Nobody will ever know the difference."

They pay me fifteen dollars an hour to go out, door to door. Two bucks an hour just to be on-call. A month of free money passes before my first dispatch at ten after ten on an icy Thursday night.

The caller says the patient has been a closet drinker for a long time; there was a dramatic intervention and the family wants him in rehab — tonight. "We're counting on you, sir," Caller says. "It's pretty near life or death at this point."

A fallen angel from the psych ward once told me if I ever

felt scared or insecure to just become someone else. "Like an actor," she said. I pull on my lambskin coat and a black cowboy hat and set out to meet the patient at the far end of the Rite-Aid parking lot.

The green Camry described by the caller waits. I park at the Quik Stop down the street and sit for what feels like a long time, staring at the car. *God*, I pray. *Little help here for the Midnight Rider or I'll mess this up real bad.*

Gathering my act, I walk across the lot and look down through the car window at my parents' next-door neighbor. Friendly guy, blue collar, gentle with his kids and wife. Helped my dad build a fence. I start to tell him I stopped at the store for some Funyuns and a coke and happened to see him there.

"Oh no," he moans. "It's you."

"Chris," I say. "This ain't your car."

"My brother-in-law's," he says. "Guy that called. I didn't want nobody to come with me. I haven't been drinking today. Been trying to straighten up but it's . . ." His forehead drops to the steering wheel and he starts to sob. "F*ck, man," he says, punching the dash.

I look down the street towards my truck. I don't know what to do. It's too late to leave.

"Hey, brother," I say, hunching down, elbows on the door-frame. "It'll be all right. I'm gonna get you to a better place."

"You don't know how bad it is."

I climb in on the passenger side. "Trust me. Been doing this stuff a long time. You're here now. You made the right choice. Things can be okay." These words, I don't even know where they come from.

"Ain't nothin' okay," Chris says. He turns to me and holds out a shaking hand. His fingernails are caked with grease from a part-time job at Eastside Tire and there's a purple welt beneath his eye. "I'm broke. My wife's ready to leave. I tried to quit a thousand times. But I can't man, I just can't."

"If you're ready, I'll help you get in," I say. "But you gotta want it. It's up to you."

Chris nods like he knows what I'm saying is true. He leans against the wheel. We sit in the sounds of passing traffic and the drone of yellow streetlights. The car smells like old books and Armor All. Dog hair on the seats. The emotion dies down a bit. "So what's with the get-up?" he asks.

"This is my first real call," I confess. "And this lady at the psych ward said if I was nervous to become somebody else, like in a movie or something."

"Really?" he says.

"Really," I reply.

"Counselor told you this?"

"No. A patient."

"And this is where you're gonna send me?"

"Pretty much, yeah."

Chris sits back in the seat and rolls his head from side to side. Even though it's cold and his window is open, sweat runs in rivulets down his face. "I don't know. I don't know if I can make it tonight."

"Let's just go one step at a time," I say, eyeing the neon Bacardi sign in the Rite-Aid window. "First, let me check your pulse . . ." I press my fingers to his wrist for fifteen seconds. "132," I tell him. "How do you feel?"

"Like hell."

"Dude, you're in detox. Let's go in the store, I'll buy you a bottle. Whatever you want."

Chris ducks down and studies the signs. Starts to say something then bites his lip. "No," he says, handing me the keys. "If we're going, let's go right now."

I'm driving the Camry towards rehab, figuring I've got a good excuse for barreling down the expressway with the needle on ninety-five. Chris has the passenger seat laid all the way back and his arm over his eyes. "Blaine," he grunts as we near the exit.

"Yeah?" I say.

"I'm glad it was you."

Orangutans Will Hug You for Skittles |

Standard deviation, bell curve, mean. Operant vs. respondent conditioning. Rat labs. Once you pass 101, this is the substance of college Psych.

Stimulus, response or response, stimulus? Which comes first? We have three-hour-long lectures on these subjects while I sit in the back and write storyboards for *KISS Visits Planet of the Apes*. I've got this brainstorm for a graphic novel series where pop culture icons collide. I don't want to give too much away but Prince saves Evel Knievel near the end. In Advanced Stats, I use graph paper to draw diagrams of the finale stage show in which Space Ace and Star Child band together with the Maker of Purple Rain to rock the Ape City Jamm. If I can just get my idea off the ground then maybe I can cut school and become an artiste, like Man Ray or Stan Lee.

"Sure you're in the right class, Mr. Blaine?" Dr. Glenn asks as he passes and glances at my notebook.

"It's *all* psychology, right, Doc?" I reply.

"Fair enough," he says. "See you at the zoo."

I pull down my clown mask and slip into the monkey's cage.

Even though he could tear me apart, Hooter cowers in the far corner. I speak his name sweetly and hold out the bag of Skittles. Hooter dashes up a tree, covering his eyes with his hands. I reach out and call to him. He presses into the tree limb, whimpers and hides his head beneath his arm.

Exiting the cage, I remove my coat and mask, wait five minutes and enter again. Hooter gazes down, his eyes suspicious.

"Come on, Hooter," I say.

Hooter scampers into my arms. He studies my face and pokes the candy bag with his long fingers. I shake a few out in my hand; Hooter takes them gladly, bounces a bit on my hip and flashes his million-dollar monkey smile. Zoo visitors coo from the other side of the glass.

Hoo Hoo Hoo, Hooter hoots.

Studies in racism as a conditioned response. My grad assistantship. The material is never published.

Dr. Glenn comes out to watch and is elated when I wrap a Gibbon around his neck. "How'd you get in here?" he asks. "We've been doing research for years now and they barely let us near the cages."

"Zookeeper's a buddy of mine," I tell him.

"Do all the study you want," says Glenn. "You got free rein."

A school group rushes the cage where I am feeding apple slices to Trixie and Dixie, twin lemurs in an outdoor cage near the zoo's lake.

I'm telling the students about the lemur species, the difference between ring-tailed and red-ruffed and the skunky-looking monkeys clinging to my arms and neck.

"They're cute and sweet," I tell the group, "but not very smart." I hold a piece of apple between my teeth and Dixie gnaws at the opposite end until our mouths touch.

"Ewww," says one girl but right on the tail of that, two more say, "Coooool. . . ."

Trixie bounds across the bars, causing the students to flinch back and shriek. She totters back to me and with a tiny black and white hand, takes firm hold of my crotch. Then, she offers something of a jig and impish snicker to the group of ten-year-old kids gathered around her cage. The raucous laughter of fifth graders fills the air. Their teacher stares as if I'm some sort of zoological pervert.

"Sorry," I say to her.

"C'mon, class," she says. "Let's go see the elephant."

Help Hope Hello |

Roller rink Friday and Saturday night, strobe lights and cotton candy, blacklights and birthday cakes, limbo rock and couples only, bleep out the curse words and pump the bass, smoke machines and disco balls, the smell of stale popcorn and dirty shoes, grape Bubble Yum and little girl perfume.

"We're getting swamped on parties," the rink owner, Mr. Ric, tells me. "Want to come DJ Saturday afternoons too?"

"Yeah, absolutely," I reply.

I'm driving reckless on the interstate back home, blaring the Misfits' "We Are 138." It's one step away from total noise and chaos, terrible and electric in the most epic way possible.

At my exit, I notice a new billboard. There's a responsible-looking woman, blandly attractive in an advertising sort of way, holding up a phone receiver with a look of professional concern on her face.

DEPRESSED? SUICIDAL? ADDICTED? THERE'S HELP. THERE'S HOPE. CALL 1-800-TALK-NOW.

It takes me a minute to realize the number rings to my hospital. Nurses screen the calls and patch them through to me. I am that woman.

Help. Hope. *Hello?*

I can't be that woman. I'm neither responsible nor blandly attractive nor conscientious enough to show a professional level of concern. *I* probably need help. And I hate drama. Who am I to get involved? Maybe I should just DJ and forget mental health. I back the track up, crank it louder and shout along,

IS IT TIME TO BE AN ANDROID / NOT A MAN

A few weeks later I'm called to the ER at two a.m. to see a reedy Los Angelite with jet black hair, his arms riddled with ink.

"Good luck getting much out of this one," the doctor says before I enter the patient's room.

Jet Black Angelite and I talk for a while — I try at least. He's skittish and shy, shaky from the meth, a long, long way from home. Then I notice a tattoo near his left wrist. The Misfits logo.

"138," I say, pointing to the skull.

He turns and makes eye contact for the first time. "You *know* that song?" he asks.

Brother Jumbo Thin Mint
& the Jaundiced Chimp

"But God chose the foolish to confound the wise."
— 1 Corinthians 1:27

The local Christian television station asks me to be a guest. Fascinated by the genre, I cannot resist and am booked for a Tuesday evening in the last hour of a three-hour show.

Before I appear, the musical guests are up, a church group from Albania. A swarthy man with an apple-shaped head plays an instrument, something resembling an end table with a handle on the side. He cranks his handle and a sound like kazoos in a meat grinder oozes forth while a spooky-eyed woman bangs a sporadic tambourine and atonally sings a three-note chorus for roughly nine minutes.

In the background, a sort of Latino-looking Yao Ming is folded into a school desk, hand-drumming on the lid with the sort of facial expressions that might accompany playing through the Angry Sun level from *Super Mario 3*.

They wheeze to a finish as the camera pans to fourteen men in cheap brown suits holding hands and singing "How Great Thou Art" in their native tongue, in unison.

While their last note dies, the show's host, a whaleish man with a bad toupee, rallies his fist and says, "Well, Halle-*lu*-jah!"

I'm standing there like I've just seen Father Abraham do the funky chicken when the stage director waves me onto the set.

As I stagger towards the host, trying to come up with an honest opening line to express astonishment sans profanity, a thought rushes into my head, so loud and alien, I know it must be the voice of the *LORD*.

This is where you will always belong.

"Great," I tell Jesus. "Of course."

The TV lights are hot and overly bright. I'm sweating from the heat and nervous energy. In a mint green jacket with black shirt and tie, the show's host reminds me of a supersized Girl Scout cookie. I don't mention this on air.

"You know," he brays, "through good times and bad . . . my life verse has been Romans, eight and twenty-eight: *And we know all things . . . work together. For the good . . .* Share with us, brother, if you will, *your* life verse."

It's a live three-hour show, on five nights a week. The host paces slow.

I shift in my seat and scratch behind my neck. "Psalm 2:4: *God sits in the heavens and laughs*," I tell him.

"Well, Glory," he replies. "That is a new one. On me."

"When I die," I say, "God'll tell me what he's laughing at. When he does, I'll laugh too. And everything will finally be all right." There's a bit of dead air. Then I say, "I hope."

He turns to the camera and carefully repeats my verse, as if viewers might be learning impaired. "Ha, *ha*," the host says. "That's an *incredible* impartation. From the Word. What a wonderful, inspired *hope* we have as joint heirs . . . with Christ."

"Now and then," I add, "I just go ahead and laugh with God now."

A ringing silence. The cameraman sneezes. I smile like a kindergartner on picture day. The girl who cuts my hair will later say I looked like a jaundiced chimp.

"The man who laughs . . . with God, ha *ha*," the host finally says as the brown-suited men and El Yao Ming and the Spooky

Daughter of the Clown College Dean |

I change my grad school track to Counseling. Why? No thesis. This is true.

Marathon classes now consist of group discussions on family systems, emotional dynamics, healing the inner child and application to personal issues.

The average student is at least twice my age, divorced, weepy, struggling with sobriety and deeply involved in dysfunctional relationships. Holiday sweaters and macramé necklaces. Flowbee haircuts and *Cat Fancy* magazine.

Sitting near the back, I look something like a third-rate Vegas magician or a clichéd Jesus in a tourist trap's Passion play.

I listen passively and outline my script for *Jason Meets the Dukes of Hazzard.* The hockey-masked psychopath nearly bloodsplatters Enos and Daisy's Duke Barn picnic when Bo and Luke race to the rescue in the General Lee (!). I put in a false finish, of course, where Jason certainly bites the dust at the hands of a Duke Boy dynamite-laced arrow — only to have the monster crash back in his own dark blue Dodge Charger with double sixes down the side. And Jason's horn plays Edgar Winter's "Frankenstein." There's a twin jump cliffhanger over zombie alligators and a wrestling cage match between the ghosts of Ulysses Grant and Robert E. Lee. Doctor X run-in? I never quite finish the tale.

The instructor, a waifish fellow with frail wrists and a frizzy ginger afro, pulls me to the side after class to say he has spoken with other faculty and feels I am not a good fit for the counseling program.

Shoulda been couple skating with the daughter of the clown college dean.

He means well, I imagine, protecting the program's dignity — but as he speaks I realize I am the only student with any real-life experience, who actually *works* in mental health. If I stay on the path, I will be one of the youngest graduates of the program ever. I've only got a year left. Plus, I've learned to read faces and Dr. Frizzy's says he's bluffing.

I prop my boots up, lean back in my chair and give him a serial killer smile. "You got me, boss," I admit. "This is only something to fall back on." In a flash, my smile is gone. "So. You think I should leave?" *Escape from New York* was on cable the night before and inexplicably, I've slipped into the character of Snake Plissken.

"Well," he says, nervous-like, "technically, we can't make you."

"Guess I'll stick around then," I hiss.

Frizzy makes a face, from concern to confusion, and then shakes it off and gives me a sigh. "I've requested you meet with the program director," he says. "He'll be the one to decide whether or not you should stay."

I report to Dr. Cryer's office the next afternoon. He's a down-to-earth country boy who doesn't seem to take it all too seriously. I think I'll be all right.

"Blaine, son?" he says, peering over his reading glasses at my file. "You made a C in Sex?"

"What can I say?" I say with hands lifted.

"You do know that one more C and you go on probation, right?" he says.

"Didn't know that," I answer.

"You realize that if you go on probation you lose your assistantship, right?"

"Um, no sir. Didn't know that either."

"Maybe if you didn't sit in the back of all your classes, distracted by whatever else it is you're working on — you might not make Cs?"

To that, I say nothing.

"Archie," he says.

"Say what?"

"When I was a kid, I liked Archie comics. Veronica or Betty, you know?" Dr. Cryer removes his glasses, crosses his arms and leans back. "Didn't read Archie in grad school though." He lets me hang awhile, then smiles.

"Yes sir," I reply.

"Oh, and Mr. Blaine? Counseling professors are a jumpy lot anyway. So watch your words, okay?"

"Will do."

I sit a little more towards the middle and try to listen and take notes. The grades improve but I'm still not sure Dr. Frizzy isn't right.

Feel Something |

Graduation looms. Student loans are coming due. I'm still not a counselor. So I scramble for an alternate plan.

I look into opening my own skating rink, take support classes in exercise science and get certified to train.

I record my own pseudo-gospel version of *Dark Side of the Moon* and make a demo tape to do voiceover work for cartoons. Reaching out to connections in the artistic business, I look for a foot in the door, for a place I could maybe fit in.

I meet a silver-haired filmmaker with Buddy Holly glasses and the dramatic habit of stressing his speech with sign language. When I mention my idea about pop culture icons colliding, he zips an imaginary line with his fingers and dashes my hopes with a one-word reply.

"Licensing."

"But you can always find or make your own icons," he adds, rolling his hands one over the other. "Art is everywhere. Living and breathing and bleeding and dying. It's not in here," he says, thumping my chest. "It's out there, it's the way —" He thumps again. "— what's in *here* meets what's out there."

"I have a deaf sister, Sara," he continues, holding up his hands. "Growing up, we never wanted her to feel left out. So we all learned to sign and used it whenever we talked. It's still a habit to this day. See, without knowing that, you think I'm just weird. But if I tell you the story, we connect through the emotion. Rock and roll is emotion. Film is emotion. Gospel is emotion. The bottom line in art that matters — is emotion."

The words ring truer than all my college lessons thus far. *Why can't grad school be like this?*

Later, I show him some of my scribblings. "Very Coen," he says, flicking the end of his nose three times with his thumb.

"The Coen brothers?" I gush. "I love them!"

"No, *Randy* Coen," he corrects. "The guy who sprays my house for bugs."

I duck my head, rejected. "Just kidding," he says, making a pistol with his fingers and clicking down the hammer of his thumb. "Don't you work in a psych ward?"

"Part time, yeah."

"Man, come on," he says. "Where are *those* stories?"

Pork Chop Almighty
& the Chocolate Apocalypse |

Passing through PICU, I unwittingly enter the Apocalypse.

A bipolar barrel-shaped man with short arms and pork chop sideburns thinks he is the Lord God. Across the room, a slim, floridly psychotic fellow with a Levi's jacket and *Grease 2* pompadour is certain he is Lucifer.

I step between them just as the war is about to begin.

"Gentlemen," I say, "y'all calm down."

Pork Chop Almighty laughs the hyena-on-helium snicker so familiar to Psychiatric Intensive Care. "This is my beloved son," he says, holding forth his stubby arms to me, "in whom I am well pleased."

Satan Fonzarelli snatches up a folding chair and smashes it across the side of my head, sort of like a cowboy movie without the gimmicked wood.

The Pork Chop Lord attacks his nemesis in my defense. I stumble and pull him away.

"Not again!" he shouts at the Devil. "Lightning on your ass! Lightning!"

The Denim Demon takes a seat at the card table and seems passive now. I hustle Porky into isolation and lock him down. He presses his hand against the window in the door. "I love you with an everlasting love," he calls as I stagger back and lean against the wall.

"Sorry 'bout that," Satan says casually, as he unwraps a package of cheese crackers. "You ain't really his son, is you?"

"No," I reply.

The psychopathic Prince of Darkness nods, bites off half a cracker and fumbles with a container of chocolate milk. "Hey, can you open this for me?" he asks.

A trickle of blood seeps down the side of my neck. "Sure," I say. I tear open the spout and hand it back. His eyes are lifeless, focused on the void. If Darkness stands, I've already got it planned. I'll pin his arms and take him down hard, clipping his skull on the TV as we fall. It'll look like an accident.

He takes a long drink, folds closed the spout and places the milk back on the table. "Thank you," he says.

Jackie, the charge nurse, drags her oxygen tank back in from the smoking porch and takes a quick look around. Two psychotic patients, one in isolation, broken chair, psych tech with glassy eyes.

"Sit down, honey," she says to me with the seen-it-all glaze of a thirty-year career psych nurse. "You dizzy?"

"Little bit."

She fills a bag with ice and presses it above my ear. "You ever had any concussions?"

"A few," I tell her.

"How many?"

"When I was seven I got busted in the head with a baseball bat. Knocked me cold. The Doc said they'd be easier to get after that. Three or four since then. Five, maybe."

Jackie takes a book down from the nurses' station shelf, flips to a page and reads, "*Symptoms of multiple concussions: mood swings, restlessness, anxiety, difficulty concentrating, bothered by bright lights, trouble expressing thoughts or finding the right words. Confusion.*"

"Hon, you ever have any of them symptoms?" Jackie asks.

"A few," I tell her.

Pork Chop taps on the glass until the Devil turns to look. With that weasel laugh, Piggy cries, *Lightning!*

Beelzebubba stands and hurls his milk carton into the isolation glass. Chocolate splatters, running down the pane. It drips to the floor as Piggy dances, fire in his eyes. He throws forth his fat little hands and shouts again.

Lightning!

"Crazy-ass patients," Jackie says. "Don't you just love 'em?"

Until the Shivers Cease |

22 y/o white female, suicidal ideation with plan and access, auditory and visual hallucinations, history of abuse, self-abuse, polysubstance abuse. Drug of choice: Klonapin.

It's Thursday and the curtains are the saddest shade of hospital blue, a dingy indigo faded by the afternoon sun and the awful weight of phantom fears and sadness, of feckless reapers and chemical bondage, harsh fluorescents and pale green cinderblock walls.

There is a vampire girl with stars tattooed around her eyes swearing I am the holy one, the chosen son, and she wants to bleed me badly but she is *so* afraid that she wants to and it is very *so very* important that I know how much she needs to bury her teeth into the softest part of my neck and slowly grind them together until they produce the richest of blue-black juices, to roll her tongue into a tiny o and drink until the shivers cease, until the room falls away in spirals and she will fly me to her home, where urchin friends are cast into stone, to the balcony of hedges so I can set the gargoyles free.

"Come home with me," she whispers. "For just one taste. Nations would fall."

"Where is home?" I ask.

"Oh. New Orleans," she half-sings sedately. For a long

moment we are quiet as I wait for the leather of her wings to fill the room like an army of umbrellas in a sudden rain.

"I live in the narrows between two townhouses near Toulouse and St. Pete, just a walled-in alley really, not much more than the width of my arms, narrow but tall, four stories in all and in the cellar beneath the stairs there is the Granite Christ who cries tears of wine, who told me . . ." Her hand rises slowly. She squints and looks down her finger like the barrel of a gun. ". . . of you and I saw those curls falling at your temples."

She stands, arms stretched and palms to the sky, eyes shut, pupils darting beneath the skin. The clock ticks creep and I wait for the leather of her wings.

"Your eyes are full of secrets, Secret," she says. "You know my real name."

I hold her gaze. "Yes."

"You know the many names of Moses and the apostle John, seven-eyed John and Azriel. You know the last words of Judas with his neck in the noose." The air in the room is still as a tomb and the words I should speak will not quite form.

She pulls the back of her hand across her lips and emits a small but desperate sob. "At all the world's end we will fade to black, my love. Thou art the Granite Christ who cries hot tears of wine. Wouldst thou fly with me to my home and save me?"

"*Elizabeth* —" I plead.

She grimaces, gasping. *We can be like they are.*

I rise from the desk and move to where she stands. "I am *not* the Granite Christ. I'm just a guy here to help make sure you are taking your medicine and eating."

Elizabeth's shoulders wilt. "Then you must know." She rolls up the sleeves of her shirt to show neat rows of strawberry gashes razored down her slim white arms. "These are for you, all my blood and tears . . ." She smoothes her fingers slowly over the scabs and says in the smallest of voices. ". . . *for you.*"

"I don't want your blood or your tears. I want you to eat. And take your medicine."

She nods slightly.

"So the meds are okay then?" I ask.

"Yes."

"You are able to sleep?"

"Yes."

"Are you going to eat?"

Elizabeth tugs at the frayed string of her Underdog pajamas and gnaws at a battered black nail. "I have to tell you something. They've been feeding us processed humans."

"I see. Well, how about soup? From a can?"

"Soup is okay," she sighs, thumb just inside her mouth.

I hold the door open and she shuffles away, her balled-up waistband cinched with a fist. In the hallway she turns, eyes dark and seriously slit. "Lie if you will," she says, sensing my chill. "But you cannot lie to me."

Her arms cross, she raises her chin, holding me in her stare, the hot rush of blood pounding in my neck. "I know who you are," she says. "Do you?"

And I wait for the leather of her wings.

Forever Eleven

I'm sitting in Family Systems class, listening with one ear, looking out the window at sporty girls playing volleyball in the campus sand. There's a lively class discussion on "What made you who you are today?" — about all the stray mismatched pieces and aimless roads that make up a life so far. Some students are discussing that national symbol of dysfunction, Michael Jackson.

"Sometimes," Dr. Cryer offers, "when you've got a person who never experienced the healthy process of adolescence, they stop growing and remain a child. As adults, they set out to regain their lost childhood, finding solace in the toys and games and movies of their youth. Some never get unstuck, they use nostalgia like an addict uses drugs, to hide from the world and run from responsibility. They stay stuck until something shakes their life up enough to push them forward."

Classmates rush to comment, spilling out the struggles and troubles of their youth.

"Mr. Blaine," Cryer says, juggling chalk from one hand to the other. "Any particular childhood trauma, or was yours pretty normal?"

The redhead with seven-foot legs flies like Jordan and spikes the ball. A shorter but spunky brunette dives to the sand and bunts it back to score. She scampers up and shakes her backside, slapping it for effect. I look over from the window and give the prof a nod. "Pretty normal," I say.

That night at the rink a banker bets me a coke I can't beat his six-year-old kid in the limbo.

"No way," he says with a grin. "Kid skates like a fox."

I lose, just barely, on a technicality really. I bring the banker a Dr Pepper, his son a Fanta Orange.

"Rematch," I say to the boy, slapping hands. "Next time you're here."

"Okay, yeah," says the kid. "Hey, how old are you?"

"Eleven," I reply. He nods, turns up his cup and skates back out to the floor.

"Man, you *almost* beat him," the dad says. "How'd you do that?"

I'm taller than the banker and sporting something of a beard.

"I'm eleven," I laugh.

Platinum Visions & Chariots of Fire |

At the all-night Piggly Wiggly, three chicks approach me by the Cocoa Puffs and ask if I want to join their band.

"What y'all play?" I ask.

"Rock and *roll*," the Amazon blonde singer/bassist says with a pumping fist and sneer. "Like a cross between Heart and Skid Row."

"I'm your man," I say. "But ain't y'all looking for a woman?"

"Nah," says the hook-nosed drummer who looks like a bulimic Bette Midler. "We wanna be three chicks and a dude."

"You know, for the chicks," adds the third girl, a bashful lead guitarist resembling the love child of Mick Mars and Roseanne Barr.

"Ladies," I say, right there on Aisle Nine, "let's rock."

Little Bette's dad runs a trucking company; we practice in the bay with the doors open, already pretending we're stars. The music chugs along but lacks spark until one night Amazon and I swap rhythm and bass guitar. Bette counts down from four to one and we slither into a red-hot version of Aerosmith's "Lightning Strikes." At the song's end we gather and slap hands, visions of platinum dancing in our heads.

Six rehearsals later they pull me to the side. "You're a cool guy and everything, but we decided our chances would be better all-girl."

"That sucks," I say, crushed. "But it's probably true. Best of luck."

Back at the psych ward, a schoolteacher tells me he makes a hundred bucks a shot playing guitar for weddings. "Easy money," he offers.

I buy a forty-dollar classical guitar and try to learn "Canon in C."

The call comes close to midnight.

"Are you busy?" It's Caleb's younger brother, Juke. Just five years before, their father passed and now Caleb is gone too. It's a lot of sorrow for a teenage boy to bear.

"Just picking guitar," I say. "How you doin'?"

After a long silence I hear his voice break. "Not good," he says. "I just want to see him. I just want to go."

"I'm on my way." I drive over and we walk that same neighborhood block. Doorbell lights on a dark street. There are no stars.

"I cursed God when he died," Juke tells me. "I cursed God and punched the wall and I didn't care. I didn't care if the whole world came down."

We walk through the night and I listen while he talks. At my truck door he asks, "Do you think if I practice really hard, I might get good enough to sing one of my brother's songs in church?"

"Maybe," I say. "I'll help if you want to try."

"I gotta try," he says.

We work at it but Juke struggles; he fumbles the chords and sings forced and off-key, with none of Caleb's grace. Frustrated, he throws his brother's guitar to the side.

"Come on," I say. "You gotta try."

The next day he tells me that he stayed up late reading the biblical story of the prophets Elijah and Elisha. As Elijah ascended in his chariot of fire, Elisha called out, *If you leave me behind, I want the double portion. Twice what you had, your life repeated in mine.*

"Jamie," says Juke, "that's what I want. For losing Daddy, for Caleb dying so young and leaving me behind. Daddy could preach and make people cry and want to change. Caleb could break your heart with his song. I asked for twice what they had. I want the double portion."

I sit there just looking, not sure what to say. The truth is, at best, he doesn't have half. "Son," I tell him, as gently as I can, "you're asking a hard thing."

"I know," he says. "Just pray for me."

Juke and I debut on a Wednesday night at his little Apostolic church. Just one song, after the announcements, before the sermon. His voice is pitchy and the tempo unsure but we make it through and the congregation is kind.

Afterwards, a big-haired Texas brunette, home on break from Bible College, approaches him. "I don't know if you believe in this sort of thing," she says, "but while you were singing I had a vision of two blankets coming down from the sky. Does that mean anything to you?"

"Yes ma'am," Juke says, his hands trembling. She tilts her head and closes her eyes, like she's trying to hear a call from far away. When she speaks again her voice is sure. "God says you asked for the double portion." Her finger is in his face now. "And you're going to get it."

We are silent on the drive back home. Juke pulls into the driveway and we stare at the dash. Finally I speak. "You tell anybody else about the Elijah thing?"

He shakes his head, slowly back and forth. "I was afraid to even tell you," he says.

Within a month Juke is ordained and on staff as youth pastor. Three months in, his congregation exceeds the main church. Not long after that, he is off to Nashville with a major label deal, on his way to becoming a country music star.

Ramble On, Old Blue |

There's an alcoholic in the intake office with slicked-back white hair wearing a field jacket, filthy sneakers and a t-shirt that says *Ask Me About My Grandkids.*

"How 'bout them grandkids?" I ask.

He tents out the shirt and turns his head, just now reading the print. "Ain't got none," he tells me. "Just a shirt somebody gimme."

There was a good spell of sobriety but then his mother died from cancer of the brain. Then the sweet potato plant where he'd worked twenty-five years shut down. Then his wife left him for a gambling diesel mechanic. He didn't go into any of this. His neighbor told me when he dropped off his suitcase at the office door.

"He's a good old guy," the neighbor said before he left. "Hope y'all can get him some help."

"His benefits are good, he smells like a whiskey barrel and he wants to go," I tell the neighbor. "That's all the criteria we need."

We're standing at the curb waiting for the hospital van. The alcoholic rocks back and forth, kicks against the asphalt a time or two and finally says, "You ever just look around at life and wonder what the *hell* is goin' on?"

"Sure. Who don't?"

"*Exactly*. Even in the *Bible*, son. Every one of them characters in that book wondered the same thing. If you ain't ever really read it close, check it out sometime. See for yourself."

When you're waiting for a ride to rehab at ten o'clock on a Sunday night, it's not hard for talk to turn spiritual. "All right," I tell him.

"Like, whose idea was all this?" He holds out his hands like Moses on the sea and pivots from the Jiffy Lube to Taco Bell. "I ain't asked to be born. Ain't asked to die. Sure ain't asked to be judged. I ain't signed up for none of this. But here I am." I like this guy. He reminds me of Blue from the movie *Old School*. Might still be a little drunk, though.

"I hear you," I reply. Waiting on the van sucks. I didn't really want to get a call tonight. But ramble on, Old Blue. Just listening can be pretty peaceful when I let it roll.

He pulls a nickel from his pocket, staring at it and shining the silver with his thumbs. "Even Jesus Christ Hissself . . . " he says, "wasn't so sure sometimes, was He?" Blue smiles easy, his face brighter, like the sun breaking free from dark clouds. "But I figure that's where that whole amazin' grace thing comes in. You know that song, don't ya?" Blue leans out on the street sign and sings the chorus starting with *that saved a wretch like me*. . . .

"I know it," I say, waving him down. "How much you say you had to drink today?"

"I told you. Just one," he says, moving his hands from six inches tall to about two feet apart.

Blue sits back down beside me. A former mate from college pulls up, waiting to turn right on red. She sees us, toots the horn and waves. We wave back. She laughs and shakes her head.

"So anyway, my point is, you see," he says, "maybe God said *Well, before I judge 'em too hard, I oughta walk a mile in their shoes.*" In Blue's world God talks a lot like the narrator on *Dukes of Hazzard*.

"So he come down to earth as a little baby," Blue continues, "fought with brothers and sisters and worked in the family wood shop. Tried to go tell people the good news and his friends screwed him over and then — them religious folks kilt him."

"Never thought about it that way," I say, paying more attention now.

"And maybe," says Blue, serious as he can muster, "when Jesus got back to Heaven he kicked off them shoes, looked at God and said *Dad, it's rough down there. Go easy on 'em.*"

I stare at him, wondering if the Lord has tricked me again. If He is showing me that truth comes from strange places, that for those willing to watch and listen, Revelation is all around and every place is holy ground. Then again, Blue is sort of drunk and I am overly dramatic and rattled in the brain.

"How'd you come up with that?" I ask.

"I got lots of time to think," Blue says. "When you said that van was coming?"

"Any minute now."

"We best hurry then," he says, pointing to the liquor store down the street, "get that half-pint you promised me for the trip."

"I don't remember promising you no half-pint."

"Oh, you did," he snorts. "Said your bossman would pay you back."

We cross the street and make our way down, Blue walking sideways and talking with his hands, singing "Amazing Grace" and preaching about Jesus' shoes, trying to persuade me that what he really needs for the trip is an entire fifth.

Riot at the Dollar Movie | Jesus Calling

Some college buddies and I go to the dollar theater. The movie is awful so we act like fools. There's a food fight, a stupid ruckus, blowing off steam. It's not so funny when the police arrive and take us to the city jail.

This isn't good, I think as the jailer walks me down the hall.

He places me in a short-timer side cell with five other guys. A squat, stocky man in a work shirt with *Juan* on the chest pocket steps up to me.

"Hey, Rock and Roll," he says. "Wha-choo in for, eh?"

For some reason I hang my head, drag my toe across the floor and say this in the sad voice of Eeyore: "I shot some Mexicans."

He leans in closer and narrows his eyes. I crouch down and stare back. The cell gets very still and quiet.

Juan cracks up laughing, hugs me and turns to the other guys. "This guy, we used to go to the same church!"

"What are you doing here?" I ask him.

"My old lady, like a fool I gave her the child support in cash. Then she claimed I didn't pay her. I had a few beers and . . ." Juan waves his hands in the air. "It's nothing, we work it out."

The other men gather round and introduce themselves. DUIs, possession of a schedule nine. Failure to yield.

"Failure to yield?"

"Lost the ticket and didn't pay the fine," No Yield Guy says. "What about you?"

"Riot at the dollar movie."

No Yield whistles as if he's impressed, as if I'd knocked off a jewelry store. "You really do it?" he asks.

"Naw, it was that other me," I tell him. "You know, the one that does stupid bad stuff?"

"I know that guy," No Yield says. "He's a total bastard."

A snowy old TV sits on a milk crate. "Hey," Juan says. "We can't catch nothin' but the Big Bird channel and *Nova* is on. We're about to get a game up if you want to play."

"Sure. What you got? Dominoes? Spades?"

Juan reaches under his bunk and pulls out a long box. "You know how to play *Clue*?"

"Are you kidding? I love *Clue*."

In the side cell of the city jail, board games with an old church brother and a few new friends. We roll the dice and tell our stories, about sin and redemption and grace and regret. About that *other me* that does stupid bad things. *Nova* drones softly in the background, the rings of Saturn covered in static and snow.

About the time I'm suspecting Colonel Mustard in the kitchen with the candlestick, there's a ring from the phone booth at the Quik Stop just south of my heart. Jesus Calling.

This is where you will always belong.

A friendgirl bails me out by the third round. No Yield says, "Aw man, you gotta go already? You just got here."

Juan grabs my hand through the bars as I leave. "Hey Jamie," he says. "Hold your head up. Don't let this get you down, friend. You're a good dude. We all capable of the worst sometimes."

"I know, brother. Thanks."

The following Wednesday, I return to the jail's church service with my guitar and an antenna for the inmates' TV. Most of the guys are gone but No Yield remains. When I ask him why, he just holds up his hands.

———

I'm in the corner getting tuned when a stooped old prisoner with a cane hands me a scrap of paper with *OLD RUGGED CROSS* scratched in pencil, the letters shaky and big.

"If you know it," he says, his voice just above a whisper.

"I know it," I tell him.

While I sing about that dark emblem he rests his forehead on the end of his cane, closes his eyes and drifts far away.

After service, as he shuffles back to his cell, I slip him my last ten-dollar bill.

"God bless you," he says.

"He does," I reply.

You Lose a Few |

"Remember that fourteen-year-old boy you evaluated last week?" Florentine asks as I walk into the outreach.

"Possum-looking kid with hair sticking up on top? Yeah, I remember. He liked the George Clooney Batman best. Said his parents were overreacting. I sent him home. You know how it goes." When I say this, I wave my hand, like *no big deal*.

"He shot a boy in his neighborhood today."

Some time passes before I ask: "Did he kill him?"

"The bullet passed through," Florentine says. "Kid claims it was an accident but the cops say no way."

"So he's in juvie?"

"No, he's in your office. With his parents. This time, you might want to hear their side."

A week later I'm booked to see a high school English teacher who reminds me of Jeff Foxworthy and that radio guy who says he'll leave the light on for you.

"So what's goin' on?" I ask.

"Mostly depression," he explains. "Tired. Just like everybody else, I guess."

He's easygoing and funny and we mostly talk about the consistency of George Strait and what the Eagles might have sounded like with Stevie Nicks and Jackson Browne.

In the parking lot, he thanks me for my time and says to stop by the school sometime and he'll buy me lunch.

"Man, I love school lunch. Those rolls," I tell him. "Yeah, I'll come by." He promises he'll be fine and we say goodbye.

A few days after, on a Sunday night, he ties one end of an extension cord to the banister and the other around his neck. He kneels down and leans away until the pain ends and his life is over.

The note says, *I'm sorry but it was just too hard.*

"Don't beat yourself up, Jamie," Florentine tells me. "It's part of the business. You lose a few."

Brother John

A speaker at Sunday service nearly makes the whole church cry.

"There's a man here tonight. Sir, I don't know your name but you've been battling a long time. In fact, you came here tonight to give God one last chance to come through. You've got the pistol to end your life in the glove compartment of your car."

Brother John steps from the pulpit to the floor.

"I've been there, friend. I drank that whiskey. I smoked that cocaine. I held that pistol."

He takes out his handkerchief, wipes away the sweat and sadly shakes his head.

"Sir, I don't know your name — but I know Someone who knows your name. And He is saying *It's not over.* You can make your way to this old-fashioned altar and get your heart and life right with God, tonight."

The air is electric and the weight heavy in our chests.

Brother John's voice breaks. "*Come home.*" In the second row, a woman cries out.

A man with big bifocals and a plaid shirt stands and walks the aisle, his face drawn and legs heavy, as if he is wading through deep water a long ways towards the shore.

"All across this room there are people who have been putting on a front and living a lie, like everything is all right," Brother John says. "But inside you fight a losing war. A war against depression, against thoughts of suicide. Some of you take too many pills, some of you drink yourself to sleep and you think nobody knows, *nobody knows. . . .*"

He pauses, his sad eyes scanning the room. "Come home."

Come home, come home, the choir sings. Slowly, people stream towards the altars.

"Come home sir, come home ma'am. Come home teenager — there is no judgment for you here, only mercy and grace, come home." Brother John walks through those gathered at the front, touching heads and shoulders as he passes by.

I lean against the balcony rail, watching. After the service I shake Brother John's hand. It is warm and soft, like well-oiled leather.

"That was awesome, Brother John," I say.

"God is awesome," he says. "John Rayburn is just a man."

Three weeks later, at nearly one a.m., I get a call from the sheriff to the psych ward's front door. They bring in a man, disheveled and shoeless, smelling like wine. He looks at me for a moment, then back to the floor.

"John," I say.

He nods. "I know you?"

I lead him back, saying nothing more. I give Brother John food and fresh clothes and take him out to smoke. I never mention church.

He stubs out his second cigarette and stares at me for a long time. A dim light shines in his eyes, like a lone porch light at the far end of a gravel lane.

"I know you," he says.

Mr. T, Nietzsche & the Rebel Angels |

"If a man have a strong faith, he can indulge in the luxury of skepticism." — Friedrich Nietzsche

It's my last semester and Dr. Cryer assigns a report based around Albert Camus' *The Stranger*. From there, I read Karl Barth and Franz Kafka. Bonhoeffer and Tillich and Soren Kierkegaard. Viktor Frankl and crazy old Freddie Nietzsche. Jesus and Ecclesiastes from a new point of view.

I ponder existential theories, confusion and futility in what often seems like a meaningless world. The paradox of God and man, beauty and chaos, freedom and loss, the significance of questioning everything and embracing the absurd.

I start studying the whole Bible, not just the parts evangelically approved. Blood to the bridles of horses and rebel angels having sex with the daughters of men. Stuttering, angry Moses, denied the Promised Land, lustful, murdering David, a man after God's own heart, Solomon's wisdom canceled out by concubines, Ezekiel's bread of humiliation and the wheel inside the wheel, kamikaze Samson and his suicide mission from On High, the prophet Hosea ordered to marry a whore, the only Son of God who brawled in church and vanished for days at a time, whose own family came to take him away because they were certain he had lost his mind.

One night, I'm going through *Twilight of the Idols* giving Nietzsche an *amen* then nearly get choked up watching Mr. T preach on TBN. I turn in a lot of rambling but passionate pages and score my first 100 A+. At the top, Cryer writes in red, *Good work, Mr. Blaine. Maybe you've finally found your niche.*

Flickering |

There's a hollow-eyed woman holed up in the back bedroom of a rundown house, wedged between the window and the bed with a .38 derringer in her hand.

"Ain't nothin' nobody can say'll change my mind," she says when I enter the room. "You really think you can stop me?"

The trim is painted mailbox blue, the walls and floor bare timber. Pill bottles and empty beer cans are scattered around. The ceiling fan is missing a blade.

"No," I tell her. "That's your choice. There is help though, if you want it."

A peace sign beanbag lies next to the bed. I sit down into it. There's a jade green vase on a shelf next to a VHS tape of *Lethal Weapon II*. Above the urn hangs a high school graduation picture of a smiling boy with sandy hair, long over one eye. Inscribed in the photo's corner, his birthday, a dash and the date of his death, a year to the day.

The woman presses against the wall with her free hand and hangs her head. "It's just so hard."

"Tell me about it," I say.

While she talks I watch the hypnotic wobble of the lopsided fan. With every revolution, the fixture shakes loose, flickering, darkness and light.

After a long while, the woman asks, "Why ain't you at home with your honey, sleepin'?"

The window by the bed is open and a breeze blows through the screen.

"I got no place to be. Talk all you want. Long as I'm home before the sun comes up."

She turns slow and looks to me. "So who are you anyway?"

The air smells like old clothes and frying bacon. There's a TV in the corner with the sound turned low. On the Late Night Show: *The Graduate*. Dustin Hoffman drifts across a pool before an infomercial flashes for Thighmaster Gold.

"I'm the guy who shows up at three in the morning and listens to people with pistols who just aren't sure they can go on."

She lays her head back and rests the derringer against the sill. "Guess somebody's gotta be," she says. A scatter of crows caw, close then farther away. She leans across the bed and hands me the gun. "Hold this for me awhile, okay?"

The pistol is mother-of-pearl and polished steel, its weight seductive. I pull the hammer back and stare at the slug. *FEDERAL 38 SPECIAL.* Shake out the bullet and roll it in my palm.

"Okay," I say.

An eighteen-wheeler passes on the highway past the field. Somewhere out the window, a radio is playing "Smokey Mountain Rain." We sit for a moment, listening.

"Ain't heard that song in a long time," I tell her.

"Always did like that song," the woman says.

Of Pomp & Circumstance |
Karl Barth Does the Cabbage Patch

I'm sitting in the second row at graduation. Several of the students around me are crying and the girl to my right grips a picture of two kids in her locket and keeps whispering *Thank you, Jesus, thank you, Lord.*

Dean Gage hands me a diploma, winks and says, "You made it." The diploma is fake, a blank page; the real one will be mailed two weeks later.

I pose for a family picture, give my blue Master's sash and dummy diploma to my grandmother. We eat Chinese food and less than an hour later I'm calling skaters into a circle in the center of the roller rink floor.

"We're the only rink in the world whose DJ has a Master's degree," Mr. Ric says. "What are you gonna do next?"

"'The Hokey Pokey,'" I reply.

I sneak back behind the snack bar and slip on the Roller Rabbit costume, racing to the circle just as the scratchy old record starts to play.

Kafka, Camus, Mr. T and Nietzsche. Solomon, Job and Jesus. This one's for you.

There's smoke and lights and loud, loud music. Happy children make a joyful noise.

"Ladies and gentlemen!" Ric says on the mic. "Give it up for

Dr. Roller Rabbit!" I spin on my skates and do a little hustle side to side. The children cheer; they laugh and sing; they hug me and tug at my tail.

Maybe this really is what it's all about.

PART III

Treasures of Darkness

"Push out into the deep." — Jesus

Secret Latch | Panic Attacks & Gentleman Jack

Numerous people, mostly university faculty and staff, led me to believe that a graduate level therapist could pull in sixty to a hundred bucks an hour.

If nothing else I figured I could earn near the low end, fake my way through a few hours a day and still make enough to live on until something else came along. Eventually, I find out that one can make decent money with a Master's — but not without a professional license.

"How long it take to get one of those?" I ask. "Couple a weeks?"

"At least three years," I am told. "And another three or four thousand dollars for supervision."

Screw that.

I check for full-time jobs because the student loan money I racked up goofing around undergrad is due, plus there's rent and I need a new car. The only jobs available are state positions for $11.75 an hour.

"You have to get your foot in the door," they say. "State benefits are great."

I stop by to hit up Prof Stephens for a part-time job at his practice. While I am there a college sophomore with an eating disorder has a psychotic break and attacks the gay psychiatrist. I lock my legs around her waist from behind, tie her arms back loosely and hold her steady on the floor until law enforcement arrive, nearly thirty minutes after the receptionist makes the call.

Her mother has a glass eye and she cries as the cops take her daughter away, tears streaming down one side of her face.

"I'm sorry," I tell her. "Sorry it happened; sorry you had to see it."

She puts her arms around my neck and says, "She needed help. You were just helping. Thank you."

I'm afraid it all seems very unprofessional, the hugging and the wrestling and there was a time towards the end, when I thought the police might never show, that I gave the girl a tickle or two, just trying to lighten the mood and bring her back to herself.

When Stephens calls me to his office, I'm pretty sure he's going to ask me to leave.

"You got us out of a helluva jam," he says in his Gee-Haw voice. "We've never had anything like that happen here."

"Really?" I say. "Happens at the hospital about nine times a day."

"Well, if it happens again," he says, "nice to have the human straitjacket around."

Stephens hooks me up with the outpatient program that rents out the east end of his hall. I'm hired to do some intake and an afternoon process group. They pay me fifteen bucks an hour. I go to the Goodwill off St. Paul and buy two pairs of khaki pants and a button-down Polo with ink stains on the cuff.

The first week I walk into the semicircle of group and face twelve of the saddest, most desperate, no-hope souls I have ever seen. This is not the Zoloft-zonked and benzo-happy people of the psych ward. These people are angry and no longer lulled by thoughts of escape or suicide. They stare at me as if I am the devil masquerading as an angel of light, daring me to even try to shine.

86

I take a serious and factual approach and it doesn't work. I try to be laid-back and that flops too. They sit silent, staring. *Daring* me. Fifteen minutes into a one-hour group I just sit and stare back, remembering Dr. Cryer's advice. *When you don't know what to say, say nothing.*

There's a librarian, transferred to group after a failed attempt to take his life by overdosing on Nexium. "Well, counselor," he says in a sarcastic tone. "This program is costing us two hundred dollars a day. You just going to sit there or you gonna counsel?"

I fight my way through twenty more minutes and break. Three women from group are smoking on the back steps. "Now I know what a panic attack feels like," I tell them. For a moment we have an effortless conversation a hundred times better than anything from group. Then I excuse myself to sit in the janitor's closet with the lights off.

I can do this, I tell myself. *I need the money.*

Early into school, I asked a therapist how he dealt with the pressure of people's problems day in and out. Beneath his bottom desk drawer, he showed me a secret latch. "Some days you grit through it," he said, fishing through the hidden compartment and holding forth a flask. "And other days, thank God for Gentleman Jack."

I consider hiding a half-pint behind the Pine-Sol. For medicinal purposes. Then, this epiphany: *Run group the same way you DJ. Every song a story, every story a song. Listen and watch, mixing one into the other . . .*

It doesn't work. A set of parents expresses concern to Dr. Stephens about my level of expertise.

"We're paying a fortune for this," they say. "What is he, nineteen?"

Stephens pats me on the back and says it takes time.

"Is there anything else I can do with a Master's degree?" I ask him.

Piston Hips & Fists |

The ticket line for the Skate City Sunday Night Party stretches past the corner, through the grass and over into the lot of El Loco Pollo. Booty shorts and halter tops, bootleg polos with collars popped, flashing pacifiers and Playboy earrings, white-frame mirror shades and thick silver chains with emblems sparkling in the light. . . .

Three hundred, five hundred, eight hundred, they pour through the front door and into the world of booming beats, fog and flashing lights. A seven-foot-tall security guard checks purses and pockets while another waves a metal detector from head to toe.

"One thousand," Mr. Ric says, holding up the numbered stub.

I wear my skates while I work so I can feel the beat, headphone to my ear, bobbing, spinning 360 on my wheels, watching the people, giving them what they want and need, telling a story with the songs, the rise and fall, passion, joy and pain, making sure that for a few hours we forget our struggles and let go.

"Twelve hundred," says Mr. Ric.

The people dance so hard that heat waves rise from the floor, pulsing knots of bodies in one accord, hands in the air, chanting the chorus to their favorite songs, a great and mighty sea of piston hips and fists fifteen hundred strong.

A girl with an airbrushed *Bad Bitch* tee and a panther tattoo four inches below her collarbone waves a do-rag at me and proclaims, "White boy the world's greatest DJ!"

At the end of the night I drive home with the windows down, the silence a balm to my ringing ears. I open the envelope Ric slipped me just before I snuck out the back door and sheriff's deputies escorted me out and down the road. For three hours' work, four hundred dollars.

Maybe I should just spin records for the rest of my life.

Whitney Houston, We Have a Problem

"Truthfulness itself is almost medicinal, even when it's served without advice or insight." — Augusten Burroughs

Thirty or so teens are gathered in the high school library's A/V room, cracking jokes and talking loudly, others twisting their hair and staring off into space. The assistant principal, a round little man in a short-sleeve shirt and brown tie, corrals their attention.

"All right, people," he says. "Now I want y'all give our speakers complete respect." He pauses for order.

"Both of them have advanced degrees and years of experience and expertise in their field," he continues. "And they've come to talk to you today about a very serious subject: teen suicide."

An awkward hush falls over the room as the first young lady rises to speak. She carries herself confidently, with a bookish air, her burgundy hair sort of feathered back, skirt black and boots knee high, plenty attractive enough to capture the attention of high school boys.

"Most of you in this room have considered suicide," she says curtly. "Some have made attempts. Pills, maybe. A razor blade across the wrist. Most superficial, some for attention, others dead serious." Sitting back on the edge of the desk, she crosses her legs and smugly tucks an auburn lock behind her ear.

I'm up next.

Wow, she's not fooling, I think, briefly forgetting that I have nothing planned to say. Dr. Stephen's lead therapist, a brassy blonde named Lynne, tricked me into coming.

"They needed an expert," she smirked. "So I volunteered you."

"The only thing I'm an expert on is playing music in a back-to-back fashion that makes people want to shake their behinds," I replied.

She stared at me until I broke into the Cabbage Patch.

"Just do that," she said. "They'll love it. Besides, one of those super-smart state people will be there too."

"Then why do I need to go?"

"C'mon, it's teenagers," Lynne said with a pleading sort of *shame-on-you* face. "They need somebody like you. Plus," she added flatly, "pays a hundred bucks."

"*Su-i-ciiide*," I sang, spinning on my toes and moonwalking back out the door. "*Just don't do it!*"

So here I am feeling not so cute and funny now. I try to think of something relevant, helpful or meaningful to say. Anything that doesn't sound like absolute adult-to-teen BS. I got nothing. Thank God the state chick does indeed seem pretty smart.

"According to statistics," State Chick says, side-firing the PowerPoint remote to show a charted pie, "at least twelve of you in this room have already made or will make some sort of suicidal attempt or gesture."

I gasp, nearly. *Didn't Bobby Brown's wife say the children were the future?* I take a second look over the crowd. Could I pick out the twelve?

Gothic girl giving me Helter Skelter eyes?

Fat boy in Batman sneakers slouching in the far right desk?

Anorexic anxiety-disorder cheerleader down front?

Once, in a seemingly unfixable and neverending totally frustrating teenage time, I stood out on the side beam of the railroad bridge and thought about how it might feel to step off into the black. Does that count as a gesture? I wasn't suicidal, just dramatic and overwhelmed and needing to feel the weight of choices. Sometimes adults forget all that emotional/hormonal anarchy, but I never did, because in many ways, I am still far too sixteen.

So how did I end up here? Am I really the guy giving the suicide talk in the high school A/V room? *I* should still be in high school. This is so not how I thought things would turn out.

Okay, so I accidentally got some sort of Master's degree in mental health but — really? I'm just a DJ who takes part-time gigs in psych to make a little extra cash. I do midnight crisis so I can work from home, wear whatever I want, duck through the ER and disappear.

I do end up seeing lots of suicidals on the late shift and I always tell them the truth: that I don't have a clue or any answers and if they really want to kill themselves there's nothing me or anyone else can do to stop them. Then I bring them a Dr Pepper and take them outside to smoke.

So why *am* I here? Is it just for the hundred bucks or can I actually muster up something worth saying? *Man, I don't know.*

Uh-oh, the tone of her voice. State Chick is wrapping it up. I tune back in as she tells the students she has the answer to depression.

"Lower your expectations," she says.

Say what?

Cocking out a hip, State Chick rattles the steel of her sterling conch belt and offers a short synopsis of her doomed dating life.

"My cats and my condo," she snips, not nearly so succinct or certain now, "really, is all I need. *Really.*" The assistant principal clears his throat and shoots me an uneasy look.

"My happiness does not depend on *Ron*," she insists, breezily referring to Ron as if he were a brand of fabric softener. "And neither should yours. Learn to be happy with what you have, where you are. Thank you." She flashes a plastic smile and fans her hand in my direction. "I'll turn it over now to my colleague, Mr. DeLane."

Who? Oh, me. Crap, my turn. Walk, think, pray. What was I going to say?

I walk over to the assistant principal, lean down and speak low at his shoulder. He nods and excuses himself from the room. State Chick gathers her materials under her arm, gives me a small wave with her keys in her hand and tiptoes behind him out the door.

"Skating Rink Dude!" a voice cries out from the left.

"Everybody make a circle in the center of the floor . . ." I call back in my DJ voice, pointing to the zit-faced fellow with a horse face and spiky hair, hands still cupped around his mouth. Laughter fractures the tension in the room. I wait for them to settle.

"Man. I mean. Um. . . . That's a tough one, huh?" I ask. "Twelve people in this room." I count off heads. "One, two, three, four. . . . Car crash. Overdose. Razor blade. Hanging from a tree in your backyard. . . ."

The silence is heavy now. I pull a chair from the desk, front and center, and take a seat, searching over their faces.

Sixty eyes on me.

"Twelve people," I repeat. "Twelve."

And I don't have the first clue what to say.

A hard-eyed blonde in Doc Marten boots breaks the silence. "Probably more than that," she croaks. I look around; heads nod slowly.

"At least," adds the baby-faced jock in a letter jacket.

"Well, what can I really tell you?" It's the only thing I can think of to say that feels real. "Except this: Never, *ever* expect less from life. Do that and you're pretty much dead already, just still walking around, breathing and wasting time."

Shouldn't have said that. Nearly every kid in the room nods.

"But you don't need to listen to me," I say. "I need to listen to you. Maybe we just need to listen to each other. All I can tell you is when you talk to people going through the same stuff as you, somehow, it helps."

The overhead lights tick and hum. Near the back, a droopy-eyed girl puffs an inhaler and drags her nose down the sleeve of her shirt.

My rabbi friend once told me that there is a cliffhanger of silence that therapists and priests know as Holy. "Eh," he waffled. "It can be Holy. It's up to the people. There's nothing you can do but wait."

I'm winging it. So I wait.

The Future.

The cheerleader bites her lip and slowly lifts her hand.

Abide |

"One thing we are very suspicious of here is ambition."
— Abbott at the Abbey of Gethsemani

Insurance companies cripple mental health under allegations of fraud and benefit abuse. These allegations, for the most part, are true. The outpatient program clamps down and chops service to the bone. Forest Hills is cut from five units to two. So long horse barn, goodbye gym. No more month-long stays. There are staff cutbacks and the work is harder for less pay. I hold on to weekend nights, carry call when I can and scramble to pay my truck note and the student loan. Sometimes, I consider a job with the state.

Do what you have to do, they say. *You get used to it.*

A Jesus-hippie buddy of mine puts together bicycles for Toys R Us. "I can probably get you on, bro," he says, trying to help. "Manager is way cool."

I go for an interview; the manager is a nice guy but he refuses to hire me. "I appreciate you coming out," he says, rocking on his heels with hands in his pockets. "But come on, man. Assembling Schwinns at We-Be-Toys is *so* not where you belong."

He's got a sort of abiding Jeff Bridges vibe about him so I ask, "Then where do I belong?" I figure the assistant manager at a toy store is as good a guru as any.

"Ah, dude — I don't know." He holds his arms out and I swear, even though we are in a closed stockroom, a gentle wind blows through his hair. "You gotta find it for yourself."

The Kingdom Is Now

Terry's the psych ward night tech, a lean fellow, sort of concave chest and belly roll, hairy as a Sasquatch everywhere, tragically, except for lonesome wisps scattered across the top of his head. The patients love him — even the redneck truckers strung out on meth — because he's easy to talk to and so down to earth.

At one time Terry was the music minister at a large church in town. He loved his job but eventually outed himself to a pastor and asked for help. Gossip spread swiftly and what was said in confidence was twisted and told throughout the church. Terry was let go.

He strayed awhile and then started his own support group, meeting weekly with other outcasts, discussing how difficult it is not to drink or drug or be promiscuous. I can tell he misses *church* church though. I'm in the break room charting while he cleans.

"Did you go Sunday?" he asks. "Is your praise team doing that *lift our hands* song?" His lily-white arms arch to the ceiling, swaying forth and back. "I love that song," he says, squeezing his eyes shut, singing a little run from the chorus. He snaps to, gazing up. "Good gosh, I've got Kermit arms. So what's y'all's summer mission project?"

"I think we're sending the youth to do mime at the Mall of America. How 'bout your group? Still going?"

"Monday nights at the dyke bar," he says, dismantling the coffee pot and washing the parts in a tiny sink. "We've been supporting this group that buys back sex slaves from Thailand, helps them start their own business or get a trade." Terry digs through his wallet and shows me a smiling picture of a brown-skinned girl. "This is Sarai. She sells real estate now." He pauses. "Okay, so maybe we don't improve *all* of their lives. But I'm hoping if I help save enough sex trade slaves God will forgive me for being a grouchy old fag."

I'm about to reply when the intercom buzzes. A sheriff's deputy on the closed circuit screen nudges a man in shackles and a hospital gown. "Do they *have* to handcuff the psych patients?" Terry asks. He stabs the call button and speaks into the panel. "Be right there."

We make our way through three sets of electro-locked steel doors, out to the circle drive. "Commitment case for you. Felix DeLeon," says the deputy, shoving papers into our hands. Bleary, weary and totally bewildered, DeLeon looks like George Carlin after all-you-can-drink dollar wine night followed by a fist fight in a dumpster.

"Come on, Mr. Felix. We'll take good care of you," Terry tells him.

The old drunk stumbles, his eyes rolling over the both of us. "And who the hell'r you?" he asks.

"Best of luck, gentlemen," the deputy says as he removes the cuffs. "He's all yours."

We escort Felix to his room and check his luggage, clothes and deodorant stuffed into grocery sacks. Terry finds a Gideon Bible and starts leafing through the pages.

"Listen to this one," he says, clearing his throat. "I tell you the truth, tax collectors and prostitutes are entering the kingdom ahead of you." He slips the Bible back into the bag. "Did you know that in Hebrew *kingdom of God* means a present day reality and not so much later in Heaven?" He pulls out a pair of grass-stained sneakers, lifts the insole and holds up a small baggie filled with pills. "It just means a better way of living right now."

"*Damn*," Felix pants, lolling his head from side to side.

Back in the break room things get quiet, the eleven to seven nurse grazing on microwave popcorn and shuffling through late-night cable in the lounge.

Once, when Terry was out sick, she told me in a low whisper that after the church disaster went down, he dressed up in a drag queen show with some friends. She said it was highly entertaining, that he put on a long black wig and sang a pretty good version of "Gypsies, Tramps and Thieves." One night two young men caught him alone in the parking lot with his dresses and wigs and just as they began to threaten and push him around, the back doors exploded and drag queens burst out, overpowering the thugs and giving them a sound thrashing. "Don't tell Terry I told you that," she said.

"Where'd you learn Hebrew?" I ask him.

"Bible College," Terry says. "Always wanted to be in full-time ministry. Was thinking of going back before the church put me out."

"They just fired you?"

"No, first they sent me to one of those de-gay-ifying programs."

"How'd that work?" I ask.

"*Pfff*," he scoffs. "You see those guys a month later back in the gay bar."

I laugh but Terry doesn't. "Serious," he says. "This guy tells his story about how he got delivered, *praise the Lord*, crying and all that. Month later I saw him at Silly Sally's in a string tank and denim cutoffs, dancing to the Oak Ridge Boys."

"Oak Ridge Boys?"

"It was country night," Terry says, slapping the desk. "Had on black boots and a cowboy hat with a purple feather in it. I went up to him like 'Aren't you Mr. Straight and Narrow now?' He said *Baby, I gotta be me*."

"Wild," I reply.

"You know how it is. Liars and adulterers, *come on in*, but if you're gay you've got two visits to get right and start liking girls." He cuts his eyes. "Unless you're a girl of course."

Terry leans against the tech's desk and takes a long breath, his chicken eyes sad and hollow. "I worry sometimes though. What if they're right?" He rustles through the drawer and digs out some Saltines. "I don't feel like I chose this . . . cracker?"

"No thanks." I reply. "Terry, I don't know, man. If it was up to me, church would say *Come on in everybody, anybody. We're all praying — God, be patient and help us figure out this crazy thing called life. First though, we're going to work on the mean people.*"

Crumbs tumble from his mouth. "Hallelujah," he laughs. "Come on, I need a cigarette."

In the middle of the psych ward courtyard there's the ghost of a swimming pool, filled with concrete after a teenage boy tied himself to a lounge chair and drowned. We walk around the silhouette of the old diving board, not saying much, Terry smoking and me drinking a Diet Coke when there's a pull at my shirttail.

"Spot me a smoke, Captain?" Felix wheezes, his shivering frame bent and frail beneath a thin v-neck tee.

"Honey, he don't smoke," Terry snaps playfully. "Here."

With the focus of a man defusing a bomb, Felix slides out a cigarette and cups it between both hands, like a fragile bird. "Light?" he begs, interrupted by a tremendous fit of hacking. Terry takes Felix's trembling fist and holds the ends of their cigarettes together, their faces close until both ashes begin to glow.

"Shanks," says the grizzled old addict, wobbling to the corner of the concrete slab and sitting with his arms across his knees.

"Felix needs to get somebody to bring him some friggin' cigarettes," Terry says. He holds his Winston between two fingers and takes a long drag. "Guess I could stop tomorrow on the way in."

"I can do it," I offer.

Terry lets the vapor slip from the side of his mouth and shakes his head. "I have to stop anyway," he sighs. "God knows, I might be in a place like this someday and need somebody to be kind to me."

We stand there on the deep end of the psych ward pool, watching Felix in the shallows, flat on his back, blowing smoke to the stars.

"Terry," I say, "maybe ministry is a lot closer than you think."

Amen in All the Wrong Places |

"Nobody realizes that some people expend tremendous energy merely to appear normal." — Albert Camus

Over at the church, Pastor Reddy is cast out due to issues of anger and control. I love him but there's truth to the charges. They replace him with a brash bully who brags from the platform about his alligator shoes. The church splits and I leave.

There's a smaller non-denominational church on the outskirts of town and I show up Sunday evenings, sitting in the short pew by the foyer door.

One night, during missions report, I pick up a pew Bible and study through Revelations, matching verses and themes to the heavy metal songs they've influenced. Still restless, I make a list of all the rock songs I can think of that have Christian lyrics. Ozzy's "Revelation (Mother Earth)." Bon Jovi's "Born to Be My Baby." I've got a ruminating Baptist buddy who says even Bon Scott can be seen as a hoary old prophet on "Highway to Hell."

Then I flip to the Good Book's other end and read through the Book of Job. As literature, it's weird and wonderfully bizarre. Theologically, regardless of the spin, the whole wager thing between the devil and God is scary and just doesn't seem fair.

I've never been very good at church. I like the wrong songs, the wrong Bible verses, laugh at the wrong jokes, ask the wrong questions, say amen in all the wrong places. Groups make me nervous. But I would like to find my place. I don't tell anybody this, but sometimes I feel like I've been called to preach. It's a bone-deep feeling, like the time between finding water with a divining rod and taking the first cold drink. I don't want to be a motivational speaker or a life coach or a scripture teacher. I want to raise hell for Heaven's sake, to say things that stir people and make them feel angry and awake and alive. I want to ride shotgun with God through this crazy thing called life. Sometimes I think my brain is too sideways to ever be saved.

I could join the monastery but all those monks would get on my nerves. Mission field? I can almost see myself teaching English in Bangladesh . . . taking my bicycle to work at the one-room schoolhouse with a rooster on my shoulder and a monkey in the basket by the handlebars. . . .

Maybe I should just go to seminary.

Man, I don't know. I wish I could win a five-minute phone call from God.

Psychologists might state this is cognitive bias, desperate magical thinking. Existential philosophers would say this is using religion to put off the responsibility of freedom. Conservative theologians could claim that all the communication a human needs exists in the Word.

Still, just five minutes.

The service ends with heads bowed, a call for those who feel drawn to service to file down front. With every eye closed and no one looking around, I slip out the back door.

Hot Pants

A well-meaning DJ friend cons me into taking his strip club shift for the night.

"Awesome money," DJ Dan says, knowing I need the cash. "And it's a classy place. The girls, they don't even take their bottoms off."

I walk in and there's a buck-toothed blonde with wind-blown hair, legs in the air, grinding on a pole to Great White's "Once Bitten, Twice Shy." Scarlet lips and stiletto heels, she twirls and pulls down the straps of her star-spangled bustier.

Pastor Reddy's words ring my ear: *God goes with you everywhere you go.*

"Don't look, Jesus," I whisper.

I make my way across the club, a low-ceiling cave that stinks of stale smoke and tanning lotion, weaving through the litter of leering old bikers and loud sweaty salesmen.

Jesus had a soft heart for trashy women. For scoundrels and rebels and crooks. Thank God, Jesus ran with a rough crowd.

"I got this," I say to myself.

A manicured nail traces its way up my arm and rests on my chest. A black-haired cupcake with her hair in a bun, big geek glasses, a shimmy halter-top and pink hot pants stands before me.

Lord, I pray. *I'll meet you at the truck.*

"I am *so* thirsty . . . ," Hot Pants coos, dropping her chin demurely.

A real man controls his desires. He treats women with respect. With value and honor. Pastor had gathered the young men and taught us these things.

Her hand slides down the front of my shirt until the crook of her finger hooks my belt. With a giggle, she pulls me in close and whispers three magical words. "You wanna dance?"

Dance, says the devil. *Tomorrow is a world away.*

"Um, I'm just here to uh . . . play the music," I fumble.

Her saucy eyes go flat in a flash. "Chad's over there." She points towards the DJ booth, a black tower looming over the stage. "I think he's looking for you." I thank her as she eyes me up and down. "Watch out for Sunshine. She's . . ." Hot Pants points to her pockets then rolls her eyes. "Never mind."

The money is decent and overall it's a pretty PG-13 affair, like DJ Dan told me. But the music is just a prop, the energy flat and confabulated. Unlike the dance club or the rink, there's no connection at all.

After close, Hot Pants knocks on the DJ booth window and asks for a walk to her car.

"Why you do this?" I ask, not in a judgmental way.

"I like to dance," she replies. "Money's good."

"That's it?"

"There's other stuff," she says, looking towards the blue twinkle of airport lights. "Nothin' I wanna talk about now." Hot Pants peels a twenty from a stack of bills and hands it to me.

"Whoa, no way," I say. "What's this for?"

"Standard for girls to tip the guy that walks you to your car."

"That's too much," I tell her.

"Take it," she says, pushing my hand away. "I know you wouldn't do this if you didn't need the money." Hot Pants smiles, genuine now, and touches my elbow. "You did a good job tonight."

In sweats and a tee, with the makeup toned down, she looks like a pretty nice girl. "Hey, you wanna go get some pancakes?" I ask. "My treat."

She stares at my face like a palm reader studying hands. "Pancakes . . . ," she says as if it were the name of a long-lost pet. There's a sad short laugh and she stares at a spot just behind me on the ground. "No thanks, baby."

"Why not?"

Hot Pants pops the lock and slides into her dirty white Pontiac. "You're sweet for askin'," she says, "but I ain't your type."

"What's that supposed to mean?"

She cranks the car and grinds into first. "You know what I mean," she says.

The stripper's Sunbird lays rubber and roars away. I spit my gum into the sewer grate and watch her disappear.

Back at my truck, Jesus is leaning against the hood, writing in the dust with his finger. Whoever does those pictures for church foyers and Christian bookstores is charitable because truth is, in person, he doesn't look like much. If Jesus were a Bee Gee, he'd be Maurice. Except for the eyes. He can say a lot without speaking a word.

"Just pancakes," I explain, avoiding those eyes. Jesus almost smiles, turns and draws in the dust again.

"C'mon, you drive," I tell him, tossing over the keys. "Let's go home."

Forever Church

As a child, I hated church. Church was a duty, dull and depressing, anti-think and anti-fun. People didn't act like themselves at church. Everything was fake sunny and blunted, like one big sappy greeting card store. I hid this secret in my heart but it was true. If God was the way church made Him out to be, I didn't want to believe.

Sometimes though, when I couldn't sleep, I would talk to the presence I felt late at night and figure maybe that was God. That God wasn't much like Himself at church either. It was easy conversation about girls at school and music and movies and comic books. If there *was* a God, I wondered what music He would like. So we would talk about it.

Okay, so God — who's your favorite band?
Hmmm. CCR, probably. . . . You?
They're a little janky for me. What you think about Ozzy?
Ah, God Bless Ozzy. He's a good heart.

One Sunday morning, the preacher assured us that movies, comic books and rock and roll music were a waste of time. He said that in Heaven there was no more night. That eternity was like church forever, forever church. After that, I was pretty much done.

The first time I stayed up all night long I was eleven years old. Just after two a.m., I snuck my bike out and rode around the empty streets. I liked the way trees looked skeletal and scary cool at night, the way traffic lights flashed instead of changing from red to green. I loved the way time crawled and the world turned slow. I liked feeling like the whole world was sleeping and I was the only person alive. In that moment, I knew that God was alive too.

Probably Dustin Diamond

"Across the street, lady in distress, can you go over?"

"Where?"

"Across the street."

"At the bank building?"

Third floor, back through some cubicles. Two ladies, a black woman in a pantsuit and a younger girl in a tight red skirt and white heels.

"What happened?" I ask.

"Jada, she got some call and started freaking out and climbed in the wall."

I hunch down and peer into the hole. "What is this," I ask, "some kind of big vent or something?"

"Yeah, she's back there," says Pantsuit. "Her and her man been having some problems."

"Jada, the guy's here, honey," White Heels calls through the hole.

"I ain't climbin' in there," I tell them. Both women shoot me a harsh look. "Y'all call the cops?" I ask.

"Look, she needs help. She don't need to be arrested," says Pantsuit, then right behind her, White Heels adds, "You're a counselor, right? She just *needs* someone to talk to."

"I ain't no counselor."

"What are you?"

World's greatest skating rink DJ. "I'm a — um, crisis interventionist," I tell her.

"Hello?" White Heels says, gesturing to the wall. "I think we got a crisis here."

I lean down and gaze back into the vent. Stand again. "I'm not climbin' in that hole."

A bulbous man with strands of white running through the sides of his hair steps up to us. "Listen," he says, with a supervisor's tone, "I'm going to have to call an ambulance."

"Kent," Pantsuit grunts. "Not yet, this here man's from crisis." There's a cell phone clipped to the belt of Kent's navy Sansabelt slacks. He looks at me and runs his hand down his face.

"I'm claustrophobic," I tell him.

"Screw it," says White Heels, twisting off her shoes and tossing them to the side.

"Jada, baby," she says, "I'm a come in there, you hold on."

She shoots me a really ugly look and tugs at her skirt. "All the days to wear a dress . . . ," she grumbles, scrunching down with one hand on the hem of her garment.

"Wait, wait," I tell her. "Y'all sure she doesn't have any weapons?"

"What's she gonna have? A stapler?"

"I mean no razor blades or knives or anything?"

A voice comes from back in the hole. "I don't have nothin'."

I look in their faces one by one. Kneel down and crawl into the hole.

Made-for-TV movie. Misfit Psych Guy saves jilted woman from the . . . collapsed mine shaft. Who will play my role? Probably Dustin Diamond.

I scooch through on my elbows. It's not so bad, actually. Not a vent, some sort of low-paneled crawlspace.

The gap gets bigger at the end. A girl sits with her back against the wall. She's pug-dog cute and reminds me of the TV chef, Rachel Ray. If Rachel Ray let herself go a little. It's kinda dim back here.

"Thanks for coming," she says, sarcastic-like. She's crying, blotting her face with a wadded-up tissue.

"I'm claustrophobic," I explain.

"I heard you out there," she says. "You didn't have to crawl up in here. I'm fine."

"Your friends don't think so."

"Yeah, well."

"What happened?"

She goes to explain and then breaks down crying into the Kleenex. After awhile she ekes out the words. "Tucker, he called and said he's leavin'. Took all his stuff, said he's leavin' me for Tammie."

"Who's Tammie?"

Jada blows her nose and takes a long breath in. "Bitch at the tanning salon," she says.

"Sorry to hear that."

"Calls me at work like he knows I ain't gonna freak out here, like what am I gonna do, right?"

"So you crawled back here."

"I was crying so hard. When I was a little girl we used to have a space like this through my bedroom closet. I used to sit there when the storms came, it calmed me."

"You didn't see this coming?"

"I been through a lot this year. Doctor got me on anti-depressants, sleeping pills. Still don't sleep half the time." Then, in a quieter voice, "Sometimes I tell the girls I'm goin' to lunch and come sit back here and pray and stuff, try to get my mind right. I'll be fine. I just don't want to go out there right now. Everybody needs to just let me chill."

"You suicidal?"

There's other voices now down the hole. Something about an ambulance on the way. One of the women says her mother's on the line.

Jada rests her head against the wall. "I don't think so," she says.

"What is this place?"

"Used to stack files back here," she says. "Not us. People here before us."

I sit back against the opposite wall and stretch out my legs. "One time I had a crush on this girl named Bekka Rooney. Invited to her my birthday party, all my friends there. I'm just smitten. Right in front of everybody she says I'm a skinny monkey with a big ugly nose. I climbed the big elm in the backyard and hid rest of the day. Birthday cake and candle time came, they couldn't find me. I didn't want to be around nobody. Needed some time."

"So she called you a monkey and you climbed a tree?"

"Pretty much."

Jada nods her head. "You remember what it feels like then."

"Sure," I tell her. "That party was just last year."

She spits out laughter and presses the Kleenex to her eyes. "What, you get paid to crawl in holes and make crazy people laugh?"

"Ah, you're not crazy," I tell her.

"Jada," Pantsuit's voice calls, "ambulance is here, baby."

"Shit," says Jada.

"Ok, look," I tell her. "We can't sit in this hole all day. You're gonna have to go with the ambulance guys. Or with me. I know I don't seem real professional but . . ."

"I know I need to get some help," she says. "So will you be my counselor?"

"I ain't no counselor."

"What are you?"

I don't answer. From outside the hole, radios squawk, more voices add to the mix. Jada laughs again and shakes her head.

Child-Sized Again |

"Original Sin was born of Original Anxiety — the terror freedom creates in us when we discover we are free and must decide what to do." — Lincoln Swain

There's a treatment team meeting at ten a.m. where we talk about patients and progress plans and *please God, send the bombs*, marketing.

We're seated in a small room with a huge wooden table, the kind where knees and elbows bump and chair backs ram into the wall, where once you are in, you are trapped. Everyone is on their third cup of coffee, downing digestive aids and fielding distress calls from their daycares while I sit in the back corner looking like a dog forced to wear a Halloween costume.

"First, let's go over the admission statistics," the director says. "Sorry about the size of these letters but I had a lot to get on the page."

I imagine myself small, very small, micro-sized and flying, zooming corpuscles and buzzing through veins and brainwaves, dwarfed by quarks, shrinking deeper, farther, down into inner space. . . .

My neighbor passes me a sheaf of papers, figures and graphs.

"As you can see on page six, the numbers are down. We need to get these up, way up," says the director.

I am tall as a house, a ten-story bank, a tower scraping the sky, one

*foot in the ocean, the other in the sea, seven thousand miles high and
rising, stepping over the black hole and knocking on the onyx gates of
God's mountain home.*

*The LORD steps out, wiping His hands on a flowered dishtowel. In
His shadow I am child-sized again.*

*He scoops me into His arms. His hair and beard are radiant, white
like a rushing waterfall. He smells like vanilla wafers and line-dried
linens, cinnamon and myrrh, the air before a summer storm.*

*"My boy, my boy," He says. The iris of God's eye is a brilliant blue
fire. "Want to go for a ride?" With the wave of a finger, the garage
doors of God begin to part. . . .*

"Blaine, are you getting this?"

The program director is a humorless old crow who would
be fortunate to work as an assistant mop swaddler in a Bangkok
sweat shop but somehow got a social work degree despite having a disposition somewhere between Harriet Oleson and
Cruella DeVil. She claims to be an atheist but is just the kind
of self-righteous, mean-spirited crank that makes good atheists
look so bad. Strangely enough, sometimes we get along quite
swimmingly.

"Yeah," I say, blinking.

I try my best to pay attention, to listen and follow along.
My coworkers paw through the ever-present box of dry, dusty
donuts and shoo away the obligatory fly. They look sick and
haunted — *as sick or sicker than the patients*, I think. *Am I the sick-
est?* My blood turns to quicksand, churning turmoil. The walls
waver, like heat on asphalt; the ceiling begins to press down. I
try to ride it out. *Can't do it.* I slap the table with both hands and
stand.

"Crap!" I say. "I left the stove on!" In a flash, I'm gone.

In the truck, I can breathe right again. For about two minutes I feel like life's biggest failure. Like I'll never be capable of
even a semi-normal life. Never grow up, never be dependable. I
can see myself homeless, wandering, sleeping in a boxcar bound
for Montana. . . .

The stagecoach winds up the summit and into the clouds. On Granite Peak, we fill from the well and pass another slow-moving train. Leaning from the rail of the very last car, Jesus sprays graffiti down my door.

LIVE FREE OR DIE

There's a box cutter in the glove compartment. I hack off my khakis above the knee and tie the scrap around my head like Stallone in *Rambo III*. Roll the windows down. I don't know what I am going to do tomorrow. But today, tonight, I'm free.

Any Color You Like |

Nikki the floor guard meets me at the roller rink door and holds up her hands. "Major crisis," she declares.

"What?" I ask. "What is it?"

"Brittany's birthday cake didn't get delivered."

I laugh like a jackal, drive to the grocery store in my skates and roll through the bakery until I find a ready-made red velvet cake with rainbows and butterflies. While I wait, the lady pipes *Happy Birthday Brittany* with icing on top.

Thirty minutes later the candles are lit and everybody sings. The music is loud and children are laughing and the disco balls are throwing light against the walls.

An eight-year-old kid with silver braces, her hair in cornrows and a tiara that says *Birthday Girl*, rushes over and jumps into my arms. "You are so cool!" she says. "My party rocks!"

I'm assistant manager at the rink now. If the coke fountain breaks down I can change the CO_2. I can doctor wheels and plates and teach little kids to skate backwards. I can bandage a skinned knee and spin cotton candy, any color you like.

After Brittany's bash ends at nine, we blow up the moonwalk, drag it to the middle of the floor and kick the smoke machines on high. Nikki and me and the rest of the skating rink staff, Jessie and Jenny and Isaac.

A mix list of favorite songs booms through massive speakers.

We jump and bounce and wrestle and dance and lay breathless and sweaty while a thousand sparkles swarm the fog around us.

"This is it," I shout as Mr. Serv-On mixes into DJ Kool.

"What is?" says Jessie, a chesty blonde tomboy.

We laugh; me laughing at her laughing at me. Scaling the moonwalk wall, I backflip over the bunch of them, bounce up and tell her again. *"This."*

She dropkicks me into the corner and scissor locks my head. "What are you talkin' about?" she says.

Come On, Crazy Diamond |

A thirty-six-year-old mother of two escapes from the psych ward, finds my parents' name in the phone book and convinces my father we are long-lost friends. I come home late and she is waiting by my door, barefoot in a sheer pink gown, with her clothes in a Barbie backpack.

"I left it all," she tells me. "Everything to be with you."

Her fingertips brush skin, sweeping back flaxen hair; she pulls against the neckline of the gown. Her eyes shine like crazy diamonds and the moon, of course, is full. She is not an unattractive woman.

Seize the night. You can be sorry tomorrow.

We stand there a full minute, like gunfighters on a dusty road.

Then another voice, smaller, like windchimes before a storm: *God goes with you, everywhere you go.*

"Come on, Ms. Staci," I say. "Get in the truck. Time to get you home."

Secret |

The guest reverend is a short, portly fellow with an easy preaching style and earthy sense of humor who can turn serious on a dime and make a statement so profound the whole room goes still. Throughout his message, he keeps giving me a look, like he recognizes my face but can't quite figure out who I am.

After service, he catches me at the back door. "I don't know you, friend," he says, "but while I was in the platform, God gave me a word for you."

Uh-oh.

I'm staring sort of blankly, not being impolite, just waiting. I've seen this sort of thing happen at church before, but never to me. It makes me nervous and I'm afraid of what he might say, that I won't know the right thing to say back.

"You're wondering what to do, where to go, what your purpose is," the preacher tells me. "Forget all that." He places his hand on my arm and looks me in the eye. "God says find the secret place."

I know humans hear what they want and need to hear. I know the tricks of psychics and preachers and salesmen. I love the mystical and am leery of it at the same time. But still, I believe.

"The secret place," I repeat, like a correspondent for the evening news.

The preacher turns up his palms and shrugs. "I'm just telling you what He said."

Far Away & Fractured
Another Night on Psych

Wednesday, 6:05 p.m.

A buzzcut mechanic with first-onset psychosis puts his foot through the lounge television screaming, "Lee Greenwood is the Antichrist!" He gives us a fight but we get the needle in, 10 mg of Haldol/Ativan/Benadryl, and within minutes he's a sweetheart again.

"Heard a lot of antichrists," I say, "but never Lee Greenwood."

A one-legged OxyContin fiend in American flag pajamas shakes her juice box at me and says, "That fool's been flipping back and forth between CMT and CNN all night. I tried to tell y'all some bullcrap like this was gonna go down."

7:30 p.m.

A female PICU patient with Einstein's hair and the physique of Mean Joe Greene wriggles free from my waist lock and sinks her teeth into my pants, just to the right of the zipper. Thank God for baggy jeans.

When we stick her, she roars like a grizzly and sinks to the floor. Before I leave, she calls me over and says in the kindest voice that I look *just* like her son, Marlon. She takes me by the hand and sings the first verse of "You Light up My Life."

8:50 p.m.

I'm knocking on doors down Adolescent hall. "Med time," I say.

Teenage patients shuffle to the nurses' station in gym shorts, oversized tees and bunny slippers. Two are missing. Second to last door on the right.

"Med time," I call, knocking at their door. I wait, listen and knock again. "Let's go, girls."

"Come in," a muffled voice says.

"Come on," I say through the door. "Get your meds."

"I need some help," a tiny voice returns.

Everyone is down at the station. I open the door. Both girls are naked from the waist up, posing with hands on their hips. The curly girl half-covers herself with one hand and gives me a hackneyed look of surprise. The straight-haired brunette just smiles. I'm frozen, caught in their trap.

"We want cigarettes," Straight Brunette says with a flirty smirk. "Or we're tellin'."

Bluff. Think quick. "Ladies, please," I say dismissively. "It's like, tits for cigarettes every other day in this place."

"Told you, Sondra," Curly Girl says with disgust as she pulls on her shirt. "Told you he wouldn't give us no cigarettes. We shoulda tried that other guy."

"Faggot," Sondra says, still smirking, shirtless and staring straight into my eyes. "What's your problem?"

9:40 p.m.

There's a call to the front, new patient coming from the local ER. "This one's pretty bad off," the lady cop says. "Blood alcohol of 390, slit wrist."

The shell of an old coworker sits shackled in the back seat, a therapist from a program I worked for in grad school. "C'mon, hon," the officer says, easing her from the car and helping her to stand.

My old colleague is disoriented, disheveled, her hair knotted and gray at the roots. She looks old and tired and I can tell she is far from herself, in a dark and awful place. For a foggy minute she doesn't recognize me, then the tiniest of lights flickers in her eyes. "Thank God it's you," she cries, collapsing against me. "I am so ashamed."

I take her through the double doors and down the back hall, her face to the floor and arms clinging to my elbow. Near the nurses' station she stops and stares at an office across the way.

"I used to work right there . . . ," she says, in a voice so far away and fractured, like an international phone call from Iceland, 1935.

Before I can reply, the loudspeaker crackles to life.

"*Dr. Strong. ADU.*"

"Sit here," I say, steering her to a chair on the other side of the lounge. "I'll be right back."

10:05 p.m.

"*Dr. Strong. ADU!*"

Over on rehab, Johnny Ray pulls down the lights.

I wrestle him down and steer him to the seclusion room while the nurse runs to fetch her twin needles of Thorazine. Johnny Ray hunkers in the corner, cross-eyed with crooked sideburns, dubiously watching my hands.

"Go ahead," he says, choking back tears. "Y'all just do whatever the hell it is you gotta do."

I pick up a chair and heave it into the wall. The legs stick; it juts out sideways from the berm. Johnny Ray tucks his head between his knees. I slide down beside him.

"That felt pretty good," I say.

Johnny Ray turns his hollow face to me, his breath thick and bitter, a filmy set of teeth bucked out over his bottom lip. "Let it on out," he says slowly, patting my arm with his clammy hand. "Don't do no good to keep it all in."

The nurse returns with her needles. "What's goin' on with the wall here?" she asks.

I raise my finger to Johnny Ray, half-laughing when I tell her, "He did it."

Pinball or Die |

"I tend to ascribe meaning to meaningless things to make myself feel more spiritual. Sometimes it pans out." — Megan Leah Power

It's 11:30 on a Tuesday night and the streets are empty and wet from an early rain. I ride my bike up to the Quik Stop, get two dollars in quarters and head back by the Icee machine to play *Phantom of the Opera* pinball. Twenty minutes or so I can go, on just on one quarter. I plug in my money; with a squeal the bumpers blaze, everything is neon and chrome.

I'd pulled a double on psych the night before — four p.m. to seven a.m. — and it was one hellish round after another of Thorazine takedowns and schizophrenic battle royales. At two in the morning an addict stepped off the porch into the community yard, disconnected the hose to the central air unit and nearly asphyxiated himself huffing Freon. Then, an hour before my shift was over, just as the sun was coming up, a retired schoolteacher was found hanging from the sprinkler head in his room. The charge nurse screamed just as I was getting morning vitals and by the time I rounded the corner all I saw were swinging feet and a bathrobe dangling loose. Another tech held up his legs but the noose was too tight and I had to cut into his neck to get him free. There was blood and he was sputtering and already turning blue.

I came home, ate a bowl of Cocoa Pebbles and slept 'til the sun went down.

When I was a kid, pinball was a hideout, a way to shut off my mind. So. Now. Better than snorting Halcion and downing shots of Jack.

While I wait for the ball, I catch my reflection in the window, just beneath the *Pick 3* lottery and malt liquor bull signs.

My old friends are buying homes and having babies and working their way up the ladder. I'm riding my Huffy to the Quik Stop to play all-night pinball. At the moment, I can't decide whether I'm on top of the world or on the bottom. I point to the figure in the glass.

There you are.

Guy comes in, rumpled suit, groggy eyes. Roams the aisles until he finds the Children's Tylenol. Takes it to the front and slides a twenty across the counter.

"Pint," he says with his eyes on the floor. I know him. Dake Kellers. College, third year. He always was a go-getter, the kind of guy I envied in a lot of ways, the sort of person who always seemed to have a positive attitude and a solid plan. Last I heard, he was married with two kids and working at the bank.

"Matter what kind?" says Sammy, the Quik Stop cashier.

"Nothing matters tonight," Dake mutters.

He takes the Old Charter and Children's Tylenol and climbs back into his Civic. Through the windshield I see him take a long pull from the liquor before he drives on.

"Storm's moving back in," Sammy tells me. "You can put your bike in the back room if you want."

Rain on asphalt. Taillights in the night. Alarm clocks and cubicles. Nine to five until you die.

Sammy keeps a radio on the liquor shelf end. *Midnight showers, drive safe and make it a . . . Slow Ride!* the DJ says in a stoned croak. Four on the floor, the bass drum thumps, Lonesome Dave's guitar wails like a siren in the night.

"Hell yeah," Sammy whispers as he turns it up.
Nothing matters tonight.
I pull back the plunger and fire.

Southern Gothic Sphinx

I'm sharing a cracker-box apartment by the college with a sloppy economics major but he's moving at semester's end. Some low-rent offices are available across from the Hey Y'all Used Car lot, right next to a bait and tackle shop. It's dumpy but there's a shower and I figure I can make a pallet on the floor. Two-fifty a month.

I'm about to put a deposit down when a coworker calls about her apartment in the pool house of a Southern Gothic mansion. "Meet me here in an hour," she says.

Iron spiral staircase. Walls and ceiling Picasso blue. Paris décor from the real Coco Chanel. Hidden gardens, ivy obelisks and statues of Venus and David. Driveway gated and guarded by twin Sphinxes.

"Warhol swam in my pool," the owner tells me as we pass the estate's peculiar lagoon. "Capote too."

One hundred and twenty-five dollars a month, all bills paid.

"I have to move soon," my coworker says. "Would you like to live here?"

The Gap Band Backing David Allen Coe |

Spike opens a record shop just up the street from my new house and I hang out on lazy afternoons and watch the counter for a little cash now and then. There's a *Galaga* console in the corner and a couch behind the front desk where we discuss subjects such as why Michael Anthony was the glue that made Van Halen so great and what Sabbath's *Heaven and Hell* might have sounded like if they had hired Roger Troutman instead of bringing Dio into the fold.

"So what's the bootleg holy grail?" I ask one day.

"The Gap Band backing David Allen Coe," Spike replies, looking a little like Alf with thick glasses. "Supposedly happened on some shows in Oklahoma." He walks to the racks and holds up a vinyl copy of *Gap Band V*. All three members sport ten-gallon hats and rhinestone fringe.

"Take it from a DJ," I say, "'Party Train' works at any wedding, any dance, any party in the world."

As customers slip in and out, we break out the guitars and work up acoustic approximations of George Jones covering "Hot Legs" and Green Day taking a stab at "Stayin' Alive." Jagger doing Little Milton's "Misty Blue." Spike's tastes are eclectic as mine and his knowledge of all genres pretty near encyclopedic. He's the only guy I know who loves music more than I do.

"Man, I should have opened a record store," I tell him.

"You know what's better than owning a record store?" He doesn't wait for my reply. "Having a friend that does."

This Is the Mattress Trick |

A nineteen-year-old patient with frosted tips and a tight Lycra tee smuggled in a steak knife and is barricaded in the bathroom, threatening to stab himself in the heart.

There are so many patients and so little staff, I don't really know him. Dual-diagnosis, depression. Addiction to Darvocet, maybe. Moody, histrionic at times. Manipulative. I might be thinking of the wrong guy.

The psych ward bathrooms are Jack and Jill and I enter from the opposite side, hands up and moving slow. Now I know this guy. Hair razored on the sides and long on top. Lantern face, zits and braces. Walks as close as he can to the walls with his head down, like a beaten dog. Moody, manipulative, he's the one.

"Easy, easy," I say in my softest voice. "Nobody's here to hurt you." There are two more techs behind me, a new kid and Heather, the star college athlete we all call Softball.

"Sick of this place. *Sick of it*," David shouts. Softball had ordered him to end his call just as phone times were over. He was already set off and things escalated from there until he stormed down the hall and slammed his door. The knife is in his right hand, upside down from the way you'd cut a steak. He isn't pointing it at me or at himself. I edge in.

"I know, I know. This place sucks," I tell him. "Look, I'm not telling you what you can or can't do. If you really want to hurt yourself there's nothing I can do to stop you."

"That's right," David says.

"Right," I affirm, taking another step closer. He's sitting sideways between the tub and toilet, the knife hand resting by his leg now. "Just talk to me a minute so I can say I tried, man, please." My heart is breaking and it shows in my face. I say it again. *"Please, David."*

"I'll talk to you," he says. "But tell her to get back." I look over and see Softball's face in the door.

"Phone time was *over*, David," she says. "You don't get special privileges."

"Shut up, Bulldog!" he says. "Take your dyke face on home!" In a tragically comic moment, he yanks the toilet paper from the holder and hurls it at her with his left hand.

She ducks and pops back in, the new tech's eyes wide over her shoulder. "David," she warns, "you better chill, man."

"Whoa. Whoa," I say in my calmest voice. "Everybody cool out. We're fine. Y'all step on back. Me and Mr. David are just gonna talk here."

Softball shoots him a steely glare. "Heather, go on," I scold. "Sit over there on the *bed* and ratchet yourself down some. Geez."

David breathes heavy, his nostrils flaring like an angry bull. The knife hand twitches, higher now.

"David, you're not going to stab me, are you?" He shakes his head, no.

"It's just us," I tell him. "Whatever you wanna talk about, I'll hear you out and help the best I can, okay?" He nods, yes.

"You mind if I sit here?"

"Go ahead," he says. "You're all right." Then louder, so Softball can hear. "Sick of *some* people in my space all the time."

"Yes sir," I reply, moving slowly down the wall with a wince. *"Agh.* Sorry. Got this knee thing playing volleyball in the gym last night. Nurse said maybe a sprain. Futch was set up and I was going high. . . ." I reach towards the ceiling.

As he watches my hand, Softball storms in from the other door, flattening him with the mattress while I step on his right wrist. He tries to pull away but I lean my weight on his arm until he drops the knife.

Softball pitches the mattress and knife to the side, straddling David, her knees on his shoulders, her hard face up close and tight. "You really think we're gonna let you stab yourself?" she growls. "This is the mattress trick."

David looks past her to me, hurt and confused. "You lied?" he asks in a pitiful tone.

"Of course I lied," I say, picking up the blade and turning it in the light. "Wouldn't you?"

"*No,*" he says defiantly. Thrashing, he catches Softball by surprise but is no match for her superior strength. She pins him back to the floor; he acts as if he's about to spit in her face. I reach over and rake my knuckles across his sternum until he yelps and goes limp.

"David, please," I say. "Be cool."

The new tech returns with the nurse. "Already got the order. Put him in restraints whenever you get ready," she says, before they head off towards a scream down the hall.

"What the *f*ck* kind of hellhole is this?" David cries.

"It ain't Disneyworld," I confess, then add in the calm voice again, "Look, it's your choice. I'm sorry, but we had to get the knife. Everything's safe now. We don't have to do restraints. We'll sit with you in seclusion. I'll listen as long as you want to talk."

The sink hangs crooked from the previous patient's midnight tryst and there's a bottle of White Rain shampoo spilled out in the corner of the floor. With a whimper, David turns to the wall.

Softball sits back, off his shoulders. "I'm sorry too," she says, taking his chin and pulling his face back to us. "Just doing my job." Then, after awhile, "But I understand more than you know. I was a patient here. I've been right where you are. Mattress trick and all."

He glances to me and I nod. "They lock you up in here too?" he asks.

"Not yet," I tell him.

David lays his head back against the tile floor, staring at the lights, wondering, I imagine, how life came to this. His face changes, lighter, like he's in on the joke. "Put me in the restraints," he says.

"You sure?" Softball asks.

"Yes," he says.

We lift him up and he rides limp against us, his arms across our shoulders, feet dragging behind.

Seclusion is the last room down the hall. A ten-by-ten cell with soft pink cinderblock walls and a hospital bed in the middle of the floor. The carpet is low pile, stained by blood and sweat and snot and tears, and the electrical sockets have all been removed. There's a camera in the corner protected by Plexiglas and a window on the far wall half covered by a sheet.

We lay David on the bed and fasten the Velcro straps, locking them with a skeleton key, wrists and ankles, another across the chest. Softball pulls a blanket over him, tucking it under his shoulders and hips.

"You okay?" I ask.

"Yes," he says. "I'm all right."

"You want me or Softball to stay with you?"

A look passes between them, something familiar I can't quite place. He says softly, "Let Heather stay."

Prayers for Mr. Kick-Ass

On the way home, I stop at the all-night Piggly Wiggly for cereal, chicken and eggs. Late-night grocery stores always feel like church to me, like there's a holy loneliness in the linoleum, the ordered peace of stacked bags of charcoal and walls of canned peas. Mama says I'm a little off.

An old *Super Zaxxon* machine is wedged between the magazines and produce. I waste a few quarters on escape, just to clear my mind from another night on psych.

A stocker passes, with long graying hair and a gnarled arm, pushing a dust mop with his good hand. "You get past a million, let me know," he says. "I'll play ya on break."

"You got it," I tell him. "Broke a million, huh?"

He leans over and taps the screen. "See that high score? KKS? That's me."

"What's KKS stand for?"

"Kick-Ass," he brags.

"Nice to meet you, Mr. Kick-Ass," I say as he pushes his mop away. Then, as he turns down the first row, "When I hit a mil, I'm comin' for you. . . ." Somewhere over the salsa, I hear him laugh.

Near the cantaloupes, there's a stack of composition notebooks, fifty-nine cents apiece. I buy two, take my Cocoa Pebbles home and begin to jot down little notes about the people I meet.

While I write, I say small prayers for peace and guidance and joy for those whose path I cross. Prayers tonight for David. Prayers for Softball. Prayers for Mr. Kick-Ass with the gnarled arm.

Cowboy Fabulous & Stardust 54

At two in the morning I am summoned to a blacked-out room in the back of a second-story clothes store. Fashion show posters are tacked to the walls, newspapers scattered on a desk. An emerald lamp glows from a low shelf filled with books on photography and art.

Propped in the corner of the floor sits a long-limbed woman, older but chic, with the face of a Nagel and the body of a Degas dancer. She's wearing party clothes, a black dress and half-kicked-off heels and her makeup is runny and smudged, like a paint fight between Picasso and Salvador Dali.

I'm standing in the door with the hall lights behind me, black Stetson and the lambskin coat, hair down to my waist.

"Come in," she says. "You look fabulous."

Become someone else the fallen angel said. One night after watching *Escape from L.A.* on HBO, I saw an eye patch at the Rite-Aid for a dollar twenty-five. I bought it but haven't had the opportunity yet. Tonight would have been the night.

"Hey there," I say to Ms. Chic.

"Where'd you get that jacket?" she asks.

"I was out riding late one night, just before Christmas and broke down on a back road long way from town. It was cold and I didn't have a coat. I said this crazy prayer and a tow truck driver showed up and pulled me home. He gave me his coat."

"Cool," she says.

Chic flicks a lighter but the flame won't come. She blows her nose and there is blood. She is a dilated wreck; a fading dial tone, hands trembling, completely come undone.

"Cocaine?" I say.

"First time I snorted coke," she says, staring through the window and raking her hair, "was with Andy Warhol in the bathroom at Studio 54."

"Warhol didn't do drugs."

"You weren't there," she says. "How would you know?"

"Friend of mine worked with Andy. Said he never did drugs."

"Maybe you're right. Might have been Jagger. Bianca, I mean. If you remember, you weren't really there, they say. . . ." Her voice is so fragile the sound starts to fade before the words are barely born.

I sit by the bookcase, Indian-style. "What was it like?"

"What was what like?"

"Disco," I say. "I used to DJ nightclubs."

"Do you miss it?"

"Oh yeah."

"Every night was like the last night of your life. It was magic. Ridiculous. Empty. Drugs," she says. "We did them in the bathroom but you didn't have to, you could do them in the middle of the dance floor. If you wanted."

There's a Polaroid pinned to a corkboard, the woman, twenty or more years ago, in a strapless red gown surrounded by beautiful people. She's posing for the camera with her arms crossed and a cocktail in her hand. Her lips are pursed in a practiced pout.

"Like magic," I say, pointing to the picture. "There you are."

"Everybody wanted to be the queen, to be important, but when you woke up in the morning you were still your same old ugly, lonely self. So you did more drugs and hoped the star-dust would sprinkle and make you rich and famous and fabulous forever." She stares at the photo again, shaking her head. "We never thought about tomorrow."

I sneeze twice and look around the room. A gray cat is coiled around the lamp, pawing empty air.

"Are you thinking about hurting yourself?" I ask.

"Yes," she says. "Yes, I am." Defiance and sadness, both are in her words.

"How would you do that?"

"I would light two road flares and jump naked into a barrel of gasoline. At night."

"Really now."

"If you're going, go big," she says. "Leave a mark. Make the front page."

"That would do it," I say.

"I still look pretty good naked," Chic says with a tilt of her head.

"Okay," I say.

She rests her head against the side of the desk and stares at the photo again. "Pills," she says. "I'd do it with pills. I've got some saved. But I'm not going to the nut house."

"How many pills saved?" I ask.

"Eighty-six Lortab. Forty Valiums. Some methadone."

"That's enough," I say. My collar itches and my hair feels like it is on fire.

"I'm not going," she says again, this time more to herself.

The thing about late-night psychiatric crisis is you can sit in the silence and try to think of the right next thing to say.

"If this were the other way around," I ask, "if you were me and I was you, sitting here at three in the morning — if I just told you what you told me — would you leave?"

A long pause. "No," she says.

"Would you put me in a car and take me to a safe place?"

"Yes."

"C'mon then," I tell her. "You know what we have to do."

She follows me down the hall. In a different light she looks older and frail and cocaine wasted. But she smiles weakly and holds up a ready bag.

"You packed?" I ask. "You knew you were going?"

"I don't want to go. I don't want to be in those damned groups and I don't want to hear those damned doctors and counselors say the same old damn thing. But I know if I don't get help I'm going to die," she says. "Do I have to ride in the damn ambulance?"

"Not unless you just want to," I reply. "I could get them to turn on the lights. It would be pretty damn dramatic."

"No more drama tonight," she says, rubbing her forehead. "I just want to sleep."

"I'll take you in my truck," I tell her. "Not supposed to but I really don't care."

"Thanks," she says with a crumpled smile. "Okay if I smoke?"

"Long as you crack the window."

"I love your outfit," she says as we cross the river. "Is that why you work at night? So you can be the Cowboy?"

I open the glovebox, take out the eye patch and slip it on. Chic takes a deep drag and flicks her ashes into the night.

"Fabulous," she says.

Save the World |

My old school buddy Noonce and I ride our bikes down Sweet Olive Lane, through the best part of a summer night, right after the heat has broken and the breeze from the bayou brushes over our skin like the breath of God himself. We park in the gazebo out back and settle by the pool for Peach Icee philosophies when the crisis center rings.

"Caller sounds anxious," the operator says. "Depressed. Says he just really needs someone to talk to."

Noonce swishes her toes through the water. I groan as I hang up the phone. Callers are often drunk, venting on all the low cards life has dealt them, taking no guidance or responsibility for their part in the sinking ship. I hate getting caught up on the phone with late-night drama divas. And I *never* know what to say.

Noonce and I linger awhile in the drive, slapping at mosquitoes and giggling until she finally breaks away to study for her next day's exam. I stand at the gate watching her lights fade then stare at the phone awhile. *Not yet.* Peach Icee remnants, lounge chair by the pool. A swim would be nice. *Get it over with.* I dial the number. Long stuttered rings, no answer.

Oh well, I think, tossing the phone onto the cushion of the lounge chair. I slip off my shirt and fall into the water.

Four days later at the psych ward.

Smiley, the sixty-four-year-old flame-haired psych nurse who barks like a drill sergeant and still mows her grass in a hot-pink bikini, points to a patient standing by the candy machine. I peer out of the station's glass at a stooped little fellow in bifocals mulling over the Zero bars and rainbow cupcakes.

"Shot hisself," she says casually. "Got him in after Mercy sewed him up." She taps his chart, slides it to me and pulls a tabloid from her bag. "Look at this idiot," she grouses, pointing to the mugshot cover of a D-grade movie star.

"Un-huh," I say blankly, running the patient's name through my brain, the date and time of his arrival.

I look back to the break room as the man slips four quarters through the slot, presses his selection and stands with hands clasped, watching the corkscrew turn. It stops just short; his candy does not fall. He stares in the machine's glass for the longest and I wait for his rage. It never comes. When he turns to the window and hangs his head, I see the clean red rip running eight inches through the bristle of his hair.

"Didn't do a very good job though, did he? Shoot at your temple and nine times out of ten —" Smiley says, her scarlet nail tracing from my eyebrow to just behind the ear "— all it's gonna do is graze."

I open his chart and read the report, how EMS busted down the door after neighbors heard the gunshot and dialed 911. He works at the car plant, was born in '59 and lists no next of kin.

"Can't these young girls keep their legs closed?" Smiley says gruffly, holding up the magazine again. She taps the counter when I don't reply. "Something wrong?"

"I was on that night," I confess. "He called the helpline. I tried to call him back." Then I tell the whole truth. "I only tried one time."

"Honey," Smiley says, licking her thumb and flipping to the crossword, "you can't save the world."

The patient stands at the window, head down, running his fingers over the scar. "Smiley," I reply, "I can't even save myself."

She reaches over and pats the back of my hand. "Twelve-letter word for Falcon Crest star. Starts with an L."

"Lorenzo Lamas?" I offer. She nods and her pencil goes to work.

"There is one thing I can do," I tell her. I walk over to the window where the patient stands, pull his sleeve and point to the vending machine.

"This thing take your money?" I ask.

"Yes sir," he replies.

"Does it all the time," I say. "I keep telling them to fix it."

"It doesn't matter," he says.

"Yes it does," I say. Grabbing the sides, I rock the machine back and forth, banging it against the wall. "Jump on, let's go," I tell him. "Everybody gets candy tonight."

He looks left, then right. Then puts his shoulder to the glass. The old charge nurse smiles, slips into the med room and doesn't see a thing. The patient laughs as candy falls like rain.

Safer Shoes |

"Beware of all enterprises that require new clothes."
— Henry David Thoreau

I get a call from a state office about an application I filled out over six months back.

"We're starting interviews for this position if you are still interested," the woman says.

"Yes ma'am," I tell her. I'm spinning my wheels at the psych ward, same job I had in undergrad school. I need something steadier. Safer. Predictable even. It might be okay.

In a windowless federal building, I report to a small office on the third floor. The room smells like Windex and burnt coffee. No pictures. No calendar. No quips or quotes or witty plaques. Everything is state regulation and gray. Behind the desk sits a woman in black slacks and flats and hose with rips at the ankle. When I enter she stands, straining as if every movement causes pain.

"Hello," she says, forcing a smile and shaking my hand like a man. She looks like a depressed John Goodman saddled with a bad perm and chronic gout. There's a half-eaten bag of microwave popcorn and stacks of files on both sides of her desk. A moldy brown stain sweats from the ceiling down the wall. Leaky asbestos, I presume.

"The position," she says, reading from the page. "Case worker for court-ordered counseling, alcohol and drug treatment, anger management and family liason work. Forty weekly hours, rotate call on nights and weekends. Starts at thirteen twenty-five hourly with benefits after ninety days. Two weeks yearly vacation. Have you ever worked with offenders?"

"Um, yes ma'am," I say, thinking back to the lumberyards and bars and psych wards. "You could say that."

She rustles through the popcorn and reads the rest of the description to herself. My foot bounces with nervous energy so I cross my leg at the knee. I'm wearing clean black Nikes. I've never owned a pair of dress shoes or a tie in my life.

"We don't allow that kind of shoe," she says, pointing with the eraser end of her pencil. "In fact, to be honest with you, just the fact that you would wear those to the interview tells me everything I need to know."

Treasures of Darkness |

A preacher friend gives me the Sunday night service after I mention I might be applying to seminary. I sing "Amazing Grace" to the melody of "House of the Rising Sun," blow a little blues harp and ramble about the Light of God shining through the cracks in our lives.

There's a part after the service where you are supposed to stand in the aisle, shake hands and make small talk but I can't do it, wondering if what I just said was true, if I really believe much of anything at all. I make excuses and rush out the side door.

In the parking lot a woman with long silver hair and the tics of a stroke victim tries to tell me something but all she can do is stutter and cry. Her chin trembles; she touches her chest and points to me. Red-faced, I thank her and drive away. In the side mirror I see her, shaking her head, hand stretched out towards me. *Wait.*

There's half a fifth of Strawberry Hill under the seat of my truck, left there by an intake patient who bolted at the four-way stop. I sit on the levee back behind my house and drink it, a sweet, vacant buzz reminiscent of days gone by. When I'm done I throw the bottle in the river and apologize to God for being so double-minded and unstable in all my ways.

And um, littering, Lord I add. *That too, I guess.*

I start to leave and a strange thing happens. The Spirit hovers over the face of the waters, like stars in the windshield on a dark country road. I stay until blue creeps into the edges of the night sky, listening to God listen, watching Him watch. By sunrise I am sleeping, the easy, dreamless sleep of peace.

Maybe it was the wine.
  I go back the next night.
  And the next.
  Every night for a month. Then two.
  The path to the levee is two streets over on Sweet Olive Lane. A dark ribbon of asphalt that threads between Graceland-style mansions and the slow-moving waters of Bayou Cachette. The road goes on beyond the dead-end sign, if you know the hidden way. There's a high spot on the levee where the bayou flows into the river, the oak trees break away and God walks in the cool of the night.
    Come by yourself to a barren place.
    Give no thought to tomorrow.
    Be anxious for nothing.
  I sell my truck and buy a used Trooper II, cash, and some hand-me-down shorts and tees from the Goodwill off St. Paul. My bills are cheap, I have no strings. Student loans consolidate. Got a little money in the bank.
  I work weekends at the rink. Carry crisis call here and there. Cover Sunday late shift at the psych ward. I stay up nights and sleep through the day. I eat Cocoa Pebbles and grow my hair. Go days at a time without speaking a word.

I try to find a way to explain to my father where I am. Growing up, he read *Walden* and admired Thoreau's work.
  "I am going the Thoreau way," I tell him, as a frame of reference. "Sort of."
  My father shakes his head. "Thoreau was lazy," he says.
  My mother takes a picture of me at Easter. "Your face looks

like a baby," a friend says. "But your eyes look a thousand years old."

I pass like a shadow with family and friends. Mostly, I am loneliest with others and perfectly satisfied to be alone. I am never truly alone. I don't know how to explain it if you don't understand.

> *Come away with me*
> *& I will give you rest*
> *treasures of darkness*
> *hidden riches in secret places*
> *so you may know*
> *that I am*
> *the One*
> *who calls you by name.*

Winter passes, then spring into fall and winter again. There is Silence. There is Peace. There is something beyond happiness. A calm knowing and deep content, wanting nothing more than exactly what you have in the moment.

And something beyond that still.

Sweet Olive Lane, past the dead-end sign, lights in the trees, stars on the water, all-night grocery stores and driving in the dark. Roller rink parties and psych ward porches and two a.m. crisis calls. This is my seminary, my monastery.

Walking with God in the cool of the night, the whole world turning slow, living in the unforced rhythms of Grace, the Love of God shining through the cracks in my life.

The Secret Place.

PART IV

Strangers & Angels Unaware

"You return thinner, stronger. You've grown accustomed to silence and thus learned of an inner voice which has begun to speak, urgent but unheard, along time. You have less patience now with the white noise of the world but this will serve you well." — John Caroll

Catch Me |

Silent night on the psych ward, Terry's got the radio on that bland sort of heartland country that sounds so soothing in the wee hours, like steel-belt tires trucking cargo across the land, farmers up before the sun cranking old tractors to life and lovers holding hands on the front porch swing.

The patients are sleeping and the paperwork is done. Smiley, the old flame-haired charge nurse, is sawing logs in the lounge recliner to a rerun of *Magnum, PI.*

Terry digs through his knapsack and pulls out a pimento on wheat. "You want half this sandwich?" he asks.

"Nah."

In the stillness there's no rush for words. The steel-barred side window is open and we can hear cicadas in the trees where Indian ghosts supposedly still roam. "Thanks, though."

"You still seeing that same girl?" Terry asks, fishing for conversation I suppose.

"Sort of," I say. "Yeah."

Terry gives a winsome little nod. "I almost got married once. Country girl."

"Country girls are the best," I tell him. "Mine's a blue-eyed farmer's daughter with a genius IQ. Good girl."

"Do you love her?" he asks.

"I don't know. Sometimes?" I reply. "It's complicated."

"When you're apart, do you think about her all the time?"

"Yeah," I confess. "Pretty much."

"It's always complicated," he says. "But if you love her, you better let her know."

"So what happened with your girl?" I say.

Terry chews slowly and stares at his shoes. "I'm gay."

"Oh. Yeah. That."

"She was in choir while I was worship leader." Terry fans his eyes with his fingers. "I don't need to talk about it," he says but then continues. "She could *sing*. Sweet girl, quality person. We could have a little house. Children."

"You ever see her?" I ask.

"In the store one day. She has kids now." His eyes lose focus again. "Maybe she didn't see me. Maybe she acted like she didn't see me. I don't know."

"I hate the way church just kicked you out, brother."

"They didn't really. I wanted to stay, but the elders said it would be disruptive. I asked if I could sit in the balcony and they said that was okay."

"Really did you a favor, huh?"

"It was a hard time," he says, brushing the crumbs from his sweater vest. "I would sit up there and try not to get too emotional. One morning it was more than I could take. I missed all my music people. Petra, God bless her, she's really overweight and shy but just a beautiful girl inside. Drags her cello center stage and plays 'His Eye Is on the Sparrow' and I tell you —" Terry puts down his sandwich and lays his hands flat on the table. "God was in that place."

Over in the lounge, Magnum's got a dealer on the run. Smiley coughs and pulls the afghan up over her legs. Terry pushes his bag of SunChips across the table. I take one and crunch lightly as he speaks.

"Then the praise band came up and played one of those happy-happy greet-your-neighbor songs and everyone is walking around hugging and laughing. Everybody's standing and clapping and waving banners. . . ."

"Ooh, I remember the flag thing." I grab a t-shirt from the lost and found and mimic the slow swaying arc of Christian banners, just noticing the owl logo over the front. "Except, like, not with Hooters flags."

"Well, Charismatics," he replies. "Either way, a little girl, maybe three years old, rushes down the steps to the flag rack by the balcony wall. I'm standing right there and you know, the wall is like this high," he chops right above the knee. "She bounds off the bottom step and just that fast goes on top of the wall. This woman behind me screams *Katie!* — but it's too late, her head and arms are over and she's going."

"What?"

Terry pulls back. "I thought I told you this story."

"No. So what'd you do?"

"I'm like, calling out *Jesus help!* And I fell against the rail, grabbing — I look over and faces are seizing on the platform but the music is still going and I just catch the back of her dress, I mean it's right there. . . ." Terry holds his fingers up, seeing the moment again. "But it's slipping. I throw my left arm over and everything goes in slow motion. I see all the bald heads below, ladies hunting through their purses for tissues. I dig my fingers in . . . but she's gone. All I can do is watch her fall. The pianist points and screams and everybody looks and Brother Roy — big, bushy beard, the old family doctor who goes on all those Africa trips for the kids?"

Yeah, I nod, even though I don't know him. *Yeah.*

"So he turns, with his whole body because he's got a bad neck — holds out his arms and catches that baby." Terry pauses for composure, raising his hand to the sky. "Checks for damage, kisses her forehead and sets her down. And you know what she does? Laughs and bounces her little legs like it's funny. Opens her arms back up to Brother Roy like *Do it again!* And the church is just going nuts."

"Whoa," I say. "You think that'd make the news or something."

"Something," he says. "I watched it all, up on that rail, the mom flung herself on the wall beside me — I thought I'd have to catch her dress next — and she sees her baby, in the arms of Brother Roy, smiling and bouncing and she starts bawling and I did too. It was just too much for me."

Terry rustles through the chip crumbs and adds slowly, "That's the last time I was in church."

Crickets chirp their two-note song over old Choctaw bones in the woods just beyond the window. Smiley snores lightly as Magnum rides away. Over on the radio, a mountain girl sings about the kindness of Daddy's Hands.

"Jamie?" Terry says.

"Yeah?"

"That's my prayer," he says. "Hey God. Catch me too."

After work I drive past her house, just to see her car, parked there on the street beneath the poplar tree.

I pull in a little ways down the road and walk over. Touch the car door and pray she is happy and well. There's a lamp light still in her bedroom window. As I step up on the walk, a police cruiser corners the lane. I dodge behind the poplar, circling as he passes. Freeze when he stops and shines his beam across the leaves.

After he is gone, I stand in the street again. Walk to my truck and back. Her window goes dark. I pace, five minutes, ten. Lay my hand against her car.

A narrow path takes me to her front step. The doorbell glows against the night. I trace it with my finger one time, two. Close my eyes and push until I hear the chimes. Her footsteps are on the stairs. She opens the door. With no makeup on, in pajama pants and an old Aerosmith tour shirt, moonlight shimmering on her alabaster skin.

"Were you sleeping?" I ask.

"About to," she says. "Not yet."

"Can you go for a ride?"

Her blue eyes sparkle before the reply, "Just let me get my shoes."

I stand at the step, watching through the crack in the door. The cadence of her hips as she walks down the hall. The little song she sings while she sits legs crossed at the foot of the stairs and pulls her high-tops on.

I'm laughing when she returns.

"What is it?" she says when she sees my goofy smile.

"Nothing," I say. "I'll tell you later."

Eclectic, at Best |

A letter comes in the mail from the state. Through a loophole, all I have to do is fill out a form and submit it to the board with a check for one hundred dollars. And they'll send me my mental health license.

I've been told that a license is the key to validity. To the real cash, because with a license you are bonded and certified, able to bill insurance companies eighty to one-hundred and twenty-five bucks an hour.

I never pursued it before because it was an intense and expensive process with lots of scrutiny from supervisors and psychology boards. It was for people a little more serious and secure about their calling than me. Still, for a hundred bucks, I'd be a fool to pass it up.

There's a question on page twelve of the form that says *Please explain your theoretical approach and orientation to therapy.*

Eclectic, at best I write.

Six weeks later, an official-looking certificate comes in the mail. I read my name in fancy script and laugh like a con man on the car ride home, just after he knocks off a bank.

I'm still goofing around at the rink and pulling psych ward nights. Chasing crazies through the alley at two a.m. Scrambled. Rambling. Living for the day. Hanging out with God on the levee at two a.m.

In the grocery store one night, I see an old colleague from the outpatient clinic. Gill Thomas looks like a cross between Sigmund Freud and a latter-day Ron Howard and has that sit-back-and-see restraint that belongs to good therapists who have been through the fire.

"Hey," I tell him, "finally got my license."

"Hmm," he says. "Interesting."

A few days later he calls to offer me a position at the counseling center of a megachurch. As an actual sit-down psychotherapist.

"We don't bill insurance," Gill says. "And I hate that this is all we can do — but I can only offer twenty-five an hour. Are you interested?"

"Yeah," I reply. "That'll be okay."

"You wanted to be in ministry, right?" he asks.

"I'm willing to give it a try," I tell him.

Like Crop Dusting or Wrestling Bears |

"I started to realize that there was a great hunger and thirst for regular, cynical, ragbag people to talk about God and goodness and virtue in a tone that didn't frighten and upset you, or make you feel that you were doing even more poorly than you'd thought." — Anne Lamott

The Christian Counseling Center sits in the shadow of the sanctuary of one of the largest per capita churches in America. It's a small southern town, Super Wal-Mart and Friday night football, the kind of place where thirty-eight-year-old grannies still tan in video store sun beds back behind the racks of *Big Buck Ruts* and *Duck Commander* DVDs and stickers on pickup trucks proclaim the gospel of the fair-haired Southern Jesus. Not the most likely place for church-based psychotherapy. Most folks here will discuss the problems of others far before their own, but the former pastor, a sweet lanky saint of a guy, had the foresight to start a ministry devoted just to listening.

They chose my old comrade Gill to get the ball rolling, giving him a rundown building off the main campus, mismatched cans of pastel paint, stacks of old magazines and some second-hand furniture.

I'm not real sure about working for the church. I'm limited to sitting in the balcony or far back, just watching really. There's

security in community and becoming part of a movement —
and though a lot of people bash big ministries, I've seen a lot of
good come from this sort of organization too. I think I might
be able to help some people and maybe even straighten myself
up along the way.

I am going to try to participate and go to staff meetings and
wear semi-decent clothes so I don't look like a ticket scalper at a
Tampa Bay Bon Jovi show. Be a team player and on board with
the church's mission statement to offer "professional counseling in an atmosphere of hope, healing and restoration" — even
though there's something about estrogen-heavy church slogans
that make me feel rebellious and insecure, like smoking opium
and running away to become a fire-breathing freak in a side-
show circus.

I've never done actual sit-down counseling but I figure I
can fake it 'til I make it and maybe they'll send me the people
struggling with the theological/philosophical meaning of life
and why the Bible seems so mean and crazy sometimes with the
whole Job and Moses thing, with seven-headed lions and wild
women driving tent stakes through the temples of men.

I black out my office windows and shut down the lights
except for a lone amber lamp on a corner desk. I've got a sea-
green Naugahyde lounger and an old couch so cushy and low
your feet barely touch the floor once you sink into its folds.
White noise to block out the world and now and then I slip on
Eno's "Thursday Afternoon" or the ambient remix of "Wish
You Were Here." And when the clients are gone and the whole
therapeutic thing is too weird to take, I blast Motörhead and try
to balance out the overemotional angst.

For a while I fear exposure, that people will figure out that
even though I work at the church, I'm still pretty messed up and
unsure about a lot of things. Soon enough I learn I'm not the only
one faking it by far. I learn that what people claim corporately
and believe privately are two very different things. I discover
when you get hurting people in a dark room — dark enough and

hurting enough to be honest, they will tell you things that make you realize we are all struggling and stumbling and wrestling with God and wondering what's really going on down here.

I'm shaky, but thankful, praying maybe I can finally find my place within the church and work thing. I realize God doesn't always call people to a conventional way. Some are called to the fringe, to the outsider and the misfit, to dark rooms, the balcony and the far back pew. My plan is to lay low, stick to the places I know and try to stay out of trouble.

When I tell people I work at a church counseling center, they often ask something like *What kind of problems do church people have?*

There's a cute girl with freckles, a pretty good kid who sings Sunday mornings, makes good grades when she wants to and just about every weekend sneaks out of her window to meet with the neighborhood boys. And lately, the neighborhood girls.

"She grew up in church. We did everything we could," the mother cries.

Last week there were beautiful bright children who cut their skin in secret places. Yesterday it was a Sunday school teacher who drinks herself to sleep and a happily married deacon who can't stop looking at gay porn. At two o'clock, a single dad with cancer trying to raise his daughter alone and after that a starving young bride going bald from eating and anxiety disorders. On tomorrow's schedule, there's an associate pastor who preaches peace but says he's never known any and a fifty-five-year-old man who just can't grow up.

Dead marriages and depressive fatigues. Ungovernable teens, phantom lusts, deviant compulsions, chemical addictions. Doubts, fears, anxiety in the night. Lost God. Suicide.

And this is what I do: listen a lot, talk a little, hear all sorts of crazy things. Try to steer and do damage control. I practice psychological magic and distraction and when that doesn't work (*often*) I pray elaborate, eloquent prayers of great spiritual depth, like *helpGodhelpGodhelpGodhelp*, and become quite certain there are easier ways to make a little money, like crop dusting or wrestling bears. I encourage, prod, provoke when appropriate. I promote reality, balance, peace and the understanding that peace must be seized and faith does not remove responsibility. I quote King Solomon and Hunter S. Thompson.

"The more you do for control, the less you do for joy," I tell them.

"Call on God, but row away from the rocks," I urge.

And still, so often they grasp frantically for control and row back into the rocks again and again.

"Me too," I confess. Same doubts and fears and anger and lust and longing for something I cannot quite describe. Same feeling that there's some unknown X in the algebra of God that I will never ever understand. That even with all the combined powers of theology, psychology, philosophy and the good guidance of the evangelical church — I am still grasping and rowing towards the rocks; doomed to screw it all up and hit every pothole from here to Heaven.

And if there is just one thing I can say that I am certain is true and just *might* be helpful it is this: *Me too.*

Sometimes though, I want to tell people to burn all their flags and throw their TVs in the street, to rise up for the absurd, to embrace the illogical and no-show the revolution. To stir them up to speak truth, raise hell and fight the power. To truly be like that rebel Jesus Christ.

I doubt the church will ever let me preach.

Jesus Laughs |

"I discovered many of the burning theological issues in the church are neither burning nor theological." — Brennan Manning

For years I've prowled the night and changing my sleep schedule has been tough. I've got a bad case of bedhead, my clothes are rumpled and in general I look like I just woke up. Gill passes me in the hall. "What happened to *you*?"

"I just woke up."

"It's one-thirty in the p.m."

"Yeah," I deadpan.

"Is that why you keep your office so dark? So you can steal a nap during sessions?" he says with a laugh.

"Ha ha." I reply.

A beanpole of a kid in too-big clothes with rabbit cheeks and alfalfa hair fidgets just outside my door. "Hey buddy . . . ," I say, sliding my arm around his shoulders, "you here to see someone, my man?"

"Her name is Amanda," the mother says stiffly. Amanda bursts into tears. Ginny, the gimp therapist, rolls out in her special-made sporty wheelchair to save the day. "Ignore him, honey, he's been hit in the head a lot. Come on back, let's talk."

I slink away and scan the lobby's couches for my first appointment. A woman with faraway eyes sits next to a man gripping a balled-up Bass Pro Shop hat, nervously working fringes into the brim. We exchange uncertain glances before I introduce myself and usher them to the back.

I hate couples.

Fifty minutes later, I slip back through the lobby and into the front office. "I'm going to work at the Christian *Television* Counseling Center," I proclaim to Tink, the office manager, a five-foot fireplug honey of a gal, wholly devout with a wicked sense of humor. "I would much rather wave my coat jacket at people and slap them on the forehead. Anything other than being trapped in a room with some bickering, miserable couple."

"Mmm hmm," Tink says, digging through her purse for chapstick. "Your three o'clock is here."

I yank a tissue from the box on her desk and drape my tone with drama. "For your love gift of twenty dollars or more you'll get this *limited-edition* miracle prayer cloth which will ease and enable you through all sorts of trials, tribulations and dastardly marital maladies. *Act now!* — and gain defeat over depressions, delusions, drug addictions and nighttime enuresis. . . ."

Tink smiles and gestures through the sliding glass. "Three o'clock," she says. "Right there."

Out in the waiting room there's a goofus-looking guy in cut-off slacks and a white wife-beater. A Castro-style army cap sits sideways on his head, MP3 player jamming tunes into his skull. He's throwing abstract gang-signs and doing a little sidestep jig while the gray-haired woman on the couch thumbs through *Guideposts* and cuts her eyes.

"What's his story?" I ask.

"Dad's a pastor. Says the boy is *purt' near worthless.* Not working, dropped out of college. Plays in a band. We had him in youth group; he's a sweet kid, just being a kid. Dad's —" Tink severs the air with a chop of her hand.

"At least this is more my speed." I gather his papers and head for the door. "I'm taking this dude to play putt-putt."

"Have fun," she says.

Once in my office he opens his eyes wide to adjust for the lack of light and gazes around at my collection of oddball trinkets and surrealist synagogue fashion. "Hey man, have a seat," I greet him, slipping into the deep green pleather of my throne.

"This a church deal — or what?" he asks, backing into the corner of the couch.

"Well, theoretically, you come in here, we close the door and you can just be who you really are. You don't have to act like you got it all together."

"No preachin', huh?" he asks.

"Nah. You get amnesty in here."

He turns his cap backwards and laughs. "All right, then."

"That wasn't too bad, huh?" Tink says when we're done.

"Yeah, he was pretty cool," I answer. "What's next?" She raises her eyebrows and points through the window.

There's a doughy boy back behind the lobby's ficus, the sparse fronds offering little camouflage. His arms are defiantly crossed, face in a big whiny pout. The mother shifts on her heels and clutches her purse before her. "Here he is," she says, as if she has brought me a precious puppy to housebreak. "Talk to him!"

"What's his name?"

"Raymond."

Raymond? An eight-year-old named Raymond? I think. *No wonder.* I walk over and offer my hand. "Raymond, what's wrong?"

He wipes his sleeve across his face and glares at his mother. "This ain't Baskin Robbins."

I turn to her and crook my finger. "You lied to your kid about ice cream just to get him to come?"

"I had to," she explains.

"What did you think was gonna happen when you got here?"

"They said you might have some puppets or something?" she says meekly.

"Lady, I ain't Kermit the freakin' Frog. Take your kid to Baskin Robbins."

After a short squabble the woman grabs young Raymond by the wrist and steers him out the door. "Come on," she says, glowering back at me. "Let's go get your *ice cream*."

Back in the front office, Holly the intern smiles sweetly. "I have a confession," I blurt out. "I do this because they pay me. I feel no spiritual calling or responsibility in the least. I do it for the money."

"Okay . . . ," she says. "Anything else?"

"I don't even really *like* people. They get on my last nerve."

"Got it," says Holly. "Feel better?"

"I guess," I say as she places the phone in my hand.

Old Felton's voice crackles the line from the church-sponsored thrift store across the street. "There's a crazy girl on drugs or something over here and she won't leave. Can you send someone to get her?"

"I have to go get some drunk chick out of the thrift shop," I say over my shoulder, on the way out the door.

Once inside I pass by racks filled with cracked Flintstones glasses, crusty one-eyed Eeyores and pictures of Christ that give me the creeps. Felton cranes his head around the corner and waves me back.

There's a little crowd of people, some staring and others, well — staring not as obviously, peeping from the corner of their eyes while casually browsing the half-off culottes. Looking like an irate Mr. Whipple, Felton pushes up his black glasses and gestures to the blonde babbling nonsense and making a mess of the Christian fiction paperback section.

As I step towards her, she drops and begins a furious set of situps, six inches of threadbare underwear flashing from the back of her jeans. The customers slowly move their stares over to me.

I hit the floor and start crunching. If nothing else, I am a faithful absurdist.

"What?" Drunk Chick says defensively, watching me match her moves. The culotte shoppers have now forgotten their pants and stand in the aisles eyeing us like hungry monkeys watching a clown juggle bananas.

"What?" I answer back. "A man can't work some abs at the thrift store?"

She lets out a big nutty Medusa-haired laugh and follows me back to the office. As we pass the front window, I wave Holly in for backup.

Drunk Chick slumps into my couch, cramming fistfuls of Doritos into her mouth and confessing that while in our bathroom, she took a bunch of pills and shotgunned a beer from her backpack.

"Pills to die or get high?" I ask.

Her eyeballs jangle like the cherries on a slot machine. "Fuuhhhhhhked up," she replies, raising one finger, then two. "S'cuse my French."

I shrug; she holds out her palm for me to slap and cackles. "You're one of them that's heard it all. That's cool. I can't look at you too long though 'cause I'm a sex addict." She turns to Holly and shakes her head sadly. "Can't look at you too long neither, Babycakes."

On the side of her backpack is a blown-up color copy of her driver's license. The photo is of a sun-kissed girl with long loose curls the color of champagne; her head is tilted back, eyes smiling and full of life.

"Crystal?" I read from the pack. "That's you, right?"

Her face goes dark. "I'm Crystal. But that's not me." She chokes a bit, her words warble. "Not anymore." Tears well up; she lifts her shirttail and wipes her face. There is a long silence while she cries, t-shirt raised and dabbing at her eyes, exposing her whale-white belly and tragic tan brassiere. I look to the wall and pray for poise. There are two tiny pictures of Jesus pinned behind my bookcase, one laughing, the other rolling his eyes.

I see you, Jesus.

Finally Holly speaks. "What can we do for you, honey? Tell us what you need."

Crystal rolls up the chip bag, brushes her hands over my couch cushions and lets out a deep sigh. "Shit, I don't know. The Lord, I guess." She reads our faces a moment before adding, "And a hundred and fifty bucks for a bus ticket back to California." She turns to me. "And will you call my probation officer and tell her I came to counseling?"

Gill taps on the door and motions me to the hall. "What are you going to do with the girl?" he asks.

Christ walked on water. Peter and Paul brought the dead back to life. Judas stole money and hung himself from the tree. James and John were called twin sons of Thunder. Thomas refused to believe until he had seen the nail prints in His hand.

"I don't know."

"Anything I can do to help?" he says.

"Can you get me a hundred and fifty dollars?"

Gill pauses, probably waiting for me to say I'm joking. "Make it two," I add.

"Give me thirty minutes," he says.

I slip back into the office. Holly and Crystal have their heads bowed in prayer.

". . . and God, just let Crystal *know* that You are always with her, *help* her to find her way and have peace in her heart and mind, amen."

"Amen to that," says Crystal, wiping away tears. She stands, stretches, and when she smiles, for a moment looks like the girl in the picture again.

"Miss Crystal," I say. "If you're goin' back to Cali, we might be able to help."

"You can?" she says, amazed. "I knew somebody was sending me over here today. You guys are, like, saving my life."

Holly points to me. I point to Holly. Holly points to Jesus, rolling his eyes.

"You think Jesus really laughs and rolls his eyes?" Crystal asks, in a hopeful kind of way.

"Oh, Jesus laughs," I assure her. "Mostly at me."

Don't Know |

"All I ever wanted was a good job, some bus fare and a rocket and a bomb." — Michael Knott

Time crawls and the clock ticks loudly. An attractive middle-aged mother of two sits before me. She has a sensible elegance, a warm smile, and her eyes are desperate but kind. She lives in a nice home, volunteers at the church, is active in the community and has just revealed to me that most every night she thinks of ways to end her life. Guns and pills and suicide leaps. Car crashes and cocktails laced with bleach.

"I've even thought of going to Alaska and falling asleep in the snow," she says with a soft laugh that breaks my heart.

When I waved her in from the waiting room she was reading the latest book from a popular female evangelist. She stood and smiled, pausing to offer words of encouragement to the man in the next chair down. In the office she spoke with pride about her children, their good grades and success in sports. She gave thanks for her husband's patience and praised him for being a good father and provider. In a whisper she said life was wearing her down. How no pill or prayer or program had given her relief.

"Do you really think all suicides go to hell?" she asks.

I don't know.

A fragile man with ragged fringes of gray sits with his head in his hands. He wears an old suit jacket, long out of fashion, the sleeves too short.

"Now, she is gone," he says, the words measured and low. "No one to cut my hair. No more crossword puzzles together. No one to come home to."

Staring at his hands, he twists the gold band on his finger. "Every night, I would iron her skirts for work so she would have them in the morning." His eyes drift up into mine. "Been three months." His voice drops to a whisper. "I still iron every night."

There is an ocean of grief between us. My arms can't reach, my faith too weak to span the distance.

"Thirty-seven years ago, we built our house. Behind every panel of sheetrock, on every brick and support beam, hearts we drew in chalk. *G loves L. L loves G.* Now L is gone. And gone hurts like hell. And there is no God in this hell, son." It is like watching a scene from some sad awful movie, only I realize he is here with me and it is all too real.

"What am I supposed to do now?" he asks.

I don't know.

I don't know why life can be so beautiful and damned difficult almost in the same breath. I don't know. It is the only honest thing I can say and I hate it. I hate not knowing, I hate the helpless way it makes me feel. You would think after all the school and study, after all the seminars and sermons, that I would have something figured out. You know what I figured out? You know what I know?

That *I don't know.*

Not knowing, an old Rabbi once told me, *is where wisdom begins.* Sometimes, I despise wisdom.

Last appointment of the day. A big bouncy woman with a bright-red bob fidgets on the edge of my couch.

"I wouldn't want this gettin' around the church . . . ," she says, her eyes giddy, the tone of her voice saucy and sweet, like a late-night lonely hearts chat line. "So, this *is* confidential — right?"

Believe it or not, some come to gossip under the guise of counsel. Hey, my job is to listen, not judge. I settle back into my chair and give her a knowing smile.

"Oh yes," I whisper in the dark.

Green Onions |

On Thursdays I go straight from the counseling center to manage the rink. Tonight, we are closed for a private party, the inter-Greek Spring Fling mixer or something like that.

It's Jessie, Jenny, a hundred or so sorority girls — and me.

I play "Brick House" and flash all the lights. KDs, Phi Mus, and AOIIs whoop, they dance, they sing. I am the only man in a building filled with fun-time girls.

"This is the greatest job ever in the history of the world," I tell Jenny, a shy education major with a runway model's twiggy physique.

A dumpy green bus from the group home rattles up to the rink's front door. A tired woman leads in a cluster of ragamuffins, awkward children with dirty faces in tattered, mismatched clothes. They press in behind the woman, holding hands and grasping at the seam of her pants, staring out to the disco blacklights and darling gaggles of roller boogie sorority girls.

"The party is private," we explain, in the kindest possible tone. Jenny is handing the woman free passes for family night when the sorority leader skates up with her second-in-command. Both have ribbons in their hair that match their shorts and t-shirts with their names embroidered on the front. *Abby. Emily.*

"Are they staying?" Abby asks.

"It's your party," I tell her. "Up to you."

Emily leans down with her hands on her knees and speaks to the children. "Y'all like to skate?" she asks. The kids nod and squeal and squiggle with glee.

"Hush, now," the woman says to the children and they do. Quiet but giggly and ready to burst. "How much is it tonight?" she asks, looking through her purse. "For a group?"

"We'll have to count and figure," Jenny says, shooting me a knowing look. "Just go ahead and let them start getting skates."

"Are you sure?" the woman says to Abby and Emily.

"Of course," they say.

I stand to the side and fan out my hand, like Willy Wonka at the factory gates. "All right, kids," I say. "Are you ready?"

In a screaming fizzy, the children rush the counter. The sorority girls meet them there, unlacing shoes and helping with skates. They hold hands and lead them around the floor. It was happy before, but everything now is one notch higher, the music louder, the mix of group-home kids and college girls, skating, helping, falling down, hooting and laughing and having fun.

I autopilot the music and pocket the wireless mic. Jessie, Jenny and I meet them on the floor for the Crazy Trio, a roller rink game where you lock arms and skate in threes to the tune of "Green Onions." When the whistle blows, the trio turns and goes the opposite direction, cracking the whip, fast as you possibly can. From the pile of bodies, a new trio begins.

"This is the greatest job ever. In the history. *Of the world*," I shout as we fling each other round.

"We know," Jessie says, just before she kicks my skates out from under me. "You told us already."

After we've fallen all over each other ten or twenty times, I end up between Abby and Emily. "Hey, just put those kids on our bill," Abby says, like it's no big deal.

"You don't have to do that," I tell her.

"We know," Emily says. "But it's more fun this way."

The funky organ of "Green Onion" grinds. The whistle blows again and again. We spin and crash and fall and laugh and laugh. . . .

As we're shutting down, Mr. Ray, the rink handyman, comes in to mop the skate floor. Ray's a good-hearted guy, sweet and patient with children — not just the cute ones like most of us are — and well-read enough to beat us all at *Jeopardy!*. For some reason he's been at the rink twenty or more years now and still lives with his mom and dad.

I walk over before I leave. "I'm gone, Mr. Ray. Hey, how long this usually take you?" With a rag mop and bucket the floor must look the size of a football field.

"Probably mop 'til four or five in the morning," he says. His eyes are bloodshot and graying hair spills from the edges of his Atlanta Braves ball cap.

"What do you do then?"

"Eat a Frito Pie in the snack bar. I'll lay down and sleep awhile then get up and mop some more."

"Sleep? Where?"

"Got a pallet behind the counter in the skate shop."

"I don't see how you do it," I say, shaking my head.

"You do what you have to," he says. "It's fun here, Jamie, but you've got an education. Do something with it, man. You don't want to end up mopping the rink floor for the rest of your life."

I turn out the last of the lights and look back as Mr. Ray polishes one tiny spot on a solid half-acre of hardwood. It seems poetic and sad, like I should turn on the mirrored ball and play some befitting song like "Wonderwall" or "McArthur Park."

"Hey, Mr. Ray. You want me to put some music on for you?"

"No thanks," he says. I lock the front doors and leave him there, pushing his mop, alone in the dark.

Signs & Wonders, Kind of Blue |

"I don't know about you, but I practice disorganized religion.
We call ourselves 'Our Lady of Perpetual Astonishment.'"
— Kurt Vonnegut

Signs and wonders, they shall follow true believers.

The front pew deacon comes back from Brazil and says revival is there, that gold dust fell like rain. Another woman says she saw an amputee's foot grow back. I am skeptical and hopeful at the same time. Miracles make faith so much easier.

The church counseling center gets a little restrictive and I don't sit still well so I set out with the missionary team on a downtown run.

"Where are we going?" I ask.

"Wherever God takes us," Martin, the team leader, says.

There's a snaggle-toothed woman in grimy sweats, wandering down the sidewalk. We pull over and talk to her. She's windswept and lost, maybe a little off.

"What can we do to help?" Martin asks.

"I lost my car," she says.

"Ma'am, God's gonna help us find your car." Martin says this with assurance.

"We're downtown," I whisper to him. "There's, like, a million cars down here." Martin ignores my comment and smiles as the woman climbs into the backseat next to me. She has a kerchief tied around her head and smells like mothballs.

"What color is your car?" Martin asks. To be honest, his confidence is getting on my nerves.

"Kind of blue," the woman mutters from her fog.

The streets are lined with cars, parking lots filled with cars. Garages, filled and stacked with cars. Most of them, it seems, are some shade of blue.

"There's no way . . . ," I say, shaking my head. The woman pats the back of my hand and beams. She looks like a babushka.

We circle town for fifteen minutes, then another ten. There are five of us in the car. No one speaks. I'm ready to suggest a more rational action when I spot a blue car with a white top over behind the bank, about a quarter mile away.

I start to say something but it seems wishful and ridiculous. There are at least ten blue cars between us but I keep coming back to the one with the white top, like the rest are muted and this car is focused and bright. I don't say anything. We make the block and everyone searches. Martin says a short prayer.

"Lady," I finally say, pointing across the lot, "is that your car?"

She squints in the distance. Martin pilots us closer. The woman claps and bounces in the seat. "It is! It is!"

No way.

We pull up next to it. Babushka jumps out, produces a key, opens the door and starts the motor. I nearly fall out in the street.

Martin kneels next to her and asks if there's anything else we can do.

"Oh no, this was all I needed," she says, then to me, "You found my car." She leans over and holds out her arms until I give her a hug. Martin looks at me with a *ye of little faith* grin.

He waves the other guys in; they pull out their wallets and produce money. I fold four ones and stack it with the rest. He piles up the cash and hands it to her. "Put some gas in your car and we'll pray you get to where you're going, okay?"

Babushka looks at us, one by one, then back to me for a longer time. "I'll be praying for you boys too," she says with a twinkle.

"Martin," I say, after she's gone. "What if she takes our money and buys wine?"

Martin gives me a sad look and shakes his head. "You've been in that counseling center too long," he says. "What difference does it make? That's between her and the Lord."

"Yeah, I guess so," I tell him. "Wow, this is crazy."

"Things like this happen all the time, brother," he says. "You need to spend more time on the street."

One of Us |

Skeeter is haggard and lean, shirt half-tucked and hand-me-down dress pants covered with mud. He reeks of booze and flop sweat and speaks with the kind of lazy southern drawl that makes every sentence sound like a commercial for hot grits and home-made biscuits.

"Why they call you Skeeter?" I ask.

"'Cause I can live right up in the thick of 'em and they don't even bite me."

Skeeter stops into the church outreach now and then, telling stories and lies and outright nonsense at times about how he thinks his daddy might be Webb Pierce and that he once rode in that Cadillac covered in silver dollars, a long time ago. He says if he just had some money for a blood test he could prove that silver dollar car rightfully belonged to him.

"One day I'm gonna git it," Skeeter tells me. "And when I do, gonna pick you up and we'll drive all over town so everybody can kiss our behinds."

"Shotgun," I declare. "I'm there."

Skeeter never asks for anything but accepts offerings grace-fully and with thanks, some pots and old clothes, beans and rice from the church pantry. Recently, the deacon with the sporting goods store donated a brand-new tent and another set him up with an appointment to get his teeth fixed.

"I been to y'all's house, you oughta come see mine some-time," he says. "Got me a nice little spot out by the river bridge."

"Sure," I say. "I'll come."

Just over the hill from the boat landing, Skeeter's got a camp-ground in a small clearing in the middle of a pine thicket. It's a tight circle of trees that offers solid protection, low profile and a good vantage point to see out without being seen. When I get there he's poking at his fire with a long stick. "C'mon in," he says. "Welcome to my humble abode."

A blue tarp is draped over some low limbs and fastened with rope. The ground is cleared out underneath and there's a sleep-ing bag, kerosene lantern and some paperback books in a milk crate. I spot Merton, Lucado and a large-print *Purpose Driven Life*.

"Good book," I say, pointing it out.

"I love books," he says, ripping a few pages from the Lucado and feeding them to the fire. I start to snicker but he rubs his hands together and holds them near the flame. Maybe he's just telling it straight. "Hey," I say, "I thought the church gave you a tent."

"They did," he says, reaching to the shadows and holding up a bottle. "I sure do appreciate that brand-new tent." He unscrews the lid and with a wink, takes a nip.

I laugh now and tell him about the time I ran away from home and slept in the woods in my Hot Wheels sleeping bag, built a pine-straw fire and woke up blind because the smoke had been blowing in my face all night. He nods like he's been there and then, without taking his eyes off the fire, hands me the bottle.

I take it and feel its weight in my hand, the curve of the glass. *Hiram Walker Sloe Gin. Premium Mixer* the label says. There's a picture of some grapes. Skeeter eyes me, waiting.

I wonder what the church might think about their outreach counselor drinking with the homeless guy by his campfire. I think about communicable diseases and Skeeter's busted teeth.

I wonder what Jesus would do.

I take a short pull and pass it back. The flavor goes down harsh and sweet, then a burst of warmth radiates like a depth charge through my chest.

"Forgot how good sloe gin is on a cold night," I say.

"Sloe gin's good any night," Skeeter shoots back with a black-gapped grin.

"First thing I ever got buzzed on was sloe gin. I was thirteen. We were playing the Christmas parade and another drummer snuck a flask out from his old man's stash. We hid behind the 7-Eleven dumpster with some chicks from the clarinet section and drank sloe gin and Sprite during the fireworks show."

"Thirteen," Skeeter says. He fastens the top back and slides the bottle into the brush. We sit and watch the fire.

"Show you that tent y'all got me, if you wanna see it," Skeeter says.

"Okay," I tell him.

He pulls out a cell phone and holds it to his ear. "Y'all at the underpass?" he says. "Wook and them down there?"

Skeeter leads me through a path near the tree line, the moon a gleaming crescent above, our breath a fog.

If it gets back that I had a drink with Skeeter, well, it might not look good at the church. *Would Jesus drink from Skeeter's bottle?* I can see it either way. I can't always figure out what Jesus would do. Maybe He would perform some kind of miracle and make everything all right. Maybe Jesus would tell Skeeter about new wine and the Kingdom and how there was plenty of room for him there. But yeah, I figure Jesus would drink from Skeeter's bottle.

The trees give way to a Stonehenge-looking set of low concrete walls at the river's edge. Three men stand around a fire built in a sawed-off barrel, hands jammed down into the pockets of their army jackets. They look past Skeeter to me and get quiet, their eyes bright in the flame.

"Who you got there?" the tallest man asks Skeeter.

"I seen you before," another man says. "One of them church folks."

"Him?" says Skeeter, as if he's forgotten I tagged along. "Hell, he ain't one of them." He loops his arm around my neck and laughs. "More like one of us. . . ."

The tall man steps up, looking like a cross between Larry Bird and Willie Nelson with his braids down. "Preacher, 'preciate you comin' out here," he says, sticking out his hand. "Been wantin' to talk to you. Everybody round here calls me Wookie."

Save a Star |

Wookie stands and waves long before I stop the car. Scrawny white arms flap from a sleeveless tee, crude ink tattooed up and down his spindly limbs. Flames and skulls, names of long-lost girls. Lonesome Jesus.

He called me at the church a few hours before, asking for a ride from the grocery store to his new campsite. Said he got kicked out of the boarding house and chased from beneath the bridge by the FBI. Stayed awhile at Snake's house but then the crack whores came over and he didn't want to be around none of that. Found a site out on Lake Felkell, seven dollars a night. Just needs a ride.

"Hey! Hey brother!" he calls out. He's covered in flashy jewelry and with his mossy hair and Manson beard resembles a caveman rapper from the dirty south.

"What's all this?" I ask, shielding my eyes.

"My lady over to the pawn shop gives me all the broken necklaces and stuff and I fix 'em up to sell." He fingers a thick cross, crusted with fraudulent jewels, holding its bling to the light. "You want this one? It's white gold, good stuff."

"No, I can't take your cross, you keep it."

"I'll get you another one. What you like?"

"Something small."

"I'll do it, I'll get you one. Tomorrow."

"No rush," I dip into my t-shirt and pull out the gun metal rosary, tempered with patina and time. "I got one."

He studies the beads, the crucifix in the dark. "That's a serious cross there. You Catholic?"

"I'm everything," I tell him. "I want all the good."

"Everything. . . ." He ponders and nods. "I like that. Me too, I want all the good I can get."

"Where'd you come up with grocery money?" I ask, pointing to his bags in the back seat.

"Cuttin' grass," he answers. "Got some lawns I keep over off Luster Lane."

I do some mental figuring. "That's ten miles from here."

"Yessir," he says. "'Bout twelve by bike."

"How do you get your lawn mower over there?"

"Drag it behind the bike," he says.

I'm searching for the right reply to towing a lawn mower twelve miles behind a ten-speed bike when he bolts forth and knocks on the glass. "Right here, right here by that RV. . . ." We turn into a dead end, a black and tan mutt barking angry in the beam of our lights. "Nope, un-uh," he says, "ain't it."

Seven or so wrong turns later we find the dirt path down to the lake where his gear is set up. Tent next to a picnic table. Electric outlet and grill, firepit on a rise overlooking the lake. "I like this," I say, telling the truth, not just being kind. "Peaceful out here."

"Yeah man, I love it. I got my sobriety, my serenity and my God."

"Good place to be."

"It is. Hey, come look at this. Check it out, brother, this is one cool-ass little tent," he boasts. "A, uh — nice tent I mean. Sorry, Preacher."

"S'okay," I tell him. "I'm not a preacher."

Wookie rolls back into his spiel. "Got cup holders in the sides and come with a sleeping bag and two pillows. Eighty bucks brand-new, Skeeter just give it to me, pretty much. Can you believe that?"

"All a man needs right here," I say, slapping him on the back. We step out of the tent and stand there surveying the land, Wookie's little world.

"Here, lemme give you some gas money," he says.

"No sir, thanks though."

"Aw, come on, I know that gas is high."

"Next time."

"Stay then, have a hamburger with me."

A Rabbi in rehab for pain pills once taught me that those in need sometimes need to give back, to keep their self-esteem. "That sounds good."

Wookie's eyes light up. "You hungry?" he asks.

"Sure am."

We sit there on the bank, eating hamburgers on smushed bread, the steady murmur of TV news bleeding from a trailer down the lane. Wookie shifts his food to the side of his mouth and traces the arc of a star falling over the waters.

"Know what that is?" I ask.

"Falling star?" he says.

I shake my head. "That's Enoch's chariot going home."

"Enoch who?" he asks.

"Enoch in the Bible. Enoch was, then he was not," I answer. "For God took him. Enoch was a friend of God."

Wookie watches the sky with awe, as if what I've told him is gospel truth. "Hey Jesus," he says low. "Save a star for me."

Crazy, Messy People |

"Just arrange whatever pieces come your way."
— Virginia Woolf

Through a fluke, I land a freelance gig with a forward-thinking Christian magazine. The third month I get a cover story and a check in the mail for sixty-five bucks. I hold it to the light, run my fingers over the watermark and stare at it for a long time.

There are other interviews and features, fallen pastors and Jewish porn stars, almost Marilyn Manson.

A major Christian publisher has roots in the megachurch. Gill and I meet with an editor there who says he saw one of my magazine pieces and thought it was good.

"We'd love to see some books born out of this movement," the editor says. "Do you have any stories from the church?"

I bring him a piece from the counseling center. He silently flips the pages, shaking his head before casting it to the side like an old banana peel.

"You can turn a phrase pretty good," Mr. Editor says with a dour face. "But you can't use words like *crap* here."

"Sometimes," I try to explain, "people who are trying really hard not to stick a twelve-gauge between their teeth, don't exactly say 'Gosh, this darn life thing is wearing me out.'"

"I'm just telling you how the business works," he says. "No

curse words. None at all."

It's pointless but I argue with him, debating that nearly everything in the Bible is outlaw, subversive, messy and earthy and real; nearly everything at the Christian bookstore is neat and nice and conventional and safe, written by Bible school valedictorians, motivational-speaking preachers and shiny happy church-y people. Where are the books about God by the outlaws? By the hell-raisers and rebels and ramblers and wandering dreamers?

"What would the Bible look like if the Christian gatekeepers got hold to it today?" I ask Mr. Editor.

"Much slimmer," he admits. "But don't give up. Get with your pastor and keep trying."

Gill and I convene weekly at the China Café to hash out plans for a book from the counseling center of a Bible Belt megachurch. Almost immediately he confesses to me that he never wanted to be a therapist, that even now, during most sessions, he fantasizes of being a forest ranger.

"See, I'd love to read that," I tell him over Schezwan chicken. "It rings true. But the church'd cut you for sure. Better keep the ranger thing between me and you."

"Good idea," says Gill.

I try to pen something that won't get us fired, that can be trumpeted from the pulpit and placed in Christian bookstores. I think through our cases and try to come up with just *one* clean story of victory and resolution, just *one* case where the client ends up like the people on the cover of all those Christian books and CDs, standing on the hilltop with hands lifted, without any hint of fists or middle fingers. I try to write the kind of faith-based book that sells. As writing goes, it is truly wretched. It is factual, but not true.

There's a writer I trust so I ask her opinion. "If you aren't going to be real," she says, "don't even waste my time."

"Yeah," I tell her. "But what if *real* doesn't sell? If all that crazy, messy truth stuff comes off as pretty *un*-Christian?"

"Then write for all the crazy, messy people," she says. "You might be surprised."

Better Than Zaxxon |

Lacey from the church choir pulls me to the side and asks if I'll go to the hospital to talk to her brother, who at age forty-eight has decided to stop fighting cancer and die.

"He's refusing chemo this time," she says, "and he's got everybody all mad and sad and . . . just worried sick. Jerry Wayne, God bless him, in a lot of ways is still just a big stubborn kid. He can be a pain but we love him. And we're not ready to lose him yet."

She shows me his profile on the internet, a sunburned redneck with a Porky Pig face, standing on the tailgate, holding a stringer of bass in one hand and a Bud Light in the other. The tag beneath his picture reads: *The Coolest Old MF You'll Ever Meet.*

Lacey smoothes her eyebrow with her little finger and gives me an apologetic look. "We're not real sure where he is spiritually," she says. "He don't care much for preachers but I figure maybe he'll talk to somebody like you."

Fifth floor, room 640. There's the hissing of machines and IV drips and the smell of disinfectants like chemical death. Jerry is propped in a hospital bed watching LSU and Notre Dame on ESPN Classic, his face concave and gray now, hair cropped close.

"You the man here to talk me outta dyin'?" he asks with a grin.

"Nah," I tell him, "I'm here to meet that cool old MF I read about on the internet."

"You got him," he says with the firmest handshake he can manage. "Better hurry though. Offer expires soon."

"I heard."

Jerry looks back as the '80s-era LSU boots it up for three. "Hundred thousand bucks to live, what?" he says. "Six more months maybe? A year? To hell with that. Ain't no quality life, either. Lacey can take that money and buy her kids some college or somethin'."

I pull a chair up by the bed. "So what are you gonna do?"

"Leavin' it up to The Man," he says looking to the sky. "See what's on the other side, I guess."

"What do you think is on the other side?"

Jerry fumbles with his IV and looks hard into my eyes. "I hope it's good," he says, with resonance. "And I hope they let me in."

"Good," I repeat. "What would *good* be?"

"You know, I been thinkin' about that." Jerry adjusts his pillow and places his hands behind his head. "You from the church, right?"

"Sort of," I reply. "But not really."

Jerry nods, satisfied with my non-answer. "I went to church a lot when I was a kid. All that streets of gold and pearl gates — what's a gold street worth when you're dead?"

"Never understood that either."

Jerry mutes the TV and turns to face me. "My old man was tough and he loved his whiskey — but he always made sure we had enough. Every Friday afternoon he'd slip me a ten-dollar bill and say: 'Boy, go spend it. Spend it like there ain't no tomorrow. You got the rest of your life to be careful.'"

"You was, what?" I ask. "In high school?"

"Early high school, yeah. Mama'd drop me off at Godfather's Pizza, meet some friends. I'd eat about ten pieces of black olive and ham, drink a pitcher of Dr Pepper and play the hell out of some Zaxxon." His eyes light up now. "I remember the night I finally beat high score. Jukebox was playing 'Rebel Yell.' Becky Brister kissed me by the bathrooms."

"I love Zaxxon," I tell him.

"You played Zaxxon? You ain't old enough to played Zaxxon."

"Big time. It's still around."

"Ah," he says. "Anyways, old memories. Young and free. Your whole life ahead of you. Not a care in the world. What you wouldn't give to feel that way again. Flirtin' with girls and laughing with your buddies. Biggest problem I had was trying to beat that — what was at the end of Zaxxon?"

"Dragon."

"Dragon was Super Zaxxon," Jerry says with a snap of his fingers. "Regular Zaxxon had a robot. His arm shot missiles."

"Robot," I reply, mimicking its firing arm. "The Piggly Wiggly up close to my house had a Super Zaxxon near produce. Cold all summer. Used to hang out with a roll of quarters trying to kill that dragon."

Jerry lets out a hoarse laugh and cuts his eyes. "You say you was a chaplain?"

"Naw."

"Lacey said you were some kind of counselor or something though, right?"

"Just some dude who used to play Zaxxon."

Jerry laughs again, shifts back and adjusts the covers. I catch a glimpse of skin and bones, bruises from purple and black to sickly green, a jagged gash zippered with stitches near the low part of his back. He sees my shudder and says, "Hey brother, it's okay. I'm not in pain."

I nod for a while, saying nothing.

"So what do you think's up there?" he asks, pointing north. "Gold streets is fine but . . . that ain't Heaven for somebody like me."

"Jerry, I hope Jesus picks you up at the gate and takes you straight to Godfather's. There'll be old friends and pizza and pitchers of Dr Pepper. Then he'll pull you to the side and say *Got a lil' surprise for you.* He'll take you out past the moon to play real-life Zaxxon, with a space ship and everything."

"Now that'd be some cool shit right there," Jerry says.

"And instead of Billy Idol on the jukebox, he'll be there live," I tell him.

"If Billy Idol makes it in, I guess we'll all be okay," he says.

"Ain't that the truth."

He lays back and stares at the ceiling; a calm look sweeps across his face. "Then maybe Jesus'll say *Hey Jerry. Your daddy's here.*"

I think about my own father and all he sacrificed for my happiness, all the money he gave me for rock music and video games. I think about seeing him young again someday where everything's redeemed and nothing is lost again. I know Jerry is thinking the same because the room is heavy with that emotion. He pulls his hand across his eyes and smiles. "Dyin' man ain't ashamed to cry," he says.

"Hey, when you see your mom and daddy again and they're young and ain't ever gonna get old," I say, "that's better than Zaxxon."

Jerry pulls himself closer by the rail of the bed. "You really believe that?" he asks.

Sometimes I wish I couldn't read people. It's a knowing born from one brief moment, a look paired with the tone of voice, the way hands move with a question or certain words.

His knuckles are scarred from bar fights and working on old junk cars. There's a woman he loved and trusted and she crushed his heart. I see him sitting alone a lot of long nights, drinking and wondering what the hell went wrong.

The echo of old hurts lingers in his eyes, disappointments and desperation, never really finding a place or a way to be all right. Maybe this is Jerry's way, his hope of finally finding his place and being all right.

"I really do," I tell him. "I believe Jesus meets us on the other side, just like we are. And He loves us. And He makes everything all right."

"Don't nobody really know for sure though, do they?" he says.

"Guess not," I say. "But I believe what you hope is more important than what you know."

"I believe that too," he says, resting his fist on top of my hand. "Tell Lacey."

"She kinda needs to hear it from you."

Jerry pauses, looking past me. "All right," he says.

LSU is first and goal, fourth quarter, late. When the ref throws his flag, Jerry coughs and says to me, "You ain't a preacher, huh?"

"Nah."

"You oughta be. You oughta go preach about Billy Idol and Zaxxon in Heaven. Then maybe folks wouldn't be afraid to die."

"Kinda help with the living part too, wouldn't it?" I tell him.

"Can I tell you a secret?" Jerry says.

"Yeah."

"Don't tell Lacey this part. Wait, okay?"

"Okay," I say.

Jerry leans to me, his eyes clear. He waits and measures his words, making sure I catch each one. "I can't explain it. But I'm more at peace than I've ever been in my life."

You hear all kinds of things listening to people for a living. But every now and then there's something so different and true that it shakes you and makes you wonder how much of our lives are spent in the shallow end of the pool, so much unspoken and unknown. When someone trusts you with words like these, there's nothing to say in return. You receive it as a gift, like you've just caught a rare glimpse of the world that lies beneath the ocean.

All I can add is this: "That's rich, brother. Thank you."

We watch the Fighting Tigers flicker and score as the final seconds tick away. Purple and gold fill the screen. "It's still good even though you know who wins," Jerry says.

As the game ends, I stand to leave and wish him well.

"If I don't see you here again," he says with a grin. "I'll see you out past the moon."

Black Belt Bible Monsters
Meet the Tattooed Hairdresser from Hell |

"I form light and create darkness; I make harmonies and create discords. I, God, do all these things." — Isaiah 45

"Hey Super Bible Boy," Tat jabs. "If Jesus is so great, why are Christians so crazy?"

Tat from Kat, short for Katherine, and she's got an ink-black buzz cut and a rainbow dragon tattooed up her back and over the shoulder. She runs a funky little salon out by the bowling alley decorated with vintage horror schlock and rock posters and the music is always up *loud*; old punk and Waylon, Whitesnake and Peter Tosh. Because I work at the church, she calls me Super Bible Boy. Despite that, I think she likes me.

"*Turn. Or burn. Heathen*," I intone, lurching towards the nape of her neck.

She feigns a swoon and shrieks like Elvira, Mistress of the Dark. Then, in a growl straight from the tagline of a Tarantino film, "*Black Belt Bible Monsters Meet the Tattooed Hairdresser from Hell! Zombie Christians! Trying — to EAT MY BRAIN!*"

There's one other person in the shop — a gawky teenage girl with an overbite, in checkered tights and a denim mini sitting in the hair chair. "He better not be too hungry then," zings the girl, guffawing like a cartoon horse.

"Ooh," I say, giving her points for the slam.

"Shut it, you two," Tat threatens, wielding her clippers. "I'll skin you bald. The both of you."

Tat's mile-a-minute mouth knows no filter — the spiritual benefits of colonics, UFO theories and unsolicited sexual advice — but she's interested too, always asking about what music I'm into, how my job and love life are going, that kind of stuff. Her tattoos and attitude have gained her a reputation around town and I've heard rumors of everything from mushroom parties to amateur whorehousing. But Tat doesn't seem to care what people say and neither do I. She's cool to me and I like the way she cuts my hair.

I take the next chair over and wait while Tat smoothes the girl's newly black-and-white-streaked pageboy. "Looks hot, doll. Your parents know, right?"

"Yeah, uh? They said if I made straight As I could do whatever I wanted and they'd pay for it." The girl presses two twenties and a ten into Tat's hand.

"Congrats, sweetie," Tat says, slipping the twenties into the leopard-print lace of her bra and pushing ten back towards the girl. "That's for the As. Go eat pizza." She spins her around in the chair. "Hey Zombie Bible Boy," she says, "I present to you . . . Jilly Beanie, the Teenage Queenie! What do you think about this hair?"

"Your hair?" I reply. "It's *awesome*."

"Yay!" Jilly cheers, clacking her retainer against the roof of her mouth. "Hold out your hand!" I reach out until our palms and fingers press together. "I give you good energy!" she declares, eyes squeezed shut.

"I receive it," I respond. Teenie Queenie hugs Tat and hobbles towards the door, dragging a withered leg behind her.

"*Love* her," Tat mouths to me.

"What's wrong with her leg?"

"Born with it," Tat says. "But girl don't let it get her down."

Jilly Bean climbs into her tiny clown car and cranks the stereo, bass rattling the windows of the salon. As she pulls away she rallies her fist out the window and puckers her face into a menacing snarl.

We raise our fists in salute; Queenie eases into traffic, off and away. "Geez, at her age I was knocked up," Tat sighs, her fingers in my hair. "Kicked out, livin' on my own. But things happen for a reason, you know. . . . This shit is getting thick."

"Excuse me?"

"Your hair, babe. Can't hardly get my hands through it." She fans out her lime-green fingernails, taps them against my skull. "All right — still growing it out in front?"

"Long and low."

"Cool," Tat says, her ruby lips smacking gum. "Hey, you in a hurry?" I shake my head and she motions me to the back alley where she cowboy-straddles a kitchen chair and fires up a Marlboro Red. "I had this crazy dream the other night. Wanna hear it?"

"People always telling me their dreams," I say in a bogus grumble, "like I can decipher what they mean. I'm not a psychic — I'm a psychotherapist at a Baptist church."

"Yeah, but you'll like this one. Jesus was there."

"Let's hear it."

She spins the chair around, sits forward and sets the scene with her hands. "Okay, so a mob was chasing me through the woods. At night. I don't know why. In the distance, I see a man working through a shop window. Oil lamps were burning and everything was like old — but new. I can't explain it. It was back then but it was right now, you know?"

"I dream that way too," I tell her. "Past and present all mixed together."

"So I banged on the window and yelled *Help!*" she continues. "And he let me in. It was Him."

Most everything in the alleyway is some shade of brick-red or gray, flyers from a payday loan company scattered in dead grass, the dirt path between spilling into a side street two spaces down.

"What'd He look like?" I ask, leaning closer now.

"Kinda like Grizzly Adams, but thinner," she says.

"What else?"

Tat sits back, lost in the dream. "And He smelled like sawdust and WD-40. I love that smell . . . ," she says. "I stayed there a long time, until the mob was gone. At the door as I was leaving He said *Katherine, you can hide here anytime.*"

"Man, I always dream I'm like, trapped in a maze underwater," I confess. "So what happened then?"

"He gave me his cell phone number."

"Jesus has a cell phone?" I ask.

"It was a dream, dude. But you know, I wouldn't tell this to just anyone — but that feeling stayed with me. That's the first time I'd thought of Jesus where he wasn't mad at me. He was nice. He said I could call him anytime."

A school bus passes, the tangle of voices and laughter louder, then fading away. Tat tilts her head to me. "So. You believe in dreams?"

"I don't know," I tell her. "What do you believe?"

She runs her fingers through the side of her hair. "Sometimes I feel like God and Church and the Bible, like that stuff isn't for people like me. Like I'm too screwed up or somethin'." She sucks a good half-inch off the cigarette and blows her haze into the air. "You know?"

"Tell you the truth," I say. "I don't believe real good most of the time either."

"I guess I believe a little," she says, holding her thumb and forefinger a hair's width apart. "Sometimes."

"Me too," I tell her. "A little. Sometimes. I think that's where we start though."

"Hope so," she says.

Blackbirds light in the alley. A slow wind rustles the papers near our feet. Tat drops her cigarette and crushes it beneath her heel. "Let me show you something," she says, fumbling with the buttons of her blouse.

"Whoa," I say, reeling back.

"No, silly," she laughs. "This. A new one." She points to a small tattoo of a bearded man near the bottom of her breast-bone. "You know," she tells me. "They say this is where the heart really is."

> The folds in his shawl are filled
> with darkness
> his eyes a piercing fire
> thorns around that
> rugged cross
> where blood & water
> flow
> friend of sinners
> scarred sacred heart
> come unto me
> just as I am
> for the darkness is
> my closest friend

Jesus, Half-off

After a few awkward fiascos, the counseling center no longer sends me couples or children. I have a loosely defined position in outreach now and have become the go-to guy for misfit gay and cutter kids. Because of this, I've been pressured by staff to check out the new edgy and relevant college and youth service. For perspective, I bring along my buddy Wes. At six-foot-two, two hundred and twenty pounds of attitude and Wolverine hairdo, he's a local nightclub bouncer who never fails to speak his mind.

"What's the hot club song now?" I ask, as we wait out front for the service to begin.

"All that *boom-boom-boom* stuff sounds the same to me," Wes says, waving his hand. "I don't hear it, I'm watching for fools. Friday night, I was taking some trash out back and these two guys I threw out were waiting for me. One of 'em pulls a knife and stands there pointing it like he's tough."

"What'd you do?"

"Told him, 'You better be good with it, dude, 'cause I'm gonna take it away from you and stick it up your behind.'"

"What happened then?"

"They left."

"Come on," I tell him, as the sound of synthesizers swell. "It's starting."

The room is dim and the music way too loud. Quick-cut videos fill the flat screens around us. Grainy images of barren flagpoles and empty school desks, all very attempted artsy and abstract metaphor, DVD footage of filmstrips rattling off vague symbols of inertia, hubcaps on the carcass of antique cars, fire hydrants aging in the sun.

Attractive white-bread youth with perfect teeth and airbrushed tans mostly stand with hands in pockets, shifting from foot to foot, covertly checking their smartphones. Some, up front near the stage, hold up their happy hands and sway.

"What is this? An Abercrombie ad?" Wes asks.

"Church," I tell him, watching the scratchy montage of dashboard Jesuses on the monitor nearby.

Wes faces me, the flickering screen casting shadows across his scowl. "Church?"

"Church," I nod, squinting to see a nearby flyer, the minimalist, hipster font hard to read. *For the generation longing for meaning and community, for a people desperate for a heart-felt, meaningful message, an oasis of hope in a lost and dying world.*

"Who the hell talks like that?" he asks, a little too loudly.

"Shhh," I say, half-muffling a laugh. I grab the flyer and hand it to him. "Read it yourself. It says this is church for people who *don't like* church."

He looks over the leaflet while the slim, somewhat sexually ambiguous singer rocks back and forth, bathed in a green glow of stage lights, and breathlessly beseeches the scattered mass. *"Press in*, people. You know we just need to *press in. . . ."*

"Do we really need somebody to get us excited about Christ?" Wes grumbles.

Wes is a classless loudmouth much of the time but I can always count on him to cut straight to the heart. He's got a point. Should Faith, Hope and Jesus be marketed and sold impulsively like blue jeans, lip gloss or diet cola?

The preacher begins a vaguely pretentious ramble through Greek philosophies and the epistles of Paul, peppered with dozy jokes and theological rabbit trails. We watch and listen, until the final amen, when the slim singer takes the stage and exhorts the crowd to just *press in*, again.

After the service we sit in Wes's truck with the windows down, the first cool breeze of dusk washing us clean.

"So, what'd ya think?" I ask. He's exactly the kind of person the service aims to reach so I'm interested in what he has to say.

"They played one song for, like, seven minutes, the preacher said a bunch of stuff that didn't make any sense — then they played a ten-minute song that sounded just like the one they played before."

"Well, they're trying to reach the young people, y'know."

"*We're* young people," Wes says. "You can't get away from the gimmicks at church? Sing 'Amazing Grace,' give a quick message about living right and say, 'We're going to Chili's if you want to come. If not, God Bless, go home.'"

"Yeah, a lot of people feel that same way."

"Well, you *work* at this place," he says. "So, what's the deal? You just here for the money or what?"

"Eh, I don't know . . . ," I say, pulling the hair down into my eyes. "Wanna go get some Chinese food?"

"Yeah. But gimme the shoot first, Cowboy," he prods. "Let's hear it."

"Dude, I don't know about all that stuff. I don't push nothin' on nobody." Night has fallen and there is a chill in the air. I reach out the window, dipping my hand through it. "Only church I know is to treat people the way I want to be treated. And I can't even get that right half the time."

Wes drapes his arms over the steering wheel and stares into the windshield. "Well, we all know good people who don't go to church or talk about God all the time. Then there's those who are *always* going on about church and Jesus who you know really don't give a damn."

An ambulance passes slow, the cadence of its lights flashing

---

red and blue around us. "Maybe," I tell him, "church could just be wherever people get together and talk about God and life and how to live without being fake or going crazy."

Wes starts the truck and eases it into drive, guiding us towards the China Café. "Maybe this is church right here," he says.

Pretty Dang Sweet |

A six-year-old girl in pigtails and pink pants stands at the edge of the DJ booth, holding her pockets and twisting from side to side.

Nikki bumps my elbow. "That kid wants you," she says.

I wheel over and lean down. She's wearing tortoiseshell glasses with tape around the hinge and a Yosemite Sam band-aid across her left elbow. She is so tiny.

"Will . . ." She takes a nervous breath and looks back towards the picnic tables scattered through the snack bar. Her mother nods her on. "Will you come skate with me?" the little girl asks.

We all skate with the kids now and then but the rink is packed and the night is peaking fast. I really don't have time.

"Pleeease," she says.

I stand and look to the girl's mother. She's heavyset and tired around the eyes, in knit pants and a polyester blouse. Her hair is chopped in the style common to middle school teachers and discount accountants working the fast tax booth by the Wal-Mart checkouts. Despite that, there's an air of cheerfulness about her as she nods that it's okay and gives a little shrug that says *my kid's kind of a strange bird but what can you do?* Seems I've seen that look on someone's mother before.

Please? the mom mouths. The kid fidgets and chews her little finger, her face like a Chihuahua locked in the car.

"Go," says Nikki. "I'll DJ, you watch the floor."

I step over the chain and hold out my hand. The tiny girl takes it and we make our way out. She jerks her feet along, tipping forward and then back, hanging from my arm, *skritch skrtich skrtich*–ing in Fisher Price skates, blue and yellow with the wheels locked.

"What's your name?" I ask.

"Dani," she says. "But Mama calls me Daffy."

"Which do you prefer?"

"Sir?"

"What name do you like best?"

She smiles. Her front teeth are missing and there's some Strawberry Fun Dip spilled down her shirt. "I like Daffy," she says.

We shuffle along; she pulls at my hand. "What's your name?"

"My mama calls me Daffy too."

"Oh," she ponders. Cuts her eyes. "Really?"

"Nah, I'm kidding," I tell her. "My name is Jamie James."

"I'm in first grade," she says, holding up a finger.

As we ease from the carpet to the hardwood floor, Nikki calls for couples only. "Moooonlight couple skate," she says, covering the mic to giggle.

Thanks, Nik.

The other skaters straggle away leaving only two other pairs on the floor. Daffy pedals and totters, trying to keep up. She kicks off with her right foot, wobbles, then falls back. She stands, grabs at my fingers and falls flat again. Over in the snack bar, Mama cranes her neck to see.

A teen couple slides by in graceful arcs. Daffy stares longingly as they pass then shifts her sad eyes to me. "I'm sorry," she says. "I can't skate too good."

I start to help her over to the carpet and back to her mom

when Celine Dion and R. Kelly hit the chorus of "I'm Your Angel." Reaching down, I catch Daffy beneath the arms and lift her into the air. Her face freezes; she grips at the sleeves of my shirt.

"Are you scared?" I ask.

"N-No," she says, pointing to the couple. "I wanna skate like that."

"Then you better hold on," I tell her.

We dip and sway, sweeping across the floor, lost in the sparkle and twirl, mirror balls throwing a thousand tiny shards of light, the music all around. Like gliding over glass, we weave beneath the disco glow and through the purple smoke. As I circle and swoop backwards, she throws out her arms and soars.

Celine's and Kelly's voices weave together as one. Daffy sings along, about clouds in the sky, faith and grace and angels, no matter who or where you are.

The teen couple cruises beside us; we figure eight and intertwine, mirroring each other's moves. Just before they drift away the teenage girl reaches out and touches Daffy's hand.

It's the kind of moment when time slows and every detail bleeds living color like Instamatic film, when your throat catches because for a brief few seconds life is as beautiful as you'd always hoped, when God shows up in the smile of a shy child and shows you something ten years of church Sundays couldn't contain and when God arrives that way there's something between laughing and crying, sweet as both at the same time, the notion that maybe, just *maybe* if that's what God is like, then things could be all right.

I pivot towards the middle of the floor, beneath the biggest mirror ball, spinning us round and round, becoming one with the blur of fog and lights and loud music. She closes her eyes, flutters her hands from side to side and laughter bubbles forth like springs of pure joy. . . .

Standing at the snack bar wall, her mother waves and claps her hands. "*Whoo*, Daffy!" she calls.

As the song ends, with one last spin, I set her gently at her mother's feet.

"Mama, did you see, Mama?" Daffy says.

"I saw, baby," Mama answers. "What do you say?"

Daffy hugs me, tight as she can. "Thank you, Jamie James."

"Thank you," her mom seconds, pushing the hair from Daffy's face.

"Thank *you*," I say.

"Aw," Nikki sighs when I make it back to the booth. "Now how sweet was that?"

"Pretty dang sweet," I say.

Strangers & Aliens |

"It has always been the prerogative of children and half-wits
to point out that the emperor has no clothes. But the half-wit
remains a half-wit, and the emperor remains an emperor."
— Neil Gaiman

Let's get this over with.

I have committed theft, set mine eyes upon false gods and
a time or two coveted my neighbor's ass. I've been guilty of
both murder and adultery in my heart. I have forgotten the
Sabbath. I have loved self far more than neighbor or God. I
have been guilty of all these things *since* the hour I first believed.
Sometimes I wonder if I even believe at all.

I doubt too much. I think too much. I'm too much of a con-
trarian. Every time I try to be spiritually confident or cool, I put
my foot in the mop bucket. A part of me has always wondered if
God just looks at me and shakes His head.

*Sorry, Lord. Guide me, oh Mercy and Grace. Each day, trying to
do better.*

So it helps me to see firsthand that the church is constantly
stepping in the mop bucket too.

Truth is, I sort of need the hypocrite guy who can't quite get
his actions and beliefs on the same page. The narcissistic little
preachers and showboat singers and Ponzi scheme evangelism

programs that impress no one outside the fold. Bandwagon mentalities and bait-and-switch sales pitches. Pop culture ripoffs, sappy songs and tacky t-shirts. All the distant, distracted, professionally religious and politely practiced church staff.

You see some nutty stuff working in a church, some really crazy people. And then, if you watch, you see some of those same crazy people do beautiful things. The arrogant deacon feeds the hungry, the hypocrite cares for the sick, the religious bigots band together to serve the poor. And I realize that whether I am at a bar or a psych ward or a megachurch — people are just people and in the dark, lonely places we are all pretty much the same, frightened and confused and mostly feeling like we're doing the best we can. Knowing that the beautiful shiny church-y people are just as messed up as the rest of us — well, it gives me a strange kind of hope. The feeling that maybe I can make it after all. That maybe Grace really is amazing.

It helps me see that from Moses to the Revelator John, from Adam to the last man who will ever live — we are all screwups, stumbling through, rising and falling back to dust, lusting and loving and trying and killing and giving and living and dying and wondering why.

God in broken vessels, the Almighty come to earth as a man, existential Jesus choosing that troublemaking Peter — *of all people* — to build his church upon, Jehovah the carpenter, the one they called Mary's bastard, crucified between criminals and promising Paradise to the thief who pleaded *Remember me.*

The emperor is naked; children and scoundrels shout the news; *Long live the King.* God help us all to be naked and unashamed, to watch and listen, to laugh at ourselves and confess that the only thing we are sure of is how little we really know. To admit that Mercy and Grace and Hope and Faith and God and Heaven had better be far larger than we have made them out to be.

I love the silly crazy beautiful broken busted-up church. But I don't know if I should work in one.

Christmas Crazy |
Amazing Grace at the Dollar General Store

"People wear more masks at Christmas than they ever do at
Halloween." — Manic-Depressive at the Psych Ward Holiday
Party

It's the night before the night before Christmas.

"She didn't OD on much, but we gave her the charcoal hard,"
the nurse tells me. "She's a wreck but go on in."

I push through the ER doors and locate my charge. A gaunt
girl in black galoshes and candy-cane pantyhose, puking furi-
ously into a metal pan.

Her face is pasty, clothes covered in smudge. Ebony tresses,
streaked with green and red cascade from her head. An earring
dangles; Jack the Pumpkin King from *Nightmare Before Christmas*.

I take a seat and roll up to the bed.

"*BLARRRGGG!*" she hacks, heavy necklace lock and chain
banging against the stretcher's rail.

If I lower my head and pouf out my hair I can look a bit like
Edward Scissorhands with Stallone in the lead or Joe Perry if he
joined The Cure. It's my best goth move so I give it a shot, holding the pose until she looks up.

"*BLEECCHHH!*" she retches, toes curled, with a little con-
vulsing writhe at the end like an exclamation. Middle finger

crooked, she swabs a string of drool from her mouth and into the pan. She rolls over, arms splayed, and tries to catch her breath.

Kohl-blue eyes creep open, she spies me, watching like a crow.

"Merry Christmas," I say.

She laughs, a weak little sticky laugh, and curls into a ball. "F*ck Christmas," she replies. "I hate it."

"No you don't," I tell her. "You love it too much and it lets you down. Lots of people feel that way."

"Christmas shouldn't be so hard," she says, just before gagging again. "God should call a truce or something."

It's Christmas Eve and the congregation is swooning as a mother/ daughter duo over-emote their way through the awkward carol "Sometimes Christmas Makes Me Cry."

Except for me. Maybe it's that I've played with the kind of singers who could cut loose with a verse and chorus of "Jesus Paid It All" that would make Chris Hitchens weep. Eyes crossed, I chime in on the bass part, a little flat. *Sometimes Christmas makes me crazeeee. . . .* Sad glances are exchanged around; no one is amused.

Maybe I'm just a jackass.

This afternoon I went to a family Christmas dinner and they didn't have any Diet Coke. They had *cola* but it was that off-brand, flat-tasting stuff — Dr. Packer or something like that — and I was in that frame of mind where your skin is crawling and you feel thirteen again, hormonal and alien, like everything is okay, but nothing is all right. So I snuck behind the nativity scene and huffed some gas from a paper sack. Actually, I just excused myself and drove to the corner convenience store. But the J-Mart had chinchy fountain cokes with funky ice and not enough carbonation, the kind that makes you feel syrupy sick after you drink it.

I was in a black mood by that point and then I thought of all the poor children, of the broken soldiers, of all the lonely, hungry, sad Christmas people with no family and friends and then I was in a bad mood for *being* in a bad mood, for not being grateful or gracious or capable of glad tidings and cheer.

"What's wrong, baby?" my aunt Mimi asked.

"Nothing," I snapped.

Broadway big, the duo's weepy carol ends and the congregation rises to applaud. The pastor walks to the pulpit, clapping along; the people are seated and his message begins:

Some two thousand years ago, a child was born . . .

I read a study the other day that said Halloween was now America's favorite holiday. Evangelicals might be quick to blame Satan but scratch the surface of that fact and you realize it's probably because Halloween is all about fun and pretending and becoming someone else with none of the emotional weight and sentimentality that family-based religious holidays hold. Family and religion make a lot of people very nervous. Don't get me wrong. I love Jesus and I love Christmas and sometimes it's amazing but other times the holidays have got me a little crying and crazy too.

All the restless thoughts, the accounting of another year's end.

Why are my relationships so complicated?

What happened to my dreams?

What's wrong with me?

Expectations and emotional roller coasters. Longing for something magical, for beauty in a world of chaos, the secret wish that maybe just this *once* everything would be right. For something good to hold on to. For someone good to hold.

The goth girl was right. Christmas shouldn't be so hard.

I hit the side door and cut out early. It's the Season of Epiphany and mine is this: *Outside of my comfort zone, I am rotten.*

Dollar General is the only store open so I pull into the lot for some rations. There's a ramshackle house not ten yards away and the front door opens as I step out of my car.

A teenage couple argues on the porch. Just inside I can see a younger girl, fifteen maybe, bouncing a baby on her hip in the TV light.

With a slam of the door, the couple rambles through the gravel towards the store. I walk in behind them and gather my things. Grape G2, carton of eggs.

Tending the register is an effeminate teen with a receding hairline and a rhinestone stud in his right earlobe. I pay. He grunts and moves my goods to the end of the counter.

The young couple steps in behind me, loading their items onto the belt. Dollar Store diapers. Ramen noodles. A few packs of tuna. The girl's hair is dark at the roots, straggling out into a matted mess the color of mozzarella cheese. Her breath is heavy with congestion, her eyes like glass. Skinny and pale with scattered acne and a shock of black hair, the boy hangs like a scarecrow behind her. Both wear K-Mart versions of Hot Topic fashion five years removed.

I watch them as I bag. His face strains with the math as their purchases are scanned. When the total flashes he pulls out four ones and some change, gives the girl a panicked look and counts his change again.

I slide a ten to the cashier. "Here you go. I got some left over." I say this quietly, matter-of-fact.

The boy stares at the bill awhile before speaking. "We don't need yer fukin' money."

His girl turns, her face sour. "What you think, we're trash or somethin'?"

The cashier glares as if I've offered kindergartners cocaine. I fumble, no words come.

"Go put them diapers back," she orders the boy. "I can get some from Mama in the mornin'."

"Okay, then," I say. I sweep up the ten, grab my things and head out to the car.

The younger girl waits in the front screen door, crying baby in her arms, watching for the couple's return.

"Hey," I call to her, "the cashier gave me too much change.

You want it?"

Angling the baby inside, she cautiously looks me over. I realize my proposition could be misconstrued so I stand with hands down and the most harmless look I can muster. "It's Christmas," I say, holding out the money. "For the baby."

She steps out and smiles. In the porch light she glows, awkwardly beautiful in an innocent sort of way. Her green eyes match the child's. "Heck yeah, I want it," she says.

I walk over and pass her a twenty through the porch rail. She turns it twice in her hand. "Wow," she says, pulling a strand of auburn hair from the corner of her lips. "What are you, an angel or somethin'?"

"Or somethin'," I reply.

We share a quick laugh before I leave. As I'm pulling away she takes the baby's arm and waves goodbye.

In the rearview mirror I see her do a bouncy little jig and hold out the bill as the couple climbs the steps. With a short bleat of the horn, I return the wave.

Some 2,000 years ago a child was born
to a teenage girl on the poor side of town.
Dubious men arrived bearing gifts.
This is Christmas, the season of redemption and hope.

Come to Tennessee |

I'm driving home from Spike's record shop with the radio on when the DJ announces a brand-new song from a local boy done good. It's Juke, singing about love and God and loneliness, the ache in his voice like aged leather and cross-cut maples in the spring.

Late one night, he calls me from his tour bus. We small talk about the road and the thrill of a top-five song but there's still a sadness behind his words.

I tell him about the church, how the people are sweet and crazy and the whole thing is a mess behind the scenes but that sometimes amazing things happen anyway. I tell him it's good work but just doesn't seem to fit me anymore and how I need direction and wonder which way to go. I tell him I really miss the music. That I love our hometown, but sometimes it seems so small. I tell him about the blue-eyed farmer's daughter with the genius IQ.

"She's got dreams too," I say.

"Jamie," he says, after a long pause. "Come to Tennessee."

She is patience and grace. I am still so sixteen.

Juke loans me his best boots and suit coat. The bride wears a dress from Sears. She is beautiful beyond compare. I have never been so afraid.

At a little brown church on the outskirts of Clark County, we exchange vows at a quarter past ten p.m., just the preacher and the two of us.

He rings the steeple bell as we drive into the desert night.

My wife is accepted to Vanderbilt University. We find a little house right out of Nashville, with a hidden drive, on a hill just up over the ponds.

I take a full-time job with the county crisis team, responding to mental health emergencies throughout the region. The work is mostly based from home but when the alarm rings, you grab your gear and jump in the fire. Five counties, hundreds of miles some nights from emergency rooms to jail cells to suicidal drunks in the last house trailer off the gravel road.

The pay for a licensed crisis worker with six years' experience is fourteen-fifty an hour. It's a state job and the benefits are good.

PART V

Seven Doors

"... and now he was settling into his life's work, which was the study of things themselves in the streets of life and the night." — Jack Kerouac

When Judas Tied the Noose |

"He appeared first to Peter, and then to the twelve."
— 1 Corinthians 15:5

With the black hat and lambskin coat on, I buzz through the last of the metal doors and pull at the handle of the side cell. There's a scrawny man strapped in the restraint chair at his wrists and ankles, a thick leather band cinching his chest. He's wearing Hamburglar coveralls and orange canvas shoes, his hair white at the roots and sprouting about in wild shocks.

"Mr. Banks," I greet him, my voice echoing around the tiny cell, the room reeking of bleach and sour sweat.

"You the doctor?" he asks in a razor-harsh rasp. To the half-dead and desperate in the hour of need I have been doctor, priest, rabbi, kinfolk and friend.

"Something like that," I say, shaking his hand through the restraints. I motion to his throat, banded by rivets of purple-black bruises. "Tell me what happened."

Banks tells the story of his wife who had taken their children and moved in with the tattoo artist. She had sworn to stay true while he served his sentence for schedule II possession and armed robbery. "Had an old jackknife in my jeans," he explains.

His drunken daddy disowned him long ago and lately his deceased mother appeared in his cell and told him he'd be better off dead. He fought the notion, knowing she would never say such, but still spent each night in his bunk braiding the rope.

"Made it from strips of blankets and sheets I slipped out of the laundry. While I worked I'd read from that Gideon Bible until sleep overtook. Some nights sleep never came. Finally the rope was long enough and Mama kept calling me to come. So I did," he says, his voice in broken sobs, tears streaming into his beard. "Mister, I wasn't even at my own mama's funeral. I was in jail."

I wave to the deputy. "Cut my man loose an arm, if you don't mind."

"Whatever you say, Doc," the young officer says, stepping up and pulling keys from his belt, loosing the straps at the inmate's right wrist before slipping back out the door. I hand Banks a warm washcloth and water in a Styrofoam cup.

"I'm not really a doctor," I confess.

He presses the rag to his face and hands it back to me. "You're a Christian man though, aren't you?" Banks asks.

"By grace, a little more each day, I hope."

"Me too. Was. Tryin'. But you are one, I can tell," he says. "You might not believe this but I was raised up in church." He looks past me, through the tiny window laced with iron, over the Cumberland and into the hills. "Reading that Bible the other night, I came across something. . . . Can I ask you a question? Won't nobody else answer it for me." He studies my eyes, waiting.

"I can try."

"Where was Jesus when Judas tied the noose?"

The question hangs, bouncing off the cinderblock, filling the room with its weight. I don't know what to say.

"Seems Judas needed him the most," he continues.

I clear my throat. "Mr. Banks, I don't know. But I have to think He was there."

"Judas, he was the money man, right?" he asks.

"I think so. Yeah."

"Let me hold the money, I'da messed everything up just as bad or worse," Banks says with the hint of a grin.

"I'm totally capable of pulling a Judas," I admit, jabbing myself in the chest. "If there's no grace for that guy, there's none for me either." I lean in close, one hand on his bound wrist. "But sometimes living with yourself, it's just hell though."

Banks shakes his head slowly, tears welling up again. "Man, I don't wanna die," he says, drawing a long breath. "I gotta get right. Get myself together. For my kids." He slicks back his hair and looks me over, trembling. "What you going to do with me?"

"Send you to the hospital, let you rest awhile. Get you on some medicine so you'll stop seeing and hearing things that aren't there."

"Thank you, thank you. Sir, do they let people smoke over there?"

I hold the answer a moment, let him anticipate it. "They do."

He throws his head back, blows out his breath. "Thank you, God. I haven't had a cigarette in three damn weeks."

I pat my coat pockets. "You got cigarette money?"

Finally he smiles. "I got some money, good buddy. But thanks. How about some more water though?"

"Absolutely," I say, moving over to the shallow drain and faucet topping the steel commode. "You hungry?"

"I could sure eat something," he says.

I slip around the corner, grab a honey bun from a discarded tray and hand it to him with the water. He places the pastry in his mouth, breaks it with his free hand and hands half to me. I sit and we eat in silence. The air is thick with the Presence and I think weird and wonderful thoughts.

This is my body, this is my blood. God with us in this cell, in communion and fellowship, in brokenness, in joy and sorrow, in the quiet empty spaces of the night.

"Good honey bun," Banks mutters, crumbs scattering into the straggles of his beard.

"The best," I say, holding the moment a little longer before standing and offering my hand again. "Well. Better go get the paperwork going."

He holds my grip. "He sent you up here, didn't He?"

"I don't know," I laugh, pulling my hand free and patting his shoulder. "Maybe so."

"Yeah, well, you're doing His work coming up to some country jail in the middle of the night, to help some crazy old drunk that tried to hang hisself."

"Maybe you're here to help me," I offer and we both laugh a little.

"Maybe we help each other," says Banks. "But I appreciate you coming, I do." I return the thanks and reach for the door when he stops me. "Hey son, you got a mama?"

"Yes sir."

"Love her while you can. Appreciate her."

I nod. "I will. I promise."

"You got a wife?"

"I do."

"Don't let her go to the tattoo shop alone."

The city at night is silent as I make my way out and down through the hills back home. It's here where I best reflect, in the car, the engine's drone below and soft glow of dashboard lights. *Banks. Jail. The Presence.* For what is communion but giving thanks and remembrance? When we recall the only righteous privilege we have is to help another up and along, knowing we may well need the same help soon? Maybe this is why Jesus drew near to the poor in spirit and had only harsh words and hellfire for those so sure their hearts were pure. Sometimes you give the living water, other times you drink from another's cup. We are all as different as we are the same and all in need of the same things. To give Grace, Hope and Love. And to receive the same.

Witch Black & Baby Blue |

Anarchy everywhere in the five-county region and by the time I creep into the last ER I've had more than my fill of manic-depressives and opiate suicides gone awry. I drop my gear and sift through the patient fridge for a Gatorade G2.

"No grape?" I ask Jody, the nurse.

"Sorry," she says.

"Figures," I tell her. "So what you got?"

"Well," she sighs, puffing bangs from her eyes, "by the time she got here she'd already shucked off all her clothes and throwed them out the cop car window. Then when they dragged her through the doors she tore off the sheet they wrapped her in and shouted, '*I AM THE ARK OF THE COVENANT — do not touch meeeeeeeeeeee . . .*'" Jody gnarls her hands into claws and screeches the last line.

"All right then," I respond.

"Bed nine," Jody grunts, tossing over the chart. "Took six of us but she's strapped down and in a hospital gown. For now."

"What's her name?" I ask.

"Anna," Jody says.

I knock against nine's wall and pull the curtain back. The girl is mid-twenties maybe, with witch-black hair, baby-blue eyeshadow, and a face ravaged by acne scars. She's upright in bed, latched to the rails with straps and scowling me down with the cackle of the damned.

Jody's on my tail. "Wanna see this," she clucks.

I stride forth and hold out my hand. The patient flinches back and pulls against the straps, eyeing me like I'm Gacy offering balloons. "I do not shake hands with the devil's son," she says with disgust. Jody lets out a whoop and exits the room.

Pulling a stool over, I sit by the bed. She slowly swivels her head towards me, as if it is turned by gears.

"Hey," I tell her. "I'm just here to help."

Her laugh sounds like the quacks from a crazy pack of mallards. She cuts it abrupt and lowers her head. "You," she commands, "look into mine eyes and know what it is to be loved."

I slide in. We lock eyes. "Okay," I say, playing along.

She stares intently, like trying to bend metal with her mind. *Don't smirk*, I think. *Monster be nice.*

A minute seems endless when you are staring into the eyes of a stranger. *Maybe the monster is me*, I consider, *toying with the acutely psychotic. Be nice*, I recall. *Be kind. Do no harm.*

Time crawls and two minutes pass slowly as the waters beneath the Silver Creek Bridge. She moves closer. Her breath is hot and smells of SweeTarts, nails chipped black and filed to a point. *Peace*, I pray. *Mercy. Lord, let the straps hold.*

Three minutes, four. Silence, save for the soft blips and hum of medical machinery.

Closer still, she comes, until our faces nearly touch.

I see her in a tattered old shack with the curtains drawn and the TV always on, alone night after night, crying over the baby that died and there is nothing now. Nothing.

I see evil men and shadows and blood and shame. I see a sadness I cannot fathom.

Closer.

The emerald of her eyes flickers in the light. She blinks and tears roll down her face and it breaks me. I want to tell her that we are all so damaged. That the darkest heart hopes for beauty still. That somehow things could be all right.

But there just aren't any words.

"Anna, I'm sorry," I say softly.

She bites her lip and looks away. "You can go now."

Her gown is torn. Imprints of the buckles and leather mark her arms. I loosen the straps and lay them to the side.

"Anything I can do?" I ask.

She shakes her head. I stand to leave.

"Juice," she says.

"Juice?"

"Juice."

"That it?"

She shrinks into herself and in a tiny voice asks, "Do you have any extra underwear?"

There is no rush to speak in jails or emergency rooms. "Juice. Underwear. I'll see what I can do." I turn to go. At the door she calls out to me.

"Hey mister."

"Yeah?"

"Do you feel more loved now?"

Sometimes the job is a blessing, other times a curse. Sometimes it's sport, other times all too serious. Sometimes I don't have the first clue and other times I know I am exactly where I belong.

"Yes ma'am," I tell Anna. "I do."

Northbound Down & Beulah Land Bound

"County Crisis, come back."

"This is Crisis, go ahead."

"Forty-seven-year-old white male, disoriented, delusional, possible suicidal ideation, found roadside by a local church group who are there with him now. Got a lady on the line."

"Put her on."

"Hey there!" a bubbly voice says.

"Ma'am," I reply. "What's goin' on?"

"Well. We were out knocking on doors telling people about the Lord and come across this homeless man who says he's walking to Washington to save America from the sky butchers and the diesel bomb apocalypse. To be honest, he smells like he's been drinking. Talks kinda weird — but a real nice fellow. Think you can come up here and help us out?"

"Oh, absolutely," I reply. "Where you at?"

"You know where Beulah Land is?"

". . . Ma'am?"

"Beulah Land Trailer Park," she chirps. "Just off 309 'bout fifteen miles 'fore the Kentucky line?"

"By the Four-Way Grocery?" I ask.

"Oh yes," she says. "But now — if you pass the Dairy Dip, you done gone too far."

"On my way."

I see them sitting on the banks of a sewage ditch just beyond the trailers, sipping on Sonic slushes as the summer sun dips over the hills. A gaggle of women dressed in Sunday's best gathered around a rail of a man wearing a too-big cowboy shirt with duct tape on his boots. I pull in, walk over and introduce myself. The women are quite pleasant. Jehovah's Witnesses, they tell me.

"Jesus would sit by the ditch with a homeless man. Probably buy him a cold drink, doncha think? I'm Terri, by the way. Talked to ya on the phone." She's wearing white Reeboks with a deep purple dress dotted with tiny red cherries and is irresistibly adorable in a way only plump little women can be. Her eyes are wide and flirty and the left one wanders when she laughs.

"I imagine He would," I tell her.

"Well," she says, clapping her hands together, "let me introduce you to Jacky." The women part and there he stands, like a skinnier, *Bandit*-era Burt Reynolds after a rough bout with the flu.

"So, Mr. Jacky . . . ," I begin, motioning him to the side to get the story.

"Jacky Didem," he says before I can finish. "But boss, you can call me JD."

"Um, okay . . . JD, tell me. How does a fellow find himself on the side of the road in the backwoods of Tennessee surrounded by Jehovah Witness women?"

"Cousin," JD says in earnest, "I was just walkin' to Washington, D.C. I am on my way. Hail to the Chief called me hisself this morning." JD holds up a trash sack full of clothes and an old school cassette player.

"The Prez called you?" I ask. "On your cell?"

JD shakes his head and points to the cassette player.

"Oh. Called you on your Walkman," I say. "Well. What's the president got to say?"

"He said, 'JD, get your ass to D.C. ASAP.' See, I got the answer to some top-secret stuff I can't talk about just yet. But

I know why the food's all tainted and the sun's too hot and I know how to fix it."

We nod at each other awhile then turn to watch a Domino's delivery driver take the corner on two wheels.

"Ever want to hurt yourself?" I ask, eyes still on the lighted sign suction-cupped to the cab of the pizza man's Chevy Cavalier.

"No. Well, sometimes." He says this matter-of-fact, as if I had asked did he like cheesy bread.

"Wanna hurt anyone else?"

"Naw."

Terri walks over, sashaying her hips and batting that lazy eye. "Sir," she says sweetly, "we'd love to stay and help but I need to get the sisters back 'fore it gets too late." She rests her hand against my arm. Her group stands thick in the shadows behind her. There is giggling.

"Don't you worry, ma'am," I say, in a dashing actor-y sort of way, "Mr. JD and me, we'll work it all out. You take care of the sisters."

JD leans in and claps me on the back. "The sisters," he confirms.

"We'll run on now, then," she says, sucking blue slush through the straw. "You will call and let me know how we can follow up? Won't you?"

"You bet, thanks so much for your help," I tell her. She lingers, starts to turn and I pull her into a big hug, the kind we used to share after service at the Pentecostal church. It's completely inappropriate and absolutely fun. She makes a little Pillsbury whinny noise, rocks side to side and nearly squeezes the breath out of me. Over her shoulder, JD gives me a thumbs-up.

"Take care now, okay?" I tell her as we part.

Sister Terri totters off into the whispers of her women. They pack into the van and drive away. At the corner they honk and we wave.

"Damnation, thought they never would leave," JD says, not unkindly. "You ain't got a cigarette, do ya?"

I hand him the last Camel from my crisis stash. He lights up quickly, draws deep and lets out a long slow breath. "Nice ladies though. Doin' the Lord's work, they are. All part of the plan. You gon' send me to that state hospital by the river? My meds is *all* screwed up . . ."

I nod as their taillights vanish down the ridge. JD smokes while I write up his papers.

"Bossman, what we waitin' on?" he asks.

"Ambulance," I tell him.

"You ain't comin'?" he asks, kind of sad-like.

"Yeah, I'll follow y'all down there."

"Good deal," he says, then with the rib, "I think that lil' chunky one mighta been sweet on you."

"Think so?"

"Heh," JD says. "Hell, it's hot out here. You want to walk over to the Sonic, get a coke?"

"Sure," I say. "Let's go."

We ease across the empty lot and take a picnic table by the Sonic front door. A bubblegum-popping black girl skates out to take our order.

"Why y'all ain't got no car?" she asks, sassily smacking her Juicy Fruit. Her nametag says *Brianna*.

"We don't need no car," says JD. "Why's your behind look like two basketballs in a gunny sack?"

"Boy, you crazy!" Brianna screams, nearly toppling off her wheels in a conniption of laughter.

"Crazy as a nekkid tom in a polecat whorehouse!" JD cries.

"Nekkid *Tom*!" Brianna shouts. She levels her ink pen at me and shuts one eye. "And your poofy-ass ain't right either, I can tell."

Delirium reigns; I stand and raise both hands. "Bring me the Flapdoodle," I command, "No applesauce."

There is an embarrassing silence. Brianna digs in the back

of her slacks and waves away a wasp. "Dr Pepper," JD says flatly. "One for my partner here, too."

"Uh, Diet, no ice," I call out as Brianna skates away. JD licks his thumb and counts out ones from a wad of crumpled bills.

"Here, let me get that," I say.

"Money ain't gonna be worth nothin' in another month or two," JD says, waving me away. "You won't be able to buy shit without the Mark of the Beast. I got this."

"Appreciate it," I tell him.

"Ain't nothin'," he says, untying the twist tie on his garbage bag and rooting out a brown paper sack of cassettes. "You know what we need? Some music while we waitin'. What you say, Cowboy?"

"Turn it on," I tell him. *Just along for the ride, brother.*

He digs out a sun-faded tape and pushes it towards me. "You like Conway?"

"Who don't like Conway?" I reply.

JD smiles like Richard Petty and presses PLAY as I dial the local EMS.

"Crisis here," I say when the person picks up on the other end of the line. "Got a 404 at the Sonic off Shady Lane. Need transport."

"Yessir," the voice says back. "Got one out on a tree fallin' but I'll have somebody to you quick as I can."

Brianna rolls back with our cold drinks. JD stands, slaps four dollars in her hand and slides another four into her apron.

She does a little roller boogie hustle and sings it like an old blues shouter: "That's what I'm *talkin'* about!"

"No rush," I tell the dispatcher. "No hurry at all."

Conway growls about that tiger in them tight-fittin' jeans. JD and the carhop do a little bump and grind just as a family pull their station wagon into the slot before us. A giant woman in a plaid jumper opens the back door, releasing a ruckus of moon-faced joy as five special-ed children rush the table next to ours. In the distance, sirens whine.

"What you oughta do," JD yells to me, right between the Electric Slide and Cotton-Eyed Joe. "You oughta just walk with me to Washington."

Ten Million Beautiful Years

"Cigarette?"

"No sir, sorry," I say, patting at my pockets. "Just give my last one away."

It's eleven p.m., just outside the emergency room doors. The old man wears a blue jean jacket and black fedora, white tufts of hair curling from the sides. He's unkempt but in a classy sort of way, like an old jazz player or a character actor on *Touched by an Angel*.

"I ain't asked if you had one, I asked if you wanted one." He scowls but his tone is playful.

"Oh — no sir, no thanks. You go right ahead."

He lights up and points through the window at the TV, the funeral for a pop star. "You see somebody like that die, make you realize you can die too."

"Sure does."

"You young folk don't think 'bout no dying," he scoffs.

"Death knows no prejudice." I think I heard that in a Steven Segal movie or something.

"Son, you right," he says, nodding at the images on the screen. "You got one life to live, then we all go to Justice."

I nod back and we eye each other in the glass. "I hope when I meet Justice, Grace is close and ready. 'Cause I'm gonna need some help."

He lets his smoke out slow and shakes his head from side to side. "I sure heard that."

We stand there and watch while the show unfolds. People crying. Lionel Richie singing about the helping hands of Jesus.

"You believe in Heaven?" he asks.

"Yes sir."

"What you think Heaven is?"

"I think you get back everything you ever loved and lost. For good."

A jet plane streams across the sky, its wing lights softly blinking. The old man watches it climb and for a long time is silent.

"How 'bout you?" I ask.

He pauses a beat before smiling. Some of his top teeth are gold. "I wanna make love to ten million beautiful women for ten million beautiful years."

"Ten million beautiful years," I repeat, the words like snowfall in a dream. "Then what?"

"Then," he says, in a determined sort of way, "I guess I'd like to make love to all them good-lookin' cartoon women."

I turn to the old man and he stares back like he has trusted me with a great insight, something deeply personal and profound.

"You mean like Nancy from the Sunday comics?" I'm laughing as I ask.

His look turns sideways. He shakes his head. "*Hell* naw," he replies.

Piffle |

I'm on psychiatric crisis with no backup, driving from one end of the five-county area to the other, snarled in suicide and psychosis, winging it and doing the best I can. I don't mind the work but thus far the company has been less than supportive.

Judy, the local supervisor, a former Avon shark with a drive-thru university degree, asks to meet with me at the office. She comes in guzzling a sixty-four-ounce Pepsi and dragging her purse like it weighs two hundred pounds. A stack of folders is jammed beneath her left arm; some papers fall out in the hall behind her.

"Corporate is just not pleased with your paperwork," she says with a heaving sigh.

"Like what?"

"Well, for starters, spelling errors."

She produces a stacked printout of my recent reports and flops it before me. The page is covered with red circles and yellow highlights.

"Oh," I reply.

"And you put things in the wrong place. . . ."

I listen as her complaints continue but it sounds like nit-picking to me, like the old management scheme of using fear and criticism to keep the sheep in line. On the other hand, I suck at minutiae and I know that with the state, minutiae are crucial indeed.

Maybe a local rink needs a DJ.

When she finishes, I nod politely and tell her that maybe it's best we go our separate ways.

"Oh gosh, no," she says, waving her hands. "We don't want you to leave."

"I drove over two hundred miles last night and saw more people alone than the entire day shift combined. I do that all the time — and you guys can't say something nice now and then?"

Judy frowns and lowers her eyes, her face like a beagle caught stealing weenies.

"What's going on here?" I ask.

"Listen," she says, her tone changing from business to personal. "I don't know what crisis was like where you came from, but here it's mostly third-rate social workers and . . . piffleheaded administrators with zero people skills and nowhere else to go. And most of them need mental health intervention themselves."

Then, with a long slurp from her jumbo cola, she switches on a dime to a smile, yellow teeth and a crimson lipstick smear, sick as the Joker's grin. "But . . . ," she adds, "you've got a wife at Vandy and last I checked, Vandy wasn't cheap. Besides, what other place will let you work from home?"

She's got a point. We barter to stay and Judy agrees to switch me to two sixteen-hour shifts — four p.m. to eight a.m. Sunday and Monday — with the last eight on Tuesday night.

It'll be three days of hell but I'll have the rest of the week to freelance and try to find something a little more rewarding to do. After all, this is Nashville. . . .

440Hz: The Albatross & Whale |

"The power of one finger across a few strings with the root
wipe open . . . " — HP Toze

Pen lights in the dark, find your mark in the fog machines and
amplifier sizzle, *gronk* from the jack as guitars plug in, feedback,
such sweet tease —
   check 1, 2, 1, 2
   and the show begins . . .
   It's a gray wintry Nashville night, the Has Beens are live at
the infamous Exit/In and the house is packed. I'm playing bass
on roller skates, rocking a medley of Van Halen's "Ain't Talkin'
'Bout Love" into "Push It" by Salt N' Pepa. People are pointing
and laughing, dancing with hands in the air and I am stoned on
the adoration of strangers.
   I joined forces with a group of music industry boys to form
a Nashville party band, an antidote to the serious business of a
town filled with talented people desperately trying to get discovered and signed. Scojo and Toze, Chops and Bodi and me,
the five of us becoming someone else in the practice lab of the
Music Row Firehall — rockers and rappers, riff-drunk junkies
and show-stopping posers, goofus superstars with tongues in
cheek and a trove of musical trivia and aptitude between us.
   We play covers only, but in the way I've always wanted to

play — like a DJ, finding the common groove, making one song become another, telling a story one hook at a time, taking the people on a ride, making them dance and feel free and alive and forget their troubles, even if just for a little while. . . .

A guy with fuzzy sideburns and felt antlers in his hat tells me he's pretty sure Tipper is in the house. Up in the balcony, *perhaps*. Squinting past the spotlights, I see big hair, hips and earrings shimmying in the dark. I send a friend to fetch her but neither return. I could name other stars scattered about the bar — after all, we are Music City's second-hottest good time classic rock and old school rap production — but Porter Wagoner once told me it was classless to drop names.

"Are there any cun-tree music fans here tonight?" I plead in my best Johnny Rotten just before we crash into a mash-up of Judas Priest and 2 Live Crew.

Chops shreds methodically; Toze hopping, locks in. Scoj is steady on the one. I roll the bass like Lemmy meets Bootsy while Bodi rocks the running man in his silver lamé suit.

Some glassy-eyed chick in a Commodores tour shirt stumbles on stage and trips in the cables, splattering her Amaretto down my neck and guitar.

"*HEY, HEY SORRY,*" she screams in my ear, "*NOW Y'ALL PLAY SIR MIX!*"

Fade In |

Juke's Hollywood agent wants to steer him towards TV and film so we meet with her and end up spinning old stories of full gospel churches and kinfolk from the rural south. We talk about all the places music has taken us and I even tell a few tales from late-night psychiatric crisis.

"*Love* your stories," the agent says. "You guys totally need to write these down."

"Jamie could," says Juke. He brags on me a bit, mentions the magazine articles and that we recently wrote a song for a secretly gay cowboy that nearly went gold.

"We did an entire concept record based around the produce aisle of Piggly Wiggly," I boast.

There's a quizzical look then she shrugs. "Can you write a screenplay?"

"I can sure try," I tell her.

'Til I See Your Lights |

FADE IN:

INT: KITCHEN — NIGHT

Box of COCOA PEBBLES sits on the counter by the sink. In the background Bon Jovi SINGS about going out in a glorious blaze. Wall clock reads 10:45.

In walks BLAINE, the scatterbrained, late-night psychiatric crisis guy. Looks confused. EXITS. A moment later, RETURNS. Pours the cereal into a mixer bowl. The phone RINGS.

> CALL CENTER (Off-Screen)
> *Call for Country Crisis, come back.*

> BLAINE
> Crisis here.

> CALL CENTER (O.S.)
> *Thirty-two-year-old male threatening suicide*
> *following breakup with significant other.*

Blaine shoulders the phone and opens the refrigerator door. Stuck to the front there's a photo of him in giant sunglasses and teased-out hair, pouting and pointing a black guitar to the sky. Stage lights and smoke swirl around him.

> BLAINE
> What's his name?

> CALL CENTER (O.S.)
> *Hershaw McCall.*

> BLAINE
> Cool. Really?

Blaine takes out a carton of milk. Gives it a sniff.

> CALL CENTER (O.S.)
> *That's what he said.*

> BLAINE
> Put him on.

Blaine pours the milk. There's a sharp CRACKLE before the voice.

> HERSHAW (O.S.)
> (country drawl)
> Hell-o?

> BLAINE
> Hello?

> HERSHAW (O.S.)
> Anybody there?

BLAINE

Yeah, this is crisis. Go ahead.

HERSHAW (O.S.)

(urgent now)

I'm gonna jump, I swear I will. I'll do it! I'm gonna jump this time!

Blaine sets the milk down and closes the fridge door with his foot.

BLAINE

Whoa, partner. Ease up. Talk to me. Where you at?

HERSHAW (O.S.)

Tennessee.

With a roll of his eyes, Blaine sits back in a kitchen chair.

BLAINE

Where in Tennessee?

HERSHAW (O.S.)

Oh. Out south of Pleasant Shade.

(urgent again)

I swear, *that bitch Julie*, I'm jumpin'. This is *goodbye*. Y'all better send somebody out here *right now*. And prob'ly all they gonna find is my dead carcass.

BLAINE

Okay, okay, easy. Ain't nobody on but me. I'll come see you but might take me awhile to get there. Where exactly are you?

———

237

EXT. NIGHT — CLOSE UP

HERSHAW McCALL, raw-boned and greasy with shoulder-length hair and a two-day beard. A fistfight scar marks his cheek and his right hand is wrapped in a filthy cast. He's talking on an old cordless phone, his eyes darting like a cornered coon.

> HERSHAW
> Out on the damn roof.

> BLAINE (O.S.)
> Just where is this roof?

> HERSHAW
> You know where Nickajack Road is? Right off 80?

> BLAINE (O.S.)
> I know where 80 is.

> HERSHAW
> 'Bout a mile past Key Hollow. Right there on Peyton's Creek.

> BLAINE (O.S.)
> Then what?

> HERSHAW
> You'll see an auto shop on the right and behind that some old trailers. I'm last one in back. Look for pink.

> BLAINE (O.S.)
> You're on the roof of a trailer?

> HERSHAW
> Yeah and this is *goodbye, Julie.*

(shouts)
GOODBYE, BITCH!

                    BLAINE (O.S.)
              Is it a two-story trailer?

Beat.

                    HERSHAW
     It's on a ridge. And there's a bunch of glass and car parts and
                    shit down there.

                    BLAINE (O.S.)
                    (dubious)
                    Un-huh.

Hershaw lowers the phone, slaps the cast to his forehead and
mouths a silent curse. Slowly brings the receiver back up.

                    HERSHAW
     Listen man, I don't know what else t' do. She's gonna take the
                    baby and leave.

                    (sobs)
              Will you please just come help me?

INT. — BLAINE'S KITCHEN — NIGHT

Blaine stares into his bowl of Cocoa Pebbles. Then to the clock.
Clears his throat.

                    BLAINE
              Uh, sure. Just hang tight, okay?

HERSHAW (O.S.)
Mister, I'll be right here on this roof 'til I see your lights.

Blaine stands and walks to the . . .

HALL CLOSET. Opens the door, grabs a black cowboy hat and ragged old coat.

BLAINE
I hope you got a coat.

HERSHAW (O.S.)
Should I put one on?

BLAINE
Yeah. You should definitely put a coat on.

EXT. — HERSHAW'S TRAILER — NIGHT

HERSHAW
Hold on.

Hershaw walks to the corner of the roof, just above the open bedroom window. A skinny STRINGY-HAIRED WOMAN stands at the dresser, shoving clothes into a paper sack. A FAT-CHEEKED BABY clings to her hip, chewing on a bottle of shampoo.

HERSHAW (CONT'D)
(yells down)
Julie! Throw me a jacket . . .

JULIE
(shouts)
Hershaw, yer sorry ass kin freeze!

Hershaw lays flat and hangs his head over the edge.

INT. — TRAILER BEDROOM — NIGHT

Hershaw's head pops into view at the top of the window.

> HERSHAW
> Aw, come on, Julie. The crisis man sez I need a coat.

The baby perks to the sound of his voice and begins to laugh and wave. Hershaw makes a silly face and waves back.

> JULIE
> Oh, all right.
>
> (trails away)
> Which one you want . . .

INT. — BLAINE'S KITCHEN — NIGHT

> HERSHAW (O.S.)
> She's going to get me one. You comin', right?

Blaine pulls down the hat and grabs his keys.

> BLAINE
> On my way.

EXT. COUNTRY ROAD — NIGHT

Headlights split the darkness. Up ahead in the distance, a hand-painted sign says TOMMY'S PAINT & BODY. Just next to a shack of a garage lies a gravel lane sparsely populated with ratty old trailers. A crooked sign riddled with bullet holes reads PINK STREET. At the end of the lane sits a dirty single-wide with no siding. On the roof, a shadow paces the ledge.

The Last Song |

Thursday, 1:56 a.m. Black night. Silent. Storms rolling in.
Crisis call on the line.

"Sing me one last song before I die."

"What you want to hear?"

"You pick it," says the caller.

"Hold on," I tell him, "let me get my guitar out of the closet."

I almost always roll with the drama. Helps me deal with the business of crisis psych.

"Go 'head," he says. I hear a glass lift, the distinct clink of liquor bottles.

I could already tell he was drinking from the way his words laid thick and lazy; the way *die* at the end of his first sentence didn't rise or fall but came at the same rhythm as the rest. There was no pause between *song* and *before* and no tremor or lilt that would lend weight to the words.

None of these things meant the caller wasn't suicidal. Just that he was most likely drunk. Still, on the late night crisis line, you never know.

Holding the phone away, I write down his number off the caller ID then pick up my guitar, making sure to rake the strings.

"Okay," I tell him. "Let me catch this E string."

"S'all right," Caller says.

243

With one hand I type in his number and message *trace this, send cops* to my call center buddy via IM, then give the E string a quick tune up and back down.

"Ready?" I ask.

"Yeah," he says.

"I got one just for you."

"Make it a good one," he says. "Make it count."

"You got it."

I hit a D and jump right into the old Haggard classic about the prisoner's last request as he's being led down the hallway to his doom. I sing it slow and desperate and even though I don't believe for a moment this man is about to die, I imagine guards strapping him to that splintered chair and pulling the black hood down over his eyes. I sing it like it's the last song he'll ever hear in this life. I sing like I'm singing back home.

After the final chord, I pick the phone back up and listen to his breath and the slow draw of another taste of alcohol.

"What'd you think?" I ask.

"Purt' good," he says. "Hey hang on, somebody's at the door."

"I'll wait," I tell him.

In the background I hear sturdy voices, polite but firm. After a couple of minutes the caller returns.

"Sunamabitz, you done tricked me," he says, more amused than angry. "Damned po-lice is here."

"Yeah, I tricked you," I confess. "How 'bout that song though?"

"Good song," he says. "But you ain't no Haggard."

"Probably not," I reply, "but good luck gettin' Haggard to sing for you at two in the morning."

In the background there's the sound of walkie-talkies and deep voices talking.

"Well, they say I gotta go now," Caller says. "Thanks for the last song, good buddy."

"Anytime."

Jesus Is Alive & Well at the
All-Night Kroger Off Old Hickory Road |

"Everything is meaningless." — King Solomon, Ecclesiastes 1:1

Have you ever felt like nearly every decision you've made in life was
wrong — that you are now so far from yourself that you don't have
a clue as to who you really are, that you are doomed to be wandering
and restless for the remainder of your days?
Do you feel like life is a long dark hall and all the doors are locked?
Have you ever
driven slow through
empty streets near
midnight & dreamed
you were the only
person left
alive?
Really? Oh. Um, well then. Never mind.

Late-night grocery store.

Milk, eggs. Grape G2 — forty-nine cents if you buy ten.
On aisle five Wham is whispering carelessly but by the time I
get to hair care, Sebastian Bach is raging about the youth gone
wild.

A skinny little dude in denim cutoffs and a *Flirtin' with*

Disaster tank top high-steps through the magic doors like he's just been elected mayor of McDonaldland. I'm in no rush so I follow him.

Hey God, I pray, *Life should be more like that. Grocery store doors.*

The skinny man's salt and pepper hair is shorter on top, parted down the middle and hangs in loose ringlets over bony shoulders. He's got a Wyatt Earp mustache and the wild-lit eyes of a cur dog scattering trash. Looks like road crew for Black Oak Arkansas, like the guy who tunes their guitars and warms up the crowd with a *Ever'body reddy t' party gimme a he-lllll yeah*. . . .

He rambles down the cookie aisle until he finds the packs of yellow Hydrox, with the white creme filling and a big neon sticker on the front that says 2/99¢. I didn't think he noticed me trailing behind but he turns and smacks the package, the plastic wrapper rustling under his fingers.

"These are some good-ass cookies right here," he brags with a lusty rasp, like he just won Powerball or married Britney Spears.

"Well, all right," I reply.

"Man, if you like cookies, oughta get you some," he says. "Hell, fifty cents."

"Might do that," I tell him, a little nervous now and looking for a way to slip out of the scene.

"Bring some home for your old lady." He pins me with the twinkle in his eye. "My old lady, she loves 'em." Smiling like we share old secrets, he taps the package again and walks away.

I make a lap around produce and past the magazines before running my groceries through the self-checker.

A Jheri-curled lady in a Kroger smock hobbles over from her register and looks me up and down. "Big-hair white fella. You him," she announces before handing me a folded paper towel. "Man said give you these when you come through checkout."

I open the napkin. Two yellow creme cookies. "He uh, told

me these were really good," I explain.

"I like 'em okay," she says. "Likes the orange ones better, though."

I thank her, bag up my things and swoosh through the doors to the curb out front.

Cookie Man motors by in a black and tan Ranchero with the back jacked up. Laugh lines crease the corners of his eyes as he tells some story to the peroxide blonde riding shotgun. She hangs her cigarette out the window and gives me an easy smile.

"Hey there," she says as they pass. He ducks down and gives me a little wave, then reaches for a cookie from the open pack in the console between them.

Life's not so complicated and it doesn't take a lot to be content. Sometimes it's a fifty-cent package of good-ass cookies and somebody who'll listen to your little stories and laugh.

At the red light at the far end of the Kroger parking lot, he revs the Ford's horses. When the light turns green the Ranchero lurches, then sputters before the engine dies.

"Come on, gal . . . ," Cookie Man croaks as he grinds the starter. "You ol' tan sumbich." The blonde cackles and blows a stream of smoke from the passenger-side window. The car cranks back to life, turns right and slowly drives away.

The nights are cooler, stars brighter in Tennessee. The air feels good on my skin. A happy wife waits for me at home. I unwrap the cookie and take a bite.

Neil Peart Jr. in a Double-Wide Trailer Just Past the Paper Mill |

Squiggly from the call center rings with a dispatch to a trailer park out past the paper mill. History of schizophrenia, mania, depression, anxiety. Patient's mother called.

I don't feel like going, don't feel like talking, don't feel like listening, don't feel like getting involved. I want to stay home, lie on the floor and read trash or theology or trashy theology. Watch a stupid movie. Play Sabbath riffs and Frehley licks on my guitar. Stay in my own world. I hope they get help but I don't want to be in the middle of it.

"Squig, why does it always have to be some trailer on the low-rent side of town?" I ask.

"Because that's our people?" she replies.

I call and the lady sounds nice and sort of desperate and worried about her son. I make good money when I leave the house and I've got this gadget I want. If I go, I can rationalize buying it. So I grumble, pull on appropriate clothes and tell her *Sure, I'll be right over.*

When I pull up to the trailer the front door is open and the mother waves me inside. "Watch that bottom step, honey," she says from the door frame. "It's loose."

The mother is squat and spunky in a flowery housecoat with silver showing through the roots of her squirrel-brown hair. "I'm Larry's mama," she says.

"Nice to meet you, ma'am."

"Can I get you somethin' to drink?" she asks. "Just made a fresh batch of tea."

"No, thank you." I give the place a quick look-around. Cream-colored sofa covered with a sheet, console television. Dog. Dusty old family photos. "Footprints in the Sand" plaque. "So, your son is here?"

"Baby!" she hollers down the hall. "The man's here to see you. . . ."

"Larry, he's a good boy, just got troubles in the head. Doctor says it's that schizo-free-nia," she says to me, poking at the black lab lying on the couch. "That's Rufus. Don't pay him no mind. Thinks he runs the place." Rufus raises his head, regards me briefly and appears unimpressed.

Larry comes out looking a bit rumpled, a dirty white apron tied around his waist. "Aw man, you didn't have to drive all the way out here. Mama offer you some tea or somethin'?"

"I'm good," I say. "Just come out to see what we could do to help."

"Well thank you, man. You mind talkin' back here?"

I follow Larry down the narrow hall. He's a big dude with a walrus mustache and hair balding up front and long in the back. Smells like bourbon and fajita steam.

"You been drinkin'?" I ask.

"Drinking? Oh. Naw, I'm a cook over to the Bok Bok Wok. That new buffet place they built next to the dollar store? Just got off. Helps to work but hell, with my mind spinning, it's been hard. Come on, we can talk in here."

Larry flicks the light on to a room not much wider than a walk-in closet. There's a twin bed and a turntable stereo on a shelf. And taking up every other conceivable space in the room, a massive set of Pearl drums.

"Whoa," I say. "That is one *awesome* drum set."

"Thanks, man," says Larry. He sits on the drum stool and points to an old school tapestry of the RUSH logo draped over his window to block out the sun. "Rock and roll," he says, nodding his head. "Gets me through."

I edge past the crash cymbals and rototoms and take a seat on the edge of the bed. Two rosaries are wrapped around the bedpost and a crucifix hangs on the wall above.

"Seems every Rush fan I know is Catholic," I tell Larry. "I was raised Catholic."

"Yeah, me too," he says, turning to look at the cross. "Guess I never thought about it that way. All them heavy lyrics and such. Peart, that's some deep shit."

"I used to DJ at a gospel radio station and we carried this syndicated preacher who was seriously anti–rock and roll," I say. "He was bashing Rush one day and supposedly Geddy called in and said he was a believer."

Larry leans over and clicks on an oscillating fan. "I think I heard about that. Wasn't really him though, was it?"

"I don't think it was him," I say. "Hey, you got your meds here?"

Larry reaches down, pulls a plastic baggie from beneath the pillow in the bass drum and hands it to me. He fidgets while I look them over, clops the bass pedal a few times and apologizes. "Them pills, I don't even think they work no more."

I roll the bottles around, noting the doses and drug names. "You still taking these?"

"Yeah, but my ADD gets cranking and I'm —" he waffles his hand and raises it to the ceiling. "Just up and down. Can't concentrate, ain't sleeping. I don't wanna kill myself or nothin'. My medicines need adjusting but you know a poor boy can't get no appointment. They said the first one was, like, three months out."

I'm listening and making a few notes, mostly staring over his shoulder at what looks to be a twenty-plus-piece drum set. Larry swivels to the side and starts softly sizzling the hi-hat open and closed.

"Go on," I tell him, "cook it."

"You a drummer?" he says.

"Used to be, but . . . " I gesture to the set in a way that says *nothing like this, buddy.*

"Wanna hear something?" he says.

"Absolutely," I reply.

Larry mutters to himself a bit and counts in to the incredibly difficult drum solo from the live version of "YYZ." Eyes shut, arms flailing, the big man plays like an octopus possessed, attacking the algebraic jazz-rock rhythms of the legendary Neil Peart, peppering the piece with his own abstract improvs. In the close confines of the double-wide, fills, flams and paradiddles ricochet from every wall, at times sounding like a boxcar full of firewood falling down a mountain, an armory of machine guns misfiring at once, like the Apocalypse led by the drum corps from a million marching bands. If St. Irenaeus is right and the glory of God is a man fully alive, then the Almighty has one fist lifted chanting *LARRY LARRY LARRY. . . .*

As quickly as he began, he ends, folds his sticks and gives me a sheepish grin. I sit back slack-jawed. Rufus barks once from down the hall.

"That was crazy!" I say, realizing too late that *crazy* might not be the most appropriate word. "Dude, why aren't you in a band?"

"Ah, I ain't got nobody to play with," Larry says, wiping the sweat from his neck. "I just play with these records." There's some gray coming in near his temples and a jagged scar under his eye. He reminds me of Ben Franklin, if Franklin had been in Skynyrd, with a little bit of David Crosby mixed in.

Behind some wadded-up clothes and a fishing pole, there's a classical guitar propped in his closet. I pick it up but it's sorely out of tune.

"Been trying to learn that thing," he says. "It's tough though. You play?"

"Some," I reply, twisting the pegs into place.

"How 'bout *Moving Pictures*, man?" Larry says, holding up the LP cover of Rush's most famous release. "Never be another."

"I hope there is," I say.

"Wouldn't that be cool?" he says, his words faster and talking with his hands now. "If Rush went right back in and made *Moving More Pictures* or whatever they want to call it. Bang, seven new songs that fit in right where that one left off. Or *3113* or somethin'. . . . I know you think I'm nuts now. The way my brain works. That's my problem. I'll sit around all day thinking about stuff like that and never get nothin' done. Thank God, Mama's been real good to me."

"Tell you a secret?" I say.

"Yeah, man."

"I think that way a lot too."

"Really?" Larry says. "What do you do to stay straight?"

"Come talk to people like you."

Larry gives me that sweet sheepish grin again. "That's cool, brother," he says, shaking his head.

I give the tuning peg one last twist and pluck out the harmonics that begin "Red Barchetta."

"Aw, I know that one," Larry says, just before he joins in on the ride. "Good one."

Call me over-spiritual if you wish, or oversensitive, or given to magical thinking or allegorically clumsy or maybe even touched with a bit of psychosis myself. But I'm telling you, somewhere near the middle of the song, Jesus walks into the room. *He must have hovered though*, I think, *because with all drums and guitars and octopus arms, there's sure no place to stand.*

"Watch your elbow, Lord," I sing with the witchy Geddy Lee warble.

As we fade down the coda, Larry's mom knocks on the door and sticks her head in. She looks at us and smiles, relieved. "You sure you boys don't want some tea or something?"

"Yes ma'am, I'll take a glass."

"Larry, you want some, baby?"

"Yes ma'am," he says.

She brings in a tray, heavy old glasses with diamonds down

the side, wrapped in a napkin to keep the cold off our hands.

"Say," Larry says, after the first big gulp. "You don't know 'By-Tor and the Snow Dog,' do you?"

Occasionally I get the Epiphany, that slim instant when I see the scene removed from myself and realize how ridiculous and perfect it is for a misfit life like mine. The Epiphany of the Holy, and of the Absurd. That God still shows up in unexpected places. I wish I could cut around the edges and take this moment with me, show it to the people I love who do not understand.

"Don't know it," I say.

"How about 'La Villa Strangiato'? It's got that classical part at the start. Goes a lot like Barchetta."

I laugh, the sort of self-deprecating laugh a man might laugh were he asked to conquer Kilimanjaro on a pogo stick. "Brother, I'm no Alex Lifeson," I tell him. "But if you start I'll jump in on the middle part."

Larry grabs his sticks and looks the drums over like a road map. His mother makes a face like *let me get gone* but first reaches over and squeezes my hand.

"Hey Larry," I say while she's still listening. "I'm gonna get you an appointment this week about your meds. We'll get you fixed up, okay?"

"Sounds good," he says.

"Sure glad you could come out tonight," says Larry's mom.

"Me too," I tell her. She trots off down the hall as Larry clicks his sticks seven times.

For Southern Girls
Who Love Jesus & Skynyrd |
Dinner with a Classic Rock Jukebox Programmer

Neon Jukebox. Steaks and beer. Bold yellow letters proclaim: *Great food, rockin' tunes*. Peanut shells crunch beneath our feet as we follow our hostess through the restaurant. At a table in the middle of the floor, a child wails.

"Nowhere near the kid," Case says.

The hostess swerves, taking us to a booth in a side room near the back. "This the no-babies room?" I ask.

"Unofficially," she says, hand hiding her mouth.

Fleetwood Mac — "Don't Stop"

"Can't beat the Mac," says Case with a finger in the air. "I can play the Mac in any market, anytime."

Ray Case has the floppy silver hair and angular features of the drummer from the Stones matched with the wacky charm of Joe Walsh and the fashion sense of Jimmy Buffet.

He gets paid a ton of cash to program the tunes for classic rock stations and chain restaurants across the country. It's a field I'd love to get into so I invited him to dinner. He insists on paying however, and takes me to one of the places that pays him to pick their music.

"I like Fleetwood Mac," I reply. "But I *love* Stevie Nicks."

"Here's the thing about Stevie Nicks," Case says, pausing in thought and pressing the ends of his fingers together, "I'd love to get zipped-up and drunk in a sleeping bag with her."

"Stevie now or Stevie '76?" I ask.

"I'll take Stevie now, what's wrong with Stevie now?"

"Just askin'."

A rail-thin redhead with thick black eyeliner and boobs too big for her frame steps up to our table. "Hey, I'm Charity and I'll be your server tonight. Can I start y'all off with some drinks?"

Case thumbs through the menu. "How do you make these cocktails look so tantalizing? Hide naked chicks in the ice?"

Charity leans in with a flirty laugh. "I don't know but lemme tell you, that Sunrise Minderaser is awesome. . . ." She rolls her eyes at me in a way that insinuates scandalous stories could be told.

"Why not?" says Case. "Want one?"

I shake my head. "Water. With lemon." They both frown then Charity flitters away.

The Doobie Brothers — "Jesus Is Just Alright"

"Nobody really loves the Doobies," Case says, "but they are well tolerated."

"I hate the Doobie Brothers."

"No money in your demographic," he says dryly.

"What's that s'pose to mean?"

"You know what I mean," he says, scanning the room. Over at the bar a man with badly dyed hair downs a shot of tequila and plays air guitar against his leg. His t-shirt is tucked into his shorts and every time a woman walks by he gawks like a dog in a cage at the fancy cat parade.

"That guy . . . ," says Case, " . . . and *that* guy." He points to a long-haired man wearing greasy coveralls. The man leans back in his chair and laughs as the leathery blonde to his left flips him her middle finger.

"Hey, that's the good-ass cookie man," I tell him.

"Say who?" Case replies.

"Met him in Kroger one night. He had a pack of store-brand Oreos and told me *This here is some good-ass cookies.*"

"Exactly," Case says. "See his table? Appetizers, surf and turf. How many beers have they had?"

"At least six."

"All right, Mr. Water with Lemon who hates the Doobie Brothers, whose musical tastes are we going to accommodate here?"

Charity arrives with our drinks. "Sunrise Minderaser, whoo hoo," she says with a little kick. "And lemon water for party boy here."

"Hey, let me ask you something," Case says to her. "You like this song?"

"Well, *hell yeah*," she says, snapping her fingers and giving her hips a shake. "Who don't love the Doobies and Jesus?"

Case raises his hand across the table. "Our boy here, apparently."

"Figures," she teases.

"I love Jesus," I shout out as she's walking away.

Rick Derringer — "Rock and Roll, Hootchie Koo"

"Great song," Case says, giving a little flourish to his own invisible guitar. "Gotta love this song. How could you not love this song?"

"Because they run it in the ground?" I drop down into DJ voice. "*We play the same songs! At the same time! Every day! We're — 101.1 HOME OF THE ROCK!*"

"Hey man," he says, "gotta be universal. Play songs *everybody* loves."

"Like Billy Joel."

"Actually, people either really love Billy Joel — or completely despise him."

"So what's universal then?"

"Certain Eagles songs. 'Start Me Up' by the Stones. Springsteen." He pulls at the liquor and puckers his face. "All right, so gimme five classic rock songs you never want to hear again long as you live."

"Five, huh? Okay. 'Takin' Care of Business.'"

"Well, yeah."

A familiar bassline rattles through the room.

George Throughgood — "Bad to the Bone"
I grab the steak knife and feign stabbing myself in the ear. "This song, this song, this song."

"Buh-Buh-Buh-Bad," Case mocks.

"And I'm sick of 'Jet Airliner.'"

"Agreed, though it tests very well North, South, East and West."

"'Stairway to *Frickin'* Heaven.'"

"Stairway? Stairway's classic, dude. Why Stairway?"

"Because you guys always play it at, like, *two-thirty in the afternoon.* Who wants to hear seven minutes of draggy, druggy allegory in the middle of the day?"

"People who don't use words like allegory. You read a lot, don't you?"

"Well, yeah."

Case laughs and stirs his drink with the end of a spoon. "You know the last book our average listener read?" He doesn't wait for my response. "*Nothing.* Okay, that's four. One more."

"I could name fifty more."

"No 'Freebird'?"

"Nah, see I'm not snotty. Skynryd's great."

Case waves me off. "Lotta people hear Skynryd, they think redneck."

Charity appears. "Y'all ready for some food yet?"

"How you feel about Lynyrd Skynyrd?" I ask her.

She holds one finger up and hollers across the room. "Hey Vanessa!" A bleach-blonde server slinks over, tan and lean, wearing tight black jeans and a white dress shirt with the top three buttons undone. "Nessa, you like Skynyrd?"

Vanessa turns and holds up her hair. On the back of her neck there's a Rebel Flag tat with an eagle soaring over the stars. Underneath, the words *If I leave here tomorrow . . .*

"For my daddy," she drawls. "T'was his favorite song."

"Sorry 'bout your dad," I say, heartfelt as I can.

"Oh, he ain't *dead*," she says, pointing down the interstate. "Locked up down at Mountain City."

"What's he in on?" Case asks.

"Some manslaughter BS," she replies. "I'll be nearly forty 'fore he even gets out."

"Think I'll have the sirloin," Case says.

"I got a good ol' Southern girl tattoo too," Charity chirps in with a wicked grin. The girls exchange glances and giggle. "But I can't show it to y'all at work. . . ."

"Grilled fish looks good," I add.

"Gotcha," says Charity with a wink.

ZZ Top — *"Tush"*

"Hey hey," says Nessa. "That's my *sawwnng* right there." She locks arms with Charity and they traipse away, back pockets bouncing to the beat.

"Have mercy," Case growls, his eyebrows dancing.

"I hate this song," I reply.

Case catches my smile and matches it with his own. "No you don't."

Beauty & Chaos: Jump in the Fire |

"In crisis you call it success if nobody dies or tries to set the world on fire." — Dr. Dennis Parks

Sunday, 7:55 p.m.

Wilmoth County Jail. The client, who previously swallowed razor blades and bleach, now refuses to eat or drink. He tears the sprinkler heads down every chance he gets and has been on lockdown for four days straight.

"*Please* get him out of here," Lieutenant Beverly says.

The jailer leads in a wiry little Haitian with voodoo eyes. He spots me, pedals backwards and pulls against the cuffs. "Mossad!" he cries. "Mossad! He will pull off my ears with pliers!"

"Chill out, Haiti," the jailer says. "Blaine here's from Dixie."

"Shalom, ami," I tell the inmate, opening my coat and holding out my hands. "I got no pliers, see? Now have a seat and tell me what's going on."

He stares warily and sits. Denies harm to self or others. Denies voices or visions. We talk for ten minutes or so then the Haitian hangs his head and says *No more questions, please.*

Committal papers signed, they shackle the prisoner's hands and feet, place him in the back of a squad car and transport him to a state psychiatric facility over one hundred miles away.

"How many times this make you've sent him in?" Lieutenant asks.

"All together?" I reply. "Six."

Sergeant Ensley runs in, breathless. "Got a situation in booking and need your help."

We race back down and there's a twenty-two-year-old guy who looks like a beefy, bearded, wild-eyed Axl Rose, shirtless with no shoes, strapped into the restraint chair after he choked his landlord and kicked through the bars of the patrol car.

"The counselor is here," Sergeant announces. *Where? Oh.*

Wild-Eyed Rose howls for someone to wipe the mace from his eyes before he goes blind, says he is schizophrenic and off his meds, that he has asthma and panic attacks and is about to die.

"You gotta take him," Sarge says in a panic. "We're short-handed and a riot's about to boil. . . ."

I roll Rose into side cell 3 as hell breaks loose around us, ricocheting off the cinderblock and steel. An inmate in cell 2 has busted out the Plexiglas with a torn-down pipe and now stomps the half-wall that hides the toilet and sink. Another in 4 screeches like a Batman villain and my fire-haired patient is losing his mind.

"You gotta let me out of here! LET ME OUT!" Terror rips Rose's voice. "Don't leave me here, *please*, man — I can't see . . ."

"It's okay, it's okay," I say as the auto-locks fire and cage us in.

The call goes out for backup and one lone guard nervously eyes the hall with Taser in hand. I feel for the knife in my pocket and slide it out, ready to open with a flick.

"I'm with you," I tell Rose in a shaky voice. "You are in the safest possible place."

The sound of breaking glass bounces off the wall followed by a wail and the violent *thwack* of a body slamming against the floor.

"*Let me suck my thumb*," cries Rose, rocking the chair and yanking at the straps. "It helps, please, man, let me just suck my thumb, *please!*"

Emergency lights strobe as the sirens rage. The concrete shudders; there is laughter and screams. Through the glass, I see the jailer go down.

I turn Rose's chair backwards and back it against the door. "Brother, I can't," I apologize. "I don't even have your keys."

Rose chokes, asthma and adrenaline and fear, he bangs his head back against the window and wheezes through the spittle, *"We're gonna DIE. . . ."*

I flip out the blade of the knife. *If he seizes, I can stick a hole in his throat.*

There's a fountain on top of the toilet tank, spewing water from a break in the main. I splash a handful in his face and drag my shirt sleeve across his eyes. He blinks, struggling to see me. "If it gets too crazy," I say, showing the knife. "I'll cut your straps."

Metal clangs metal, like echoing cannons and black-clad officers pour through the booking door. More yelling and wails and thwacks of violence. I slump down next to Rose with my back to the wall.

"Breathe, dude," Rose gasps. "Breathe."

His feet are dirty black and ragged and his torso scarred with more marks than I can count. Scratches and sketchy tattoos, *Lisa Ann*, praying hands, Grim Reaper and Jesus' Barbed-Wire Heart.

"Who is Lisa Ann?" I ask.

He shoots me a sharp look, then drops his head and closes his eyes, like a cleric before prayer. "My girl," he says. "My daughter."

"How old is she?"

Rose blows out all his breath and takes another in. "Four," he says. "She's four."

10:30 p.m.

Giles ER. Skinny guy with a grasshopper face and multiple

piercings. Cut both wrists, arms and legs. Burnt himself with a lighter. He is tearful, threatens to leave and says DCS is coming to take his kids away.

His wife appears, a hearty woman who claims she has late-stage cancer and that the client threw a battery and hit her between the shoulder blades.

"Wanna see the bruise?" she asks, already raising her shirt. She stands in the hospital hall, with her elbows over her head, a hot red welt stamped in the middle of her back.

"D cell?" I guess.

"How'd you know?" she asks, lowering her shirt and turning back to me. "Oh, yeah. I bet you done seen it all. You're one of them mind-benders."

I place both palms to my forehead and close my eyes. "It wasn't a Duracell," I tell her. "I see — children crying. . . ." Eyes open now. "Happened in the kitchen, didn't it?"

"Holy *shit*," she says. "How you do that?"

I hold a finger to my lips then tell her I'll make a note of the incident.

"Can I go in and talk to him now?" she asks. "I really need to."

"You can go," I tell her. "But if y'all fight you're both going straight to jail tonight."

"I'm tired of fightin'," she says. "But you already know."

Monday, 1:05 a.m.

Dora Memorial Emergency Room. One county up, in bed 1, there's a thirty-two-year-old woman who looks fifty-five. Her face is featureless, like a biscuit with eyes. White scars mark both arms near the wrist. *History of borderline and bipolar*, her intake sheet says. *Benzo abuse.*

"How's it going?" I ask, tilting my hat to her as I enter the room.

"Sir, don't take this the wrong way," she says, "but I ain't sayin' another word until I get my shot."

"Wait, what are you here for?" I ask, confused-like and flipping through her chart.

"Tried to kill myself," she says. "And I meant it. I'll do it again."

"Works for me," I tell her, turning on my heels. "I'll let the doc know you're ready."

"Bed 1 is going straight in," I tell security at the desk. "Don't even let her know until the sheriff shows."

"Fine with us," says the nurse. "There's a lady 'round the side in room 16. Just sad, really. Would you mind sticking your head in and clearing her for us?"

"Might as well while I'm here."

Room 16 is dark, the hall light spilling in from a crack in the door. The bed is empty and I start to leave when I see the shell of a woman crumpled in a corner chair, head down and arms wrapped around herself. I walk in, turn on a lamp and say hello. She lifts her head and a bolt runs through me. She looks that much like my mother.

I put my things down and sit on the edge of the bed. I keep trying to think of something good and right to say but nothing comes out. Finally, she reaches over and touches my knee.

"Are you all right?" she asks.

2:50 a.m.

Up on floor 7, there's a cute kid named Samantha with scared rabbit eyes, just twenty-five and paralyzed for life from the waist down. She was shot by a boyfriend at age eighteen. He served three years in county, was released and lives nearby. Her sister saw him not long ago, in the dollar store behind the old junior high.

"BJ's free while Sam is stuck in this damn chair," Sam's sister says. "She might coulda walked but insurance wouldn't help us and she didn't get no rehab. Didn't nobody wanna help, they just give her more dope."

Sam's dad shambles in, gray and haunted, and tells me that Mom is at her job, that work has been slim lately and they are all so tired. He stays for a tortured moment, his eyes like a man trapped in a fire. Finally, he excuses himself for a cigarette. "Didn't use to smoke," he mumbles as he passes through the door.

"This is what she looked like before the accident." Sam's sister flips her phone to a picture of the two on them on a beach, faces pressed together, tan and smiling in the sun. "Now she's lost twenty pounds and her teeth are falling out from all the pills and she has to wear a catheter twenty-four-seven." She looks at the photo again and starts to bawl. "She used to be such a beautiful girl. . . ."

Sam bites her nails and pulls her hair down into her eyes. One tear trickles down her cheek as she reaches for her sister's hand.

I want to tear down Heaven and tell God enough of this senseless game, this experiment where billions of broken lives rise and fall from the dust, where one bastard with a gun can so completely screw up someone's life, an entire family's life, that there seems to be no hope at all. I want a real live Jesus to say *Get up and walk* and hold Sam's hand as she takes her first wobbling steps in seven years. I want to see her run and laugh and forget all this pain. I want to fix all this but I can't.

"It's going to be all right," Sam tells her sister. She catches the look in my eyes, reaches over and takes my hand too. "It'll get better," she tells us both. "It has to."

4:15 a.m.

One Horse Hospital up in the hills. It's a two-bed unit, separated by a curtain.

"Where's the doc?" I ask the young nurse on duty.

"Aw, Doc Littles ain't here, honey," she answers. "He's home, sleepin'. You want me to wake him?"

"Let him sleep."

My patient rambles about Satan and crack cocaine but her voice sounds a thousand miles away. Sometimes my brain feels feverish, like my mind won't fire right and I'm broadcasting remotely from the belly of the whale. It's all I can do to sit still and listen.

I'm shaken awake when a local group home calls. A long-term client there is crying hysterically and says that he wants to die.

"I'm sort of booked solid," I tell the resident manager. "You can wait or bring him here."

Within ten minutes they show. I wave them out back and we lean on the septic tank in the hospital yard. There's a church next door and cattle graze in the field below. It's cold out and I pull my coat around me.

The client is an older man, pleasant in a Jonathan Winters sort of way. Mentally challenged, paranoid delusions. His name is James.

"Hey, look," I tell him. "We've got the same name."

He sways and smiles sweetly. "We do?" he says, as if I've just informed him we are long-lost brothers. He's shivering in saggy carpenter jeans and the kind of thin white t-shirt that comes three to a pack.

"Where's your coat, buddy?" I ask.

"I-I, uh, loaned it to my roommate. Donnie. He didn't have no coat," James says. "And he's been s-sick. So I give him my coat."

"He bad about giving stuff away," the resident manager says, shaking his head. "Tell the man why you here, James."

"The fix-it man came?" James tells me. "Mr. Eddie?"

"Yeah," I say, pretending to know. "Mr. Eddie."

"He has that van?"

"Okay . . ."

"Our puppy, Muffins, got caught up under the wheel. I heard it and it made a terrible sound. I can still hear it. It makes me real sad and I just don't know if I want to be in this world anymore." James buries his head and cries. The resident manager looks at me like a crowd watches a magician about to make an elephant disappear.

"I'm sorry about your puppy," I say.

"I miss her," says James.

"I lost a dog that way," I tell him. "Still hurts sometimes."

"I-It does?"

"Yeah. But I figure I'll see her again someday."

"You do?" asks James.

There's a hole beneath the arm of his t-shirt. He covers it with his hand and trembles as the wind picks up. I pull off the lambskin coat and hand it to him.

"Oh . . . ," says James, his face like I've given him the Hope diamond. He slides his arms through the sleeves and slips his hands into the pockets. "I like this coat. I like it a lot."

"It's old," I tell him. "But you can have it."

In the space between the church and the emergency room, there's a small graveyard surrounded by a hurricane fence. A Purity milk truck gears down to top the hill as an old Buick slows and throws a newspaper into the hospital drive.

"Do you really think I'll see my dog again?" James says.

Two counties away, another patient waits and I've got a long way to drive.

Defeated, Tennessee |

I've been carrying around my best friend from high school's phone number for a few months now but haven't called yet.

Been waiting, waiting for the stars to align. Waiting for something but I don't know what. Waiting to see the payphone at the Piggly Wiggly near Defeated, TN.

It's just starting to sleet as I duck under the overhang and dial the number. The ring trills like a tunnel back through time. I pull my collar up against the wind and angle myself into the shallow booth. *It's all real. Nothing's real.* Man, I don't know.

Click-click. "Hello?"

"Kells."

"Yeah?"

"Hey."

"Unh-huh. Who's this?"

"JB."

"J . . . B — oh! Hey! Wow. Where you at?"

"The Piggly Wiggly payphone near Defeated, Tennessee."

There is a long pause and static on the line. In the chrome panel just over the phone, someone scrawled *FUK IT ALL*.

"There's still payphones?" Kells says.

"At the Piggly Wiggly near Defeated, Tennessee, there are."

"Huh. I guess, yeah. Are you all right? Is something wrong?"

"Naw. Just calling to . . . talk."

"So, how you been?" says Kells. "Can't even remember the last time."

"I'm all right. You?"

"Good. Married. Kids and all that."

"I heard."

"How about you?" Kells says.

Two teens impossibly dressed in tube tops and cowboy hats leans out the window of a passing pickup and yell out an extremely indecent proposal. Laughter and screams echo until the truck vanishes around the bend.

"Married," I say. "No kids."

"Yeah, oh. Okay. So, uh, what are you doing now? Hey, I heard you were writing."

"Who said?"

"Maddy Green. Saw her in Sears one day — like a year or two ago."

"Little bit," I say. "Here and there."

"Least you got outta here and did something 'sides work at the mill. So what do you write? Songs or what?"

"Right now I'm trying to figure out whether I should write another midnight story about some half-naked drunk chick in the side cell of the county jail."

"You ain't still doin' that suicide Batman crap, are you?" Kells groans.

We talk for a while about everything and nothing until the conversation trails off.

"Hey, um." The words aren't coming out right. "Remember that night we crashed your car and saw the angel?"

"Jim Beam," says Kells.

"Yeah, but . . . I mean, it's just — no way we shoulda walked out of there. No way."

There's a sound over the line, like a deep breath or a sigh. "J, baby, I don't know," Kells says. "Jesus."

Bananas are forty-nine cents a pound. A black dog near the dumpster stops and sniffs the air.

"What do you think we saw in the field that night?" I ask. Sometimes I hear myself and it sounds like someone else talking.

"Jim Beam and Jesus," my old friend says.

Kells' voice goes low and sounds another thousand miles away. "Haven't thought about that in a long time."

"I think about it all the time."

There's a hand-drawn sign on the window for the 5 for 5 Meat Special. Another says *WIC Accepted Here.* The front doors open and a woman braces her son against the cold. She shoots me a wary look but when I nod, the boy waves and she smiles back. Just past produce, a skinny old man in a short necktie leans his mop against the wall and shuts down the corner lights.

"You sure you okay?" Kells asks.

"Yeah," I say. "I'm doin' all right."

Through the Sallyport |

There's an angel-faced girl with carrot-colored hair, apple cheeks and a gap between her teeth sleeping peacefully in a side cell at the Carroll County Jail. Stripped of clothing, her elfin frame is curled into the corner and loosely secured by a pickle-green suicide smock.

"Miss Darla," the lady jailer says, giving her shoulder a shake. Zzz. "DARLA!"

Darla moans, rolls over and hikes one knee. When she does, the smock rides to her belly button. In the flickering florescent light there is a flash of freckles and naked flesh.

"Come on now," the jailer scolds, pulling the smock hem down with both hands. "This fella's here to talk to you and he don't need to be seein' your stuff."

I turn away, staring through the observation glass. The desk sergeant points at me and laughs.

"Darla a sweet person. Good-hearted as all get out," says the lady jailer. "But when she get to drankin', girl go *crazy*. Caught her up on 231 runnin' through traffic hollerin' 'bout hell is hot. Okay, she decent now, turn around. Lord, I bet you seen it all in this job."

"No ma'am," I turn and tell her, maybe smiling a little. "Ain't seen a thing."

"Yeah, right," she says, stepping just outside the armored

door. "Be out here if you need me."

Darla sits up, smacks her lips together and rubs her eyes. She's the kind of fair-haired girl that could pass for twelve or twenty-five.

"You kinda look like Jesus," she says.

"If I could just figure out how to act like him."

"Tell me 'bout it," she groans, slumping over and pressing her face to the cool surface of the cinderblock wall. "Jesus, take the wheel."

"I heard that," I tell her.

"Heard that," she sighs. "You bail bondsman?"

"Nope."

"Commissioner?"

"Un-uh."

One eye opens. "Then who are you?"

"Psych guy."

"Oh shits." She sits upright and blinks hard. "You can get me outta here. If you only knew my story, mister. . . ."

"I do know your story." Pause. This is the fun part. "That's why I'm here."

Five minutes later Darla's back in street clothes, eating a baloney and cheese sandwich on the front bench of booking.

"All aboard," I say, passing back through from the copy machine.

"What's that?" she asks, cramming in another mouthful and rattling her shackles as she swings her short legs back and forth.

Taking a seat beside her on the bench, I point and read from her bright blue Vacation Bible School tee. *"All aboard Noah's Ark."* There's a giraffe and some balloons on the front.

"Oh yeah," she says, wiping crumbs from her belly. "Church folk gimme this. They been letting me sleep in the back room of the charity house."

"Where does a person sleep in the back room of a charity house?" I ask, swinging my feet alongside hers.

"Anywhere," she shrugs. "Old couches. Pile of clothes. I was sleepin' on the porch but Brother Tom says it got too cold. I ain't picky though."

"Sleeping on somebody's old underwear. Huh. Passed-out drunk in a side cell. Jailhouse sandwich and leg shackles. I don't mean to sound judgmental but, uh, maybe you should start being a little more picky. Y'know?"

Darla goes to say something but stops. Her eyes flicker down, then away. "Yeah," she says in a quiet voice, "Prob'ly."

I hold out my hand. She studies it a second before giving a shake. "Let's try not to meet this way again," I tell her. "Okay?"

"'K," she says, crinkling her nose when she smiles. "Hey, can I get another one of them sandwiches?"

"Jailer?" I call. "Can Miss Darla have another sandwich?"

"Girl look like she could use another sammich. Yeah," the jailer replies.

"You a pretty nice guy," Darla says.

"My mama thinks I'm pretty," I reply. "Not so sure about the nice."

She breathes deep and lets out the words with a lazy Zen, like blowing dandelions over a field. "Well, we all got the best and worst in us, I guess."

There's a tug in my gut I know too well so I palm a ten from my pocket and pass it to her in another handshake, this one a little more awkward until she feels the bill against her fingers.

"Thanks," she whispers, coughing and sliding the money into her jeans.

"You get over to this place I'm sending you, shoot straight and get some help, okay?"

"Okay," she says.

"If you get in a bind," I tell her, "find me."

"I will," she says with that crinkle-nosed, gap-toothed smile.

I buzz back through and out the sally port. The sign on the outside wall states,

IF YOU ARE HERE TO TURN YOURSELF IN OR NEED ASSISTANCE PLEASE USE THE INTERCOM.

A couple waits at the door, a grim woman about five foot tall and nearly as wide, in a low-cut top and tiny white shorts with two silver bars gouged through her left brow.

A goat-looking weed of a man stands behind her in a wife-beater with food stains down the front. If you cloned him four times, they could all still hide behind the woman. He holds out his bone-white gangly arms and whines, "Well honeybunch, whut the hail you wantin' me to do?"

"I don't know, Troy," she huffs. "Ring the dag-blasted buzzer, I guess."

I slip past them to my car. Parked next to it is a beat-up mini-van with an air conditioner hanging out the back window. Two heathen children thrash wildly inside.

"I'ma come beat me some young asses y'all don't settle down!" the woman shouts.

I slide into my car seat and start the motor. The kids gather in the van's open side door and stare me down. A boy about seven, with huge nostrils and a Hitler haircut, flips me the bird. Another boy, younger, and flattop blond like a mini-Eminem, throttles his crotch and does a taunting side-to-side bounce.

I grab a handful of loose change from my door handle and fling it into the van. The hellions yelp, diving to the floor. In the melee, they knock heads and howl like jackals.

The woman lets out a growl and charges the van like Gorgon plowing down Tokyo.

Hitler boy clutches his forehead and kicks against the floor, tears streaming down his face. As the woman bears in, he points to me and wails. Spotting the change, she turns and gives me a disgusted glare. "*Jackass*," she hisses.

I give them a wink, throw the car into reverse and head west, to another call, some forty miles away.

Sad Old Laundromats, Mother's Day Payphones & Dolly Parton Pinball |

I'm halfway down the mountain when I get the feeling that something is wrong. My chest is a vacuum; a cold and awful notion that I will never speak to my mother in this life again.

Mama was a country girl, barely eighteen when I was born. Life was happy for a while, then everything fell apart. A fatal car crash. The neighbor's house burned. Mama's best friend, a sweet and loving woman who was like a second mother to me, took her own life. My parents started fighting a lot and split. I got hit in the temple with a baseball bat. All around the time I was seven years old. Sometimes it seems like a lifetime ago, other times it feels like yesterday.

I think about the old ghosts and how time slips away, about all the things we leave unsaid, the way we live so fast and busy, rarely realizing what matters until it is too late. The sort of things you might think about if you are overemotional and six hundred miles from home, driving through the hills at sundown the night before Mother's Day.

I try to call but at this place on the ridge my cell has no bars. Pretty soon I spot the payphone at a two-pump Chevron just past the county line. I pull over, stuff in enough change to get through and wait for the ring, remembering back to when I was a boy. . . .

There is nothing more depressing than a small-town laundromat on a Sunday afternoon. Broken coat hangers and hard plastic chairs. Concrete walls and hand-lettered signs for lost dogs and old cars for sale.

Mama and me were just sitting there, waiting for the clothes to dry. Pinball tempted me from the corner by the change machine.

"Mama, can I have two quarters?" I asked.

"We have to get these clothes done," she said sternly. Mama was a sophomore in college and we were living in some economy apartments just across the way.

"I hate all this," I said and I said it in a mean, spiteful way and looked at her like *and this is all your fault*. She was tough but I could tell my words hurt her.

"Watch it, boy," Mama warned. I turned and stared out the front window to the drive-thru chicken and liquor mart next door.

Mama walked over to the washers, then to the corkboard by the sorting table. She pretended to read the ads awhile before coming back.

"Jamie, son," she said, "I know you aren't happy, but this is how we have to live right now."

"I hate laundromats, Mama. I hate you have to come here. When I grow up you won't ever have to come to a place like this no more."

"It won't be *that* long," she laughed.

I turned back. "And I'm gonna play pinball all I want."

"If that's what you want," she said. "When you grow up."

I was crying a little. "Mama, I'm sorry. I didn't mean it."

"It'll be okay, my baby," she said, a little sweeter. "I'll be out of school soon enough. Things will get better."

I rested my head against her arm. "One day I'll buy you a whole Laundromat, except nice, and it'll have ten washers and ten dryers and ten pinball machines. . . ."

Mama fished through her purse and held out fifty

cents. "Here, boy," she sighed. "And you can help fold clothes when you get done."

I closed her hand over the quarters and pushed it away.

"I can wait, Mama," I told her.

The pump lights flicker then shine, drowning out the approaching night. A car pulls in, pinning me with its headlights; I cup the phone and look away. One ring, then two. A *V* of charcoal geese glides across the sky and over the ridge. Dread claws me at the third ring. Then, just after the fourth:

"Hello?"

"Mama?"

"Hey boy, where you at? This isn't your number."

"Mama. . . ." I lay back against the wall and let out my breath. "I just, I just — wanted to call you." I say. "I-uh, I'm just working and wanted to see what you were doing."

I feel embarrassed and then I feel embarrassed for feeling embarrassed. I know that doesn't make sense.

"Not much, Boo," she says. "You know."

"Yes ma'am I do, yeah." The last word cracks.

"Something wrong, my baby? What's wrong?"

"Nothing. I don't know. Sometimes it's hard living far away and . . . I don't know." There's an awkward second or two. The words, they're all tangled. "I just want to thank you for being a good mama and . . . to let you know how much I miss you up here. Things were hard sometimes and I know you did your best."

"Well, you were always a pretty good boy."

I laugh that first nervous laugh after a serious spell. "No, I wasn't."

"For the most part," she says. "We all turned out okay and that's what counts." There's so much I want to tell her when she says those words.

"Yes ma'am," I say. "I guess." In the background I hear high-pitched whistles and sneakers on a shiny floor. "Where you at?"

"Ball game," she answers.

"Are you playing?"

"Not tonight," she says, sounding alive and well and teenage mama young. "Maybe next time."

"I love you, Mama."

"Love you too, baby. When are you coming home? Soon?"

"Yes ma'am, soon."

After we hang up, I stand around trying to sort out my head. Finally, I duck into Davis' Chevron for a Diet Coke.

"Y'all got fountain drinks?" I ask.

"Back in the restaurant part we do," the girl at the register replies.

There's an add-on past the bathrooms with two red booths and a rainbow jukebox. And next to the jukebox, a Dolly Parton pinball machine.

The cafe is empty except for a woman behind the counter who looks exactly like the register girl only older, with giant hair, heavy rouge and a sweatshirt with puffy kittens on the front. I point to her, then to the machine.

"There's a Gas Station in the Hills with Dolly Parton Pinball!" The words are so delicious I have to say them out loud, like a proclamation, like I am reciting Psalm 103.

"Buford, he's a big Dolly fan from way back," the woman explains. "Had that thing twenty, thirty years now. Still works."

I nod, fill my cup and take it to the counter. "Got to be your daughter up front," I say. "Y'all look exactly alike."

"My *grand*daughter," the woman says, shaking her head. "But my daughter, she works here too."

"All of you together?" I ask. "How's that goin'?"

"Some days we drive each other plum crazy. But most times it works out fine." Her front teeth are messed up but somehow she still has a real nice smile. "You gonna see your mama for Mother's Day?"

"No ma'am. But I called her just now. Going down there in a couple weeks."

"Well, don't you wait too long," the woman says, turning back to her hot lamps. "Hey, you want the rest of this chicken? I'ma throw it out if don't nobody want it."

"Heck yeah," I tell her. "I'll eat that chicken." I slide six dollars across the counter and gesture back to the pinball machine. "Can I have some quarters?"

"You sure can, Sugar. And I'll box this up, you can eat it right here if you want."

"Lady," I say, "you are making my day."

I pull a stool up to Dolly and set my drink on the rail. Week after next, I'm going home. Think I'll take Mama shopping for a brand-new washing machine.

Down by the River of Life |

"Grace, like water, flows to the lowest places."
— Phillip Yancey

It's midnight and there's a drunk on the 309 bridge singing about the River of Life. Just a shape, a silhouette against the luminous sky, his lonesome tenor ringing through the valley below.

"Water looks cold," the broad deputy drawls.

"You'd think they could pull this sort of stunt in the summer . . . ," clips the stumpy bald cop with a thin mustache. "You can get him down though, right?"

"One way or another," I deadpan. "However, my attire is not conducive to this assignment."

"What's that?" says Bald Cop.

"Forgot my coat."

Broad Cop pops his trunk and throws me a flak jacket with three stripes up the sleeve.

"Believe it or not, gentlemen, this isn't my first dispatch to a bridge," I inform them, slipping my arms through the metallic green sleeves. "Sarge get pissed me wearing his jacket?"

"Only if you get it wet," Bald Cop says with a smile.

Their radios squawk to life. "*Eleven sixty, eleven fifty-nine in progress number nine.*" They yap back quick and pull at their belts. "Burglary at Foster's on Main, suspect firing shots. We gotta go."

"Of course you do," I reply.

"We'll send somebody out for you," Stubby says. He thumbs the button and speaks into his collar. "L.T., can you send CRT backup on the bridge?"

"Soon as I can spare one," the rattled voice replies.

"Best of luck," they bid me and roar off into the night.

I make my way down the slim walkway, sirens warbling in the distance, rough water chopping at the banks below. An eighteen-wheeler roars by, shaking the steel suspension, and I am sure the old drunk will topple but he just keeps singing.

I make my way to him and get a look. Scraggly, lanky and bent, clothes rumpled and stained with paint. He tilts back his head and echoes a hymn across the great divide.

father along we'll know more about it,
farther along we'll understand why

The business of psych crisis is not looking for well-balanced practitioners. It helps to be a little screws-loose yourself. I know the song, so why not — I sing along. When I get close enough for him to hear, he turns.

"Hey there," he calls, eying the stripes up my sleeve. "You po-lice?"

"No sir."

He pauses. "Military?"

"No sir."

"Who are you?"

I've done this job a long time now but still don't know what I'm doing. There is no way to know what you are doing. You wing it and hope for the best.

"Just a fan of good singing," I say.

"Aw, you're pullin' my leg now."

"Maybe. You mind if I come out there?"

"You ain't here to take me in?"

"Nope."

"Sure, come on."

It's a short jump down to some splintered old planks, holes

and rot around their sides. Through the spaces I can see the Cumberland battering the span's columns, white water rushing around the edges.

"How'd you get out there?" I ask.

"Step down on that solid-looking piece. It'll hold. Then come this way and over them cables."

Over them cables is a long step and there's nothing but river below. He squats down and peers through the steel. "Careful right there."

A three-foot-wide piece of iron runs the length of the bridge. I edge down and sit on a square of plywood, clinging to the rail.

"You sing that high part nice," he offers.

"Thanks."

His face is battered but he's got the sloping sad eyes of a lonesome hound and there's a kindness there that shines through the dark. A bottle-shaped bag rests on the rail beside him. "Pretty out here, ain't it?" he says low.

I shift into a secure spot and look out over the river, full moon on the waters, over the bend and into the hills, the red lights of the wire factory glowing in the distance. "It's beautiful."

"You a painter?" I ask, pointing to his splattered coveralls.

"Naw, just helping my neighbor with his porch today."

I motion to his little flowered cap. "Welder?"

"Just a fan of silly hats," he says, flashing a ragged smile. "Ah, I'm joshin' with you. Been a welder half my life. See that rebar?" He points near a column where a twisting piece of ribbed steel snakes up out of the water. "We dive down and weld them joints into the frame."

"Sounds dangerous. Good money?"

"Purdy good," he nods, taking a hit from the bag. "You a question-asking man?" he says, not unfriendly.

"Something like that. I do have to ask you this one: You come out here to jump?"

"In that cold-ass water? Naw . . . ," he answers. "I come to sing."

"You came out to the bridge rail at midnight to drink wine and sing old hymns?"

"No sir," he asserts, holding up the bag. "This here's gin." I laugh loud and we both shake our heads.

The air is charged and cold, stars winter bright. A barge rounds the river bend, splitting the shimmer cast by the moon. Dogs bark, far away.

The hymn-singing, gin-drinking man looks off into the hills and the night goes silent. "Something happen here?" I ask.

"In '83 my brother killed himself off this bridge."

"I'm sorry."

"Some say he wasn't ever right in the head. I don't know. Just never could find his place, I guess. I was two years out of high school, doing my thing. It just tore Mama up. . . ." With his right fist he wipes at the corner of his eye. "Folks round town acted like his life wasn't worth much anyways. . . . But he was a good boy." He looks to me and ducks his head. "I come up here and think about him sometimes. Talk to him. Tell him I miss him."

"What's his name?"

"Daniel."

"Daniel," I repeat.

A train passes on the parallel span. We cling to the rail as it clacks by, engines and cattle cars, graffiti down the side, over the river and down the ridge, the whistle calling as the last car fades from sight.

"Sir, any minute now sheriff's deputies will return to this bridge," I tell him. "And I'll either have to send you to a psychiatric facility or they will take you to jail. That's the only choices. Unless, that is, you somehow slip away."

He nods slowly. "I hear you, partner. Thanks."

"No problem."

"Can I ask you something?" he says.

"Sure."

"You're one of them psycho-logical people, right?"

"Not one of them regular kind." I gesture to the bridge rail and the barge. "But yeah. I guess you could say that."

"Sometimes I hear my brother talkin' to me. I mean, I really hear his voice."

"What's he say?" I ask.

"Stuff like: *Be strong, Big Brother. I love you. And I'll see you real soon.*" The man pauses and turns from the river to me. "That mean I'm crazy?"

"I don't think so," I say.

"What's it mean then?" he asks.

"Maybe," I tell him, "it just means he's still close. Closer than we can know. Maybe he finally found his place."

He looks hard into my eyes, I guess to see if I am telling the truth or just giving him a line. I believe what I said so there's no need to look away.

"I hope so," he says, his tone sober now. "Gonna shoot straight with you. I'm an alcoholic and I ain't got much in this world. And sometimes I am tempted to jump off this damned bridge, thinkin' maybe it'll take me to wherever he is." He waves his hand over the waters and points to the sky. "But I keep coming back up here and somethin' keeps saying *not tonight.*"

He kicks a loose piece of slate to the water and we watch it fall. "Not tonight," he says again.

The man reaches out to shake my hand and for a moment I hold back, knowing he could pull us both in if he wanted. "Tonight's all we got, brother," I tell him, taking his hand anyway. "So let's just stick with that."

He nods and asks, "You ever lost anybody?"

"Yes sir."

"You ever lost somebody and never quite got over it?"

"Yes sir."

"You ever wish," he says, the words real slow, "that wherever they are, you was there with 'em?"

"Yeah," I reply. "Sometimes."

"To Daniel," he says, raising his bottle and tilting it to me.

"Wherever he is tonight."

"Wherever they are," I repeat.

He tips his hat, turns and walks away.

Daniel's brother disappears into the trees, his absence so complete I wonder if he was ever really here. I sit on the bridge rail, collar of my flak jacket pulled tight against the chill. The river swirls, black and cold beneath me, as a bitter wind cuts through the steel. I stand and look over, down into the dark abyss, imagining the hole in the water where the body falls through, baptized and made new, moving strobe-like through the stars into the infinity of God.

If I break the surface will the waters take me, through the murky tunnel towards the light? Would I come out on the other side, in another world, one with no pain or loss or damage carried too long?

How does one get to the place where everything you lost awaits?

The barge creeps closer, long and wide as a runway, its rim sparkled with tiny lights. On a faraway hill the radio tower glows, one glimmer, another, then three.

Enoch was
& then he was not
for God took him
& he arrived

I release the rail and raise my palms to the sky, the thrill like blood lightning and fire in my bones. With one foot lifted, I lean out over the edge . . .

There but for the Grace of God go I, into the waters, into the night.

The wind rages then dies down to a breeze. A small voice whispers.

This is where you will always belong.

The car heater feels good against my hands as they pulse back to life. I cue up cut five and the nasal Zen of Willie carries me down the road.

grace has brought me
safe thus far
and grace shall lead
me home

The Valium of God |
Merry Christmas from the Far Back Pew

"And He shall speak peace to the heathen." — Handel's
"Messiah"

At the red light on Old Hickory, there's a liquor store with dark
paneled walls and neon flashing through the windows.

Old Charter. 7 & 7.

Season's Greetings from Malibu Rum.

The cashier slaps hands with a man in a jean jacket buying
two tall cans of beer. They point to a boxy old TV and laugh as
she slips his purchases into separate paper bags.

Once, at fourteen, I was in a tree house drinking Boone's
Farm wine with Stacy Love. She had a Snoopy transistor radio
from sixth-grade Christmas and the DJ played "I Drink Alone."

"What kinda person would drink alone?" Stacy asked.

"Beats me," I said, passing back the bottle.

My grandfather drank himself to death. He drank alone.
They say addiction runs in the family and some nights I can
hear it scratching at the door, whispering sweetly,

You can hide out here, if you want.

I understand a lot better now why some people drink alone.

The jean jacket man leaves the store and dodges around the
corner. Even from the street, I can see his shaking hands. In the

shadow of the flashing sign, he peels open a can and turns it up.

My wife slides her fingers through mine. The light turns green.

The stars hang heavy in the Tennessee night, winter dark and cold as we hustle up the steps of the little Baptist church.

A tiny old fellow with big bifocals and a powder-blue suit smiles and opens the door. He smells like fresh-baked bread and English Leather cologne, like the Valium of God.

"Welcome," he says, his coarse hands covering mine. "So glad y'all could come."

We slide into the last pew just as a man with a stiff silver bouffant invites us to rise to our feet and open our hymnals to number 259.

I stand and stare blankly while the congregation sings, thinking about how hard the holidays can be with all the expectations and emotional baggage and pressure to be joyful and triumphant and how I probably shouldn't be wrestling with the urge to shotgun Xanax from here to Valentine's Day.

Sometimes church encourages me to live justly, love mercy and walk humbly, to champion the oppressed and bless the poor. It inspires me to ruthlessly examine my own faults and strive to rise above. Other times, it makes me want to drink hard liquor in a dark room with dark sunglasses on. This is the truth.

My wife taps my knee and whispers, "Played this hymn for my dad about a million times."

I fall back into that scene — my wife as a ten-year-old girl, accompanying her father on piano at their old country church. It's a peaceful thought. *I hope Heaven is real.*

The pastor steps to the platform, lean and ready with his loose suit and thick head of hair, like a college basketball coach. With a clearing of his throat, he breezes through the announcements. Sunday school bonfire, shoes for the needy; the seniors are taking a trip to the state capitol. "Open your Bibles to Corinthians, thirteen." He begins to speak, the cadence of his baritone taking my mind away. . . .

I want a time machine with no strings attached. I want to fly. I want to see my parents young again. I want every dog I ever loved to run to me when I cross that line where time has ended and death is no more. I want to play Tokyo with Prince on the Alive II *stage. I want sex in Heaven that surpasses our wildest dreams. I want to live forever in every tiny moment. I want everything I ever lost back for good. I want all that and more and even after to hear Jesus laugh and say:*

> *we have*
> *not even*
> *made it to the*
> *front gate*

Sometimes I wonder if magical thinking is my alcohol.

A young mother carrying a baby makes her way up the aisle towards the back door. Her cell phone buzzes from her bag; she stops and shifts the infant to her hip. A tiny bare foot kicks out. I want to reach out, touch those little toes.

"Baby," says my wife.

"Oh, where are you . . . ," the mother mutters, digging through rattles and stuffed toys. The toddler swings out, away from her hip, and her fingers grasp my hair.

"Goodness, so sorry," the woman says, stabbing her cell into silence and slipping in close. "Let go, sweetie, let go."

"No trouble," I say. The baby gurgles, blue eyes staring.

"You like his curls, Emma?" the mother says, then to me, "Lucky you, got a smile. Usually, with men, she cries."

The mother gently pries Emma's hands loose and shifts her to the other hip. She cranes her head around, finding me again. Ducking her face into the back of her hands, she bounces a bit and giggles.

"Are you a flirty girl tonight?" the mother chides.

"I have found favor," I say, pointing to Emma. "Babies change the world."

"Try changing her diaper," Mom says with a sympathetic look. "That's a real spiritual experience for ya."

"I'll pass."

"Mary changed God's diaper," she says.

"Pass," I repeat. Mother and child bid farewell and make their way through the doors.

"Baby," my wife says in the high and tiny voice I so love.

"Want one?" I ask.

She pats my leg and smiles sweetly. "Got one."

In the prairies of Heaven, my wife has a cabin home. I top the hill and see her there from far away. She sits on the frozen lake, lacing her skates and, seeing me, lifts one hand to wave. I wave back and begin to run, faster and further, completely alive.

On this prairie, there are no more goodbyes. . . .

I tune back in as the pastor says, "And with this, I close . . ." He steps down to the aisle and reads his passage, slowly, as an altar call.

Love never gives up.
Love doesn't want
what it doesn't have,
Takes pleasure in truth,
Always looks for the best,
Never looks back,
Staying steady to the end.
Love never dies.

And then, with the warm tone of a Baptist preacher, "Friends, all that will matter in the end is the love you give and the love you take in. And that love — will never end. Bow your heads with me, please."

God help us all.

"You know," the music minister says after the Amen, "we should close with 'Silent Night.' Would that be all right? Stand with me and let's sing it together."

My wife leans in and lets out a contented sigh. Our hands meet at the pew back, fingers intertwine. We kiss, in church. The old man in the powder-blue suit smiles and gives us a wink.

This time, I sing.

Over the Levee

"All things are possible after midnight." — Unknown

Midnight, Jesus & Me |
Soundtrack (on Three LPs)

Side I

Hank Williams Jr. — "Feelin' Better"
David Lynch — "Dark Night"
Kyper — "Conceited (Tip Top Mix)"
Slim & the Supreme Angels — "Stay Under the Blood"
Depeche Mode — "John the Revelator (Shaffer Remix)"
Lynyrd Skynyrd — "Tuesday's Gone"

Side II

The Cult — "Black Angel"
Lenny Kravitz — "Fly Away (acoustic)"
The Singing Cookes — "Ain't No Grave (Live!)"
John Carpenter — "The Duke Arrives"
Black Sabbath — "Children of the Grave"
Rockabye Baby — "Where Is My Mind?"
Doug Packer & the Bluegrass Eruptions — "Down at the Pig"
The Cure — "Seventeen Seconds"
Porter Wagoner — "Committed to Parkview"
Jimmy Swaggart — "Room at the Cross"
Simon & Garfunkel — "The Sounds of Silence"

Side III

Zapp — "Mega Medley"
Oak Ridge Boys — "Y'all Come Back Saloon (Disco Mix)"
Motörhead — "One Track Mind"
Brandon Kinney — "Rough Crowd"
Rockell — "In a Dream"
Duran Duran — "Girl Panic (Lynch Remix)"
Sneaker Pimps — "The Chauffeur"
The Plasmatics — "Rock & Roll"
Stevie Nicks — "Planets of the Universe"
Hammock — "Wish"

Side IV

Aerosmith — "Angel"
The Glorious Unseen — "Tonight the Stars Sleep"
Godspeed You! Black Emperor — "Dead Flag Blues"
Don Was & Buddy Miller — "So New"
Tori Amos — "Losing My Religion"
Aunt Bettys — "Rocket & a Bomb"
Misfits — "She"
Waylon Jennings — "Always Been Crazy"
Anberlin — "Mother"
Faster Pussycat — "No Room for Emotion"
Joey + Rory — "Freebird"

Side V

Conway Twitty — "Don't Call Him a Cowboy"

Molly Hatchet — "Been to Heaven"

Rolling Stones — "Miss You (12 inch remix)"

Blackfoot — "Highway Song"

Rush — "Side One, 2112"

Smashing Pumpkins — "Tarantula"

Jim White — "Ghost Town in My Brain (Q-Burns Mix)"

Willie Nelson — "Changing Skies"

Amy Grant — "Tennessee Christmas"

David Phelps — "Nessun Dorma"

Apocalyptica — "Nothing Else Matters"

Side VI

Michael McDonald feat.Warren G. — "Keep Forgettin' to Regulate"

Tony Joe White & Boozoo Bajou — "Keep Goin'"

Judas Priest — "Diamonds & Rust (Live)"

Alison Krauss — "Dreaming My Dreams"

Glenn Frey — "You Belong to the City"

Black Country Communion — "Song of Yesterday"

All incidental music by Hammock
hammockmusic.com

End Notes & Epilogues |

I always loved the little section at the end of comic books and movies that told the story after the story. It was more relaxed, like when the party's over and only close friends remain, when you're just hanging out on the front porch sofa with your shoes off, talking about everything and nothing at all.

Did Ralph make it to the hospital?

What about Mr. Banks?

Is Darla okay?

But what happened next?

When friends read these stories they often ask those types of questions. And most of the time, the answer is *I don't know.*

In the spirit of endnotes and epilogues, here's a last few scattered words, the best bit of resolution I can provide.

RALPH rode away in a sheriff's car, sleepy and sweet and thanking me for my assistance.

I saw JADA not long ago when MR. JACK-O-LANTERN JOWLS had visions of blood oozing from the walls and was certain that the ghost of Johnny Cash was calling him into the trees. Jada told me she'd decided against mental health and planned to become a Physical Therapy Assistant.

"Good for you," I said. "Hey, how's Ralph?"

"Wish I knew," she said with a shrug. "He never came back."

I saw CHRIS, my parents' former neighbor, at the Tractor Supply last June. He told me he was still clean and sober. "One day at a time, ever since that crazy night."

Dad called awhile back and said that PASTOR REDDY returned to preach Homecoming service at the old rift church. Water passes under the bridge, people forgive and humility has its way. It's a beautiful thing when people change for the good, like time and age redeemed.

DR. CRYER retired from the university and now lives a farmer's life. "People are hard," he told me. "Cows are easy."

Last I heard, TERRY moved back to Indiana and was going to school to be a psych nurse.

"Hey, you," a voice called from the church foyer. It was an attractive young lady, smartly dressed, a plum-lipped baby in her arms. "Remember me?"

I squinted, trying to figure out how I might know her. Then it hit me. "HOT PANTS?"

"Aw, man," she said, punching my arm and rolling her eyes. "That was long time ago. You grow up, you know?"

"What you doin' here?" I asked. "You a church girl now?"

"Nah, my nephew's in the play," she said with that same sass. "I might come back though."

I nodded at her, she nodded back and then she sort of smirked and said, "Wanna go get some pancakes? My treat."

"See that girl?" I said, pointing to the porcelain doll working the welcome desk across the way. The doll pointed back, closed one eye and kissed the air.

"No way," Hot Pants laughed. "You were straight?"

MR. RIC and the RINK roll on. If you pass through on the right Friday night, you'll find strobe lights and cotton candy, the happy sound of children laughing. Now and then, a shaggy guest DJ back on the mic. . . .

Last time I visited home, I saw WOOKIE, riding his bike over the Black River Bridge. He was laughing and talking, but I didn't see a phone. He wasn't towing a mower.

TAT married a contractor and moved to Beverly Hills. Beverly Hills, *Florida*. Someone told me she has an autistic daughter and is a stay-at-home mom now.

GILL THOMAS still talks of moving to Tennessee to be a park ranger.

I was back home last summer, stopped at the Quik Stop for a Diet Coke, when a familiar-looking fellow walked up and opened the next cooler down. He was wearing a yellow tank top with tan lines marked around the meaty part of his arms. His face was pink and round and Piggly.
Can't be.
My memory doesn't always work well, so many people over the years, so I held my tongue. He turned, reached out and grabbed me by the shoulder.
"Zaxxon preacher man!"
"JERRY?!" I was so bewildered all I could manage was "You're still alive?"
"Yeah man, yeah," he laughed.
"Thought the next time I'd see you'd be out past the moon."
"Guess The Man had other plans," Jerry said with a laid-back grin.
"— How?"
"It's a mystery," he said, stepping in closer. "Doc sent me home, said there wasn't nothing else they could do. My old granny said, *Baby, if I make chicken and dumplings, will you eat?* I told her, *Yeah, Maw, I'll try.* She was cryin' and rolling out that dough, figurin' that'd be 'bout my last meal, I guess. I ate and

man, it was fine. Got up, went fishing the next morning. Came home thinking *I feel pretty good for a dyin' man.* Kept eatin', kept fishin'. Quit taking all them crazy meds." He stepped back and held out his arms. "And here I am."

"Whoa," I said. "So you're all right now?"

"I am today, brother," Jerry said. "And today's all we got."

MR. BANKS & ANNA were both admitted to the state psychiatric hospital. At best case, they stayed a few days, were prescribed psychotropic meds and discharged back to jail or home. I pray they are in a better place.

I brought my guitar and stopped by LARRY'S awhile back, but the trailer was gone and only a rectangle of dead grass remained. I was sorry I had waited so long.

I saw SAM one night, from a distance, in the health and beauty section at Rite-Aid. Her chair was parked sideways in the aisle and she was looking at hairbrushes. She sat there for the longest, staring at the brushes, running her fingers over the bristles.

It was the tail end of summer and the storm had just begun. I wished that I was enough of a believer to pray her out of that damned wheelchair and run with her through the rain, soaking wet and laughing and crying, just like some movie where a miracle happens and everything ends all right.

Sam moved her chair a little and started looking through the clippies and barrettes. Holding them to her hair, gazing into a tiny round mirror. I wanted to go over and say something but somehow, I just couldn't.

Like many record shops facing the digital age, SPIKE'S shut down. We helped him move to Nashville where he is now one of the world's foremost experts on all things musical. Despite his influence, the Hall of Fame has yet to induct Johnny Paycheck or David Allen Coe.

JUKE'S star would rise and fall before he followed his heart back home to find his own secret place.

MAMA has a fancy new washing machine. She bought it herself.

GOD still walks in the cool dark night at the far end of Sweet Olive Lane. Sometimes I hear Him laugh.

Gratitude |

"But you can't accidentally electrocute yourself writing a book. If you could, I would have done it already." — Lisa Lutz

Occasionally, like once or twice a year for twenty minutes, writing is like reeling in sugarbaby trout from the stocked ponds of Heaven. All you have to do is tie your line and stand in the glorious stream. The rest of the time, it's like a monkey trying to carve a three-bed/two-bath bungalow from a giant boulder, using only a hammer and a butter knife.

These are just a few who helped this monkey make a book.

Divine guidance came in the form of skilled editors and teachers like Shigu Erika Rae and my Jewish birthright, Imah Irene Zion. God bless the Patron Saint of Above & Beyond, Josie Renwah. Brothers JD, Reno and Rich. Sisters Megan Leah Power, Lisa Rae Cunningham, Dawn Corrigan & Doctor Lenore. Brad Listi and all my buddies at *The Nervous Breakdown*. Blessed assurance, my super-smart and effervescent interns, Neely Baugh and Nathan Anderson. And for providing them, Lipscomb University and the ever-gracious Dr. Dana Carpenter. The Morris to my Jerome, Lee Swartz. The Music Cities chapter of Misfits for Jesus. Apostle Andrew Krinks and the blessed mother of middle Tennessee libraries, Amma Betsy. First class attorney and comrade extraordinaire, David Maddox.

Image magicians, Carter Andrews, Bridgett McBridgett and the patience, faith and furious ink of Sergio Carillo.

Moons ago, the encouragement of Ms. Laura Weldon made all of this possible.

ECW Press, home to born-again brawlers, circus freaks, punk rock junkies — and the midnight psychiatric crisis guy. Simon Ware. Crissy Boylan, Cat London, Jennifer Knoch, Erin Creasey, Sarah Dunn. Carolyn McNeillie, Troy Cunningham, Rachel Ironstone. Jack Grisham. Michael Holmes. Thank you. (Now we can go back to talking about Black Sabbath & the Junkyard Dog.)

From the stained-glass splendor of Scarritt Bennett to the neon bustle of Lower Broad . . . the back alleys of Music Row to the peak of the pyramid at ASC. . . . the shaded paths of Radnor to the Bat Building at night . . . Much love and thanks to my home-town, Nashville, Tennessee.

Every writer needs a patient spouse.

Thank God for mine who shows me Grace and loves my crazy.

Barukh atah Adonai,
bo're m'orei ha'esh —
ha'mavdil bein kodesh l'hol. —
she'hehiyanu v'kiy'manu v'higi'anu la-z'man ha-ze

חבשה לאל

A portion of the proceeds from this book goes to support the following ministries |

Vanderbilt Children's Hospital
childrenshospital.vanderbilt.org

Amazima Outreach
amazima.org

Misfit Friends of Jesus, Bay Area, CA
misfitfriendsofjesus.com

Lantern Lane Farm
lanternlanefarm.org

The Nashville Contributor Street Paper
thecontributor.org

What?

You're still here?

The book's over. You can go watch TV now. Go.

Oh. You're looking for the deleted scenes.

Well, why not . . .

Baptism |

"I want to go back to believing everything and knowing nothing at all." — Frank Warren

Holy Hannah peels off her white patent leather pantsuit and runs naked as the day she was born through the cascade of fountains in the county square. Her skin is squeaky and pink, eyes bright as stars on the first clear summer night.

The TV preacher's words tickle her ears as the water rains down.

Until you have been born again, of spirit and water, you cannot enter the Kingdom.

She babbles and sings and speaks in tongues; she makes a joyful noise, her sins laid bare before the Lord and grim men with nightsticks and shining badges. But she pays them no mind; they are the voices of dissent with devils on their hips, eyeing her with the flat wicked gaze of the serpent.

The woman cop built like a tank tucks her braid into the uniform collar and pulls on rubber gloves. "Your girl here's pretty sick," she says to me.

The lights of the fountain go blue to gold and Hannah's hands reach for the midnight sky. Her head arches back, face bathed with ecstasy, the ripples shameless upon her skin.

The corners of my mouth creep into a smile as I reply. "Maybe it's contagious."

I take off my shoes and step into the water.

To Hell with the Devil |
Halloween Is Alive & Well at the All-Night Kroger off Old Hickory Road

Curtis,
Gregg would like you to work on the potatoes and island first after you break down the truck. Do not worry about displays.
Perry

Curtis walks over and reads the sign taped to the produce back room window again. He looks into the glass until his eyes lose focus and he sees the stranger staring back. Six years now he's been a night stocker at the Kroger off Old Hickory Road. Six years and now there are strands of gray running loose through his Wolfman goatee and long stringy hair.

To hell with the potatoes.

After midnight, Curtis fiddles with the in-store music until he lands on Hard '80s. Pushing the broom through produce goes a whole lot faster to Maiden and the Priest.

The double attack of razor-sharp flying V riffs signals the intro to "Rock You Like a Hurricane." Curtis hoists his broom and jams along and for a moment is far away from store-brand bleach and stewed tomatoes, on a split-tiered stage with wicked flickers of laser light piercing the crimson fog. Teenage girls, dizzy with lust, lift their hands and scream. . . .

Perry, the night shift leader, stands on his toes and looks over from the manager's booth. "Rock on, Curtis," he calls out, shaking his head and adding a little *heh heh*.

The next night there's a note on the console to never change the station from Easy Rock again. Gregg says a customer complained but Curtis knows better.

To hell with the island.

A woman in pajama pants and an Eeyore letter jacket shuffles past, a dirty-faced baby asleep in the bottom of her cart.

"Y'all got that Jack Daniels mustard?" she asks.

Curtis stands from his shelves and stares at a spot just over her shoulder, like he's trying to think of where the item might be. Phil Collins is playing on the in-store, but not that cool song with the drums, and Curtis feels like his blood has turned cold and slow, like all his life has been an illusion and he might just now be waking to another world. He dreams of flying Vs and limousines and young girl screams. He dreams of everything that never was and will never be.

The baby coughs and shifts in its cage. Spying a price gun on a nearby box of Apple Chips, Curtis considers swiping it up and labeling the child *$1.99*. The woman would probably be less than amused.

"If we do ma'am," he says, "it'd be on aisle five."

"Aisle five," she replies, steering her cart away.

To hell with the truck.

Back in winter, Curtis made a mug from a mop bucket, molded some Styrofoam into a handle and filled it with boxes of hot chocolate for an aisle display. Back in high school, the only class Curtis even halfway liked was art.

"Pretty okay," Perry said weakly. "But what are you going to do when you need a mop bucket?"

Curtis hadn't thought of that.

"Gregg's got me in receipts tonight," Perry reminded. "I'll need you to unpack my soup pallet."

To hell with Perry.

A couple of weeks ago, Curtis had a brainstorm he figured Gregg would love for sure. Fashioning a boat from a long crate, he stacked cases of water around it to look like waves. He filled the boat with twelve-packs of beer, then made a sail from some old poster board that said *Summertime Fun!*

The next morning Gregg sighed and rubbed the back of his neck. That was never good.

"Listen," he told Curtis. "I'm hearing you need to be more of a team player. Put a little more care into your duties. The little displays are all right, but you need to make sure you're getting all your other work done." He said it nice, but still, he said it.

To hell with Gregg.

Curtis reads the sign one more time and doesn't wait to see the stranger in the glass again. He fastens his back support, pulls back his hair and begins to wash off the island.

Sometime after midnight, Curtis drives his mop bucket past dairy and down towards household goods. As he passes the haunted house built from Kit-Kat packs and cases of Coors, the power chords of Cinderella's "Push, Push" rip through the Kroger PA. Curtis lets out a howl and laughs to himself until he spots a customer coming down the next aisle.

"Oops, sorry sir," he mutters.

The customer, a bemused-looking fellow with black glasses and a shaggy tangle of heavy metal hair, raises his chin and lets out a howl of his own. Curtis nods, cuts his eyes to the side and smiles.

"Rock on, Curtis," the customer says. "Rock on."

For Ever & Story |

Late Sunday afternoon and we are driving through the country-side with the windows down just south of town. Tennessee at its finest, rolling hills and patchwork farms, creeks winding their way through thickets of hickory. The rich loamy aroma of horses and sweet prairie hay. Nobody living too close to one another. We've got our eye on some land out here.

My wife will graduate soon in a pretty prestigious program from a top-notch university. She's not exactly sure what area she wants to work in but she'll do well whatever it is.

"I might just do the baby thing. For a while," she says.

"Do what you want," I tell her. "Don't worry about the money."

She doesn't want much, some land and a cabin maybe, not too big but built just the way we want it. A good porch and neighbors not too close. Said it was fine with her if we lived in a mobile home on the land while we were building our place.

"I'd want to keep the trailer even after we got the house built," I tell her.

"Well, of course," she replies. "Our family could sleep over there when they visit, not have to stay with us."

"And we could live over there a little too," I offer. "Trailer sleeps good on a rainy night."

"Oh yes," she says. "I don't mind a trailer."

It's nice driving the back roads and looking at the land,

planning out a little cabin in the woods, maybe there next to where the water spills down over the rock and splashes into a shallow pool below.

"Look, baby, right there by the little waterfall," she says. "We could sleep with the windows open when the weather turned cool." I nod, no further words needed.

It's nice to let my mind unravel a bit and dream. Might get some overalls, an old pickup to drive around the fields, grow a little kitchen garden. Get me a tractor, nothing too big.

"Once we get settled in I want to try and eat everything we can natural," I say.

"We should," she answers.

"I could get some laying hens," I declare.

"Probably easier to let somebody else keep chickens, just buy their eggs," she suggests. My wife, you see, she knows me.

"Probably," I agree, adding this: "And goat's milk. I hear it's better. Closer to mother's milk."

"Goat's milk is, like, four dollars a quart," she replies.

"I could get a nanny goat. We could name her . . . Maudine." The words feel magical and light, like the grandest idea of all times. I see myself, in overalls, milking goats.

"You go right ahead, baby," she answers back. My wife smiles, slips her hand into mine and the whole world slows to a crawl, the sun fading red over far mountains. I ease the car down to a leisurely fifteen, hang my head out the window and breathe. . . .

I don't know if any of this will happen and am fairly certain none of it will happen just as we think or plan. My rabbi friend tells me that the Kingdom of God is near, much closer than one can imagine. That it isn't some faraway heavenly place but rather a way of living that values the good things of life today and therefore makes a better hope for tomorrow. I struggle endlessly with that sort of thinking. If what the rabbi says is true, I am far from the Kingdom. But I'm trying to do better and the rabbi says that in the Kingdom, trying counts for a lot.

"We have to keep living simple," my wife says as she digs out her file and works at the fingers of my right hand.

"I know," I answer.

"We have to give more too," she says.

I know the riches in life are now — right in this moment, a good and righteous wife whose arms are never closed, one who is wise, discerning and always charitable, who walks in kindness and patience and through example teaches me all these things.

"Absolutely," I reply.

We drive awhile, the silence easy and right. I feel her eyes on me as the day gives way to dusk. She studies me in the dark car, her hand smoothing down the sleeve of my shirt. "Had that dream again," she says. The Dream of Twin Daughters. My wild curls, her cornflower eyes. Calla Lily and Mary Madeline.

"Except last night," she adds, her brows pinched, "they had new names. Ever and Story."

"Ever. Story," I repeat. "Maybe that's their middle names. You know, Mary Ever Madeline Blaine."

She turns her head to the open glass, to the endless fields of green. "Maybe," she says softly. And then, the words barely above a whisper: "What do you think dreams mean?"

I taste and test the words a little before my reply.

"I don't know."

Riding the highway back home, the white lines take my mind to a little cabin in the pines, right next to where sweet water flows from the rock. The front porch windows glow in the distance, drawing near, laughter and love, twin girls with curly hair and pale blue eyes. Stories without end, forever, Amen.

My wife, you see, she knows things.

Fever Dreams from the Other Life |
Brother Ferris & the Cannons on the Monastery Wall

In the heaven
before Heaven
I saw myself
in another life
a casket builder
at a monastery
near the mountains
of Montana.

Oaks and Cherry and Ebony and Ash. Pink Ivory and Purple Heart. Zebrawood, Bloodwood and Wild Olive from the garden of Gethsemane.

"Make mine pine, Brother Blaine," Ferris says in his sing-song voice. "Knotty pine, with sturdy rope handles." Brother Ferris is big-bellied and mostly bald with sky-blue Converse sneakers beneath his tattered robe.

"And if you are able," he adds, his eyes like those of a five-year-old child about to blow out the candles of his birthday cake, "carry me down."

He points to the valley of white crosses and laughs, the echoing belly laugh of an old monk unafraid to die.

I thump my heart twice with my right hand and nod. Brother Ferris smiles.

"And you sir?" he asks. "I'm curious as to what wood the man who builds might choose for his own."

I hold my fingertips together and blow them apart.

"Ah . . . ," he replies.

I point to him.

"God willing, yes," he says, "I will get you there." Ferris turns to look out over creation. "Er, and where is it you'd like to be?"

Bringing my fingers together again, I point to the cannons on the monastery wall, then fling my hands out over the valley.

Brother Ferris knits his bushy brow and looks out over the field. I point to the cannons, to myself and spread my hands out over the field again.

Brother Ferris and I, we laugh together. Then, with that same finger, I tap his chest.

"Oh, brother," old Ferris says with a shake of his head, "God wills, I shall do my best."

In my left hand, there's a three-quarter-inch nail. I hand it to him and he rolls it in his palm before slipping it into the pocket of his robe.

"Memento," he says softly, his violet eyes shining like the dawn. "Memento mori."

I pick up a fistful of nails. In the field are many crosses, simple white crosses, each of them the same.

"Peace be with you, Brother Blaine," he says. "Godspeed and long life."

Brother Ferris fades into the lilies, his tonsure bobbing until he vanishes into the fire of their bloom.

From far away, I hear him whistling. "Lacrimosa," so it seems.

Or maybe it's Glenn Frey . . .

As likely to quote Axl Rose as Saint Augustine, J.M. BLAINE is a licensed sex and suicide specialist who has worked in libraries, haunted houses, psych wards, megachurches, rehabs, radio stations and roller rinks. He is nonfiction editor of the L.A. literary collective *The Nervous Breakdown*, feature writer for America's most popular street paper, *The Nashville Contributor*, and a former contributor to the world's only religious satire magazine *The Wittenburg Door*. Blaine lives with his happy wife in Nashville, Tennessee.

For more stories, rough cuts, pictures and songs:
jmblaine.com